PRAISE FOR *WHEN THINKING IS A PROBLEM: ABOUT AND BEYOND THINKING*

"Charles Eigen has collected contributions from a variety of thinkers who cannot easily be categorized, and who all made it their life's work to benefit sentient beings. This engaging book raises a topic that goes to the root of the human dilemma: suffering and liberation from suffering. Is thinking our main problem or can it be beneficial? What does 'beyond thinking' look like and is that the solution? I like this book a lot and recommend it to any serious thinker."

—**Reirin Gumbel**, resident priest, The Milwaukee Zen Center

"Charles Eigen invites us to ponder how conditioned we are to fall into thinking as a resolutive resource, being seduced by the illusion of control, unaware of how thinking can lead us away from our self and our experience. So many processes get stuck as we pretend to intellectually understand; such a waste of life! The intricacies of life cannot be solved through thinking, as thoughts can interfere with organismic wisdom, but we are conditioned to turn to thinking. We have an illusion of certainty in which challenges can be solved at that thinking level. This book invites us to a whole-body and heartfelt experience, resulting in an enjoyable ride in the here and now. The message of this book is powerful and life-changing."

—**Maria Florentina Sassoli y Ezcurdia**, counselor, certified Hakomi practitioner, certifying focusing coordinator, president of the Argentinian Civil Association of Focusing, board member of The International Focusing Institute

"*When Thinking is a Problem* is a fascinating deep dive into thinking and not thinking guided by esteemed scholars, scientists, and spiritual leaders. This beautifully curated compilation takes us from how we understand the nature of thought, both scientifically and practically, to an exploration of what is potentially beyond thought. Each essay is a jewel that will give you lots to think about!"

—**Diana Winston**, director of UCLA Mindful and author of *The Little Book of Being*

"Perception-shifting *When Thinking Is a Problem: About and Beyond Thinking* is a round-table investigation about the nature of thinking and its role in causing suffering. Through a collection of essays and interviews, rich with insights from contemplative teachers, academics, and writers, Charles Eigen creates a spacious discussion that challenges you to discern between thinking and awareness and how to use this wisdom to bring greater presence, peace, and positive impact in our world."

—**Sharon Salzberg**, author of *Lovingkindness: The Revolutionary Art of Happiness* and *Real Life: The Journey from Isolation to Openness and Freedom*

When Thinking Is a Problem

About and Beyond Thinking

Edited by Charles Eigen

ROWMAN & LITTLEFIELD
Lanham • Boulder • New York • London

Rowman & Littlefield
Bloomsbury Publishing Inc, 1385 Broadway, New York, NY 10018, USA
Bloomsbury Publishing Plc, 50 Bedford Square, London, WC1B 3DP, UK
Bloomsbury Publishing Ireland, 29 Earlsfort Terrace, Dublin 2, D02 AY28, Ireland
www.rowman.com

British Library Cataloguing in Publication Information available

Library of Congress Cataloging-in-Publication Data

Includes bibliographic references and index.
ISBN: 979-8-8818-0057-4 (cloth)
ISBN: 979-8-8818-0058-1 (paper)
ISBN: 979-8-8818-0059-8 (electronic)

For product safety related questions contact productsafety@bloomsbury.com.

∞™ The paper used in this publication meets the minimum requirements of American
National Standard for Information Sciences—Permanence of Paper for Printed Library
Materials, ANSI/NISO Z39.48-1992.

In loving memory of my parents,
Pearl and David Eigen

Out beyond ideas of wrongdoing and rightdoing,
There is a field. I'll meet you there.

When the soul lies down in that grass,
The world is too full to talk about.
Ideas, language, even the phrase "each other"
Doesn't make any sense.

—Rumi[1]

NOTE

1. Coleman Barks, "A Great Wagon," in *The Essential Rumi: New Expanded Edition* (New York: Harper Collins, 1995, 2004), 35.

Contents

Preface

Thinking and awareness, the two subjects of this book, are common to everyone, regardless of their orientation and whether or not they follow a tradition. That said, this book relies heavily on Buddhism, which has contributed so much to the exploration and understanding of the dynamics of thinking and awareness. I have divided the book into two parts, "About Thinking" and "Beyond Thinking," but the placement of some of the chapters is a bit arbitrary because many of the chapters would be at home in either part. Rather than being a comprehensive academic survey of the subject, this book is more reflective of my personal journey of coming to know, better than I had known before, my own experience and understanding of thinking and awareness.

The contributors to this book discuss aspects of thinking and awareness from their individual perspectives and therefore may not agree with the perspectives of other writers. Some are closely aligned with a tradition, for instance, and others are not; and some, such as Krishnamurti, may be opposed to any tradition. In any case, thinking and awareness are universal to our human experience.

The reader will note that some of the chapters consist of dialogues between teacher and student. I thought that this would help make the material accessible to a wider audience because many of the questions are from listeners who are new to some of the perspectives expressed by the speakers. Additionally, the informed reader will see that some of the speakers have a mentor relationship with others. For example, Francis Lucille studied with Jean Klein, David Bohm and Vimala Thakar were influenced by Jiddu Krishnamurti, and Gangaji's teacher was Papaji. However, these writers were selected for the clarity and distinctiveness of their perspectives rather than to highlight any teacher-disciple relationship. In fact, this writer encountered the writings of most of these teachers before any such relationship between them was known.

It was also a happy, though unintentional, coincidence that the writers and writings are so international, coming from India, China, Japan, Tibet, Vietnam, Ireland, Switzerland, France, England, and the United States. Additionally, several friends offered their valuable input from Holland, Germany, Argentina, and India.

Several of the chapters were written especially for this book. Those writers are Lucy Biven, Ben Connelly, Temple Grandin, Frederick Gustafson, Pierre Morin, Jac O'Keeffe, and Shohaku Okumura. Okumura's chapter includes his recent and previously unpublished translation of the "dog's buddha-nature" part of Busho.[1] The primary text for that is included in the book's appendix. Other writers who have given their permission to include previously published material include Francis Lucille, Gangaji, David Godman (for the interview with Papaji), and Raymond Tallis. For the remaining chapters, permission to include previously published material has been granted by those publishers. This writer wishes to express deep appreciation for the generous contributions of the authors, and for all permissions received. Please see the acknowledgments for further information about permissions.

Although my own understanding is limited, many of these writers have deeply benefitted me in my own journey of discovery, and it is my hope that the reader will benefit from their writings as well.

The editor's footnotes are signed [C.E.]. Unsigned footnotes are those of the original author.

NOTE

1. Bussho, Japanese for buddhatā, the buddha-nature in Zen Buddhism. *The Concise Oxford Dictionary of World Religions.* [C.E.]

Acknowledgments

I thank the writers who contributed their original essays to this project. I thank them for their contributions as well as their patience: Lucy Biven, Ben Connelly, Temple Grandin, Frederick R. Gustafson, Pierre Morin, Jac O'Keeffe, and Shohaku Okumura. Thanks to the writers who allowed their previous work to be included in this volume: Gangaji, David Godman, Francis Lucille, and Raymond Tallis. Thank you to the publishers and organizations that allowed me to include their writers: Cory Fisher, Kristy Lee, and the Krishnamurti Foundation of America for Jiddu Krishnamurti and David Bohm; Terry Barber, Tony Lulek, and Parallax Press for Thich Nhát Hanh; Catherine Torpey and the International Focusing Institute for Eugene T. Gendlin; Dharma Communications for an excerpt by John Daido Loori from *Mountain Record: The Zen Practitioner's Journal*; Wisdom Publications for Harada Roshi; Shambala Publications for Suzuki Roshi; Julian Noyce of New Sarum Press for Jean Klein; Susan Barnett, David Godman, and Avadhuta Foundation for Papaji; Georgia Niesten of the Vimala Thakar Bookfund of Holland; and Harriet Watson, Hillary Larson, and the Gangaji Foundation. Thanks to Renata Keller and Kaiser Irani for providing information about Vimala Thakar; and thanks to Hans Peter Muelllenthaler, Cei Davis, Richard Frank, and Joan Tollifson. Thanks to Mary Dudley at Sage Publications for leading me to Lilith Dorko, who embraced this book. Thanks to Scott Edelstein Literary Agency, again, for his help with the publication process. Appreciation to Arnold Mindell for introducing me to Pierre Morin; Coleman Barks, again, for permission to use another beautiful translation of Rumi; and Lilith Dorko, Sarah Rinehart, Christopher Fischer, Jonathan Joyce, and the team at Rowman & Littlefield, whose assistance and enthusiasm were invaluable. Thank you for your endorsement and encouragement: Sojun Diane Martin Roshi, Beth Jacobson, Flor Sassoli, Sharon Salzberg, Diana Winston, and

Reirin Gumble. Thank you for your help: Daigaku Rumme, Harvey Honig, Hoko Karnegis, Karen Gustafson, Samantha Young, and Jamila Yusuf. Of course, any errors are solely my responsibility. Thanks to my friends and family for their interest in this book and thanks, especially, to my wife, Mary Bernau-Eigen, for her loving patience in all things, and especially toward this book, which has lived with us, like a house guest, these many years.

Introduction

Charles Eigen

ABOUT THINKING

This book is about thinking and the problems that ensue when thinking is an inappropriate or inadequate response to life. Thinking is, of course, a natural and an important part of living, but too often thinking becomes the medium through which we experience life, and life is always more than what we think. This book is also about awareness and especially the relationship between the activity of thinking and awareness, as well as how wrong thinking affects society. We can think about awareness, but that's not the same thing as being aware that we are thinking, and yet thinking and awareness can go hand in hand, as reflected in the title of Uchiama Roshi's book *Opening the Hand of Thought.*[1]

My interest in the activity of thinking started all at once, when I was twenty-one. In between college and the rest of my life, I was confused and anxious about my direction. One day, my confusion and anxiety became so intense that I sat frozen in my chair, overwhelmed by the storm of confusion as my thoughts spun out of control. Then, suddenly, I was no longer caught up in the maelstrom of thoughts and confusion; instead I was outside of it all, observing the activity of my mind. I could clearly see that here was confusion and anxiety, but I was calm and clear, no longer identified with the confusion, but now more identified with my awareness. I was surprised to see how calm I felt, even in the presence of this confusion. I watched the activity of my mind with some wonder, and as I watched, the confusion settled down by itself.

Although I didn't immediately act on this experience by learning to meditate, for example, it was an event that changed my inner landscape or, more accurately, revealed aspects of my interior, of awareness, that had always been there but that were previously overlooked.

A few years later I had another encounter with the activity of my thinking during a first psychotherapy session, when the therapist asked me to sense my body. This was new for me. I had always thought of myself as athletic, but my relationship with my body was more about my acting without attention to it, as an operator of my body, rather than sensing or listening to its quality of being. A funny thing happened while I sat, quietly sensing my body. As I rested in the flow of sensation in my body, I became aware of the activity of my thoughts, one after another, as they arose and dispersed. Most surprisingly, I sensed that each arising thought had a subtle effect on my body, like rain drops falling on a still pond.

While this was another dramatic experience for me, it wasn't life changing, at least in the short run, and I quickly returned to my "home base" of living in my head. It doesn't take long for defenses to erect barricades against the unfamiliar. Over the ensuing years, however, my interest in the activity of my thinking deepened with my studies of various awareness-oriented practices of psychology, spirituality, somatic practice, and Zen, some of which were described in my book *Inner Dialogue in Daily Life*. Gradually, I learned how to work more skillfully with the contents of my thinking and to recognize, and rest in, the larger field of awareness in which thinking occurs. Grace Schireson says of awareness:

> Awareness is a vast topic, and it can be defined by two aspects: essence of mind and contents of mind. Essence of mind is that which is aware of what we are thinking, feeling, sensing, and experiencing. Content of mind is the specific thoughts, feelings, and impulses that arise within essence or naked awareness. It is the essence of mind, our own undifferentiated awareness, that may observe what arises in our own mind in any moment. Like the sky, this essence exists and functions whether we choose to notice it or not. While we may not increase this awareness, we may strengthen our relationship to it.[2]

There are many methods for improving our thinking, as well as numerous methods that work to quiet thinking. This book, rather, is an inquiry into the activity of thinking itself, and how thinking affects, or even rules, our lives, to the point that we do not even recognize its predominance (the emperor with no clothes comes to mind), much less question our own thinking. On the other hand, thinking can be a problem by its absence, when it's needed but not utilized. Hannah Arendt, in her seminal lecture "Thinking and Moral Considerations," makes the argument for the necessity of thinking and the moral hazard of not reflecting on our experience. She also points out that while we think about the contents of thought, the activity of thinking, itself, gets less attention.

> The whole history of philosophy, which tells us so much about the objects of thought and so little about the process of thinking itself, is shot through with intramural warfare between man's common sense, this highest, sixth sense[3] that

fits our five senses into a common world and enables us to orient ourselves in it, and man's faculty of thinking by virtue of which he willfully removes himself from it.[4]

When I mentioned the proposed title, *When Thinking Is a Problem*, to a friend, she asked, "When isn't thinking a problem?" The answer is that thinking isn't a problem when it's appropriate, and by appropriate I don't mean preconceived or acceptable notions of how and what to think. Thinking is a natural part of our everyday lives, from the most quotidian of matters to the most intellectual. When it's needed, thinking is not necessarily a problem. On the other hand, if my thinking is not clear or is drawing conclusions on inaccurate data (note the prevalence of misinformation in social media and political advertising), then thinking and its products will be a problem, even when thinking is called for.

When we think of how thinking might be a problem, what might come to mind are the varieties of mental disorders that are characterized by disordered thinking. While problematic thinking plays its part in all mental illness, this book focuses instead on how thinking can be a problem in our so-called normal, everyday lives, and on the role that thinking, whether by its presence or absence, plays in suffering. In any case, whether the degree and kind of dysfunctional thinking meets the criteria of clinical mental illness or whether it is of the everyday garden variety, the effect is to hinder our freedom to respond appropriately and spontaneously to life as we live it. An appropriate response is the hallmark of a healthy life and is relevant across the range of human experience, as reflected in the exchange, long ago, between two Chinese monks: A monk asked Yunmen,[5] "What is the teaching of the Buddha's entire lifetime?" Yunmen answered, "An appropriate response."[6]

What do we mean when we say we are thinking? The dictionary provides a variety of uses of the word, so if I say I am thinking, it can mean anything from having a fantasy, to figuring out a tip on a restaurant tab, to having errant thoughts, to contemplating something deeply. It all depends on the context. This is true for many words for which we assume a common understanding and may be especially true when we are referring to our subjective experience. For example, Daryl Sharp, writing on Jungian typology, writes about the many uses of the word "feeling":

> It is particularly important to distinguish between the "Feeling Function" as a psychological function and the many other common uses of the word "feel." Jung acknowledged the possible confusion: we say we feel happy, sad, angry, regretful, and so on; we have a feeling the weather will change, or the stock market will fall; silk feels smoother than burlap, something doesn't feel right, etc. Clearly, we use the word feeling quite loosely, since in a particular context it may refer to sense perception, thoughts, intuition or an emotional reaction.[7]

Thinking, in its content or even its activity, is often overvalued. When think-ing is overvalued, conceptions are mistaken for reality. About this, Korzybski famously said, "The map is not the territory." When thinking is overvalued, there is little room for a feeling response, and perceptions become drained of their immediacy. The psychiatrist C. G. Jung said, "We should not pretend to understand the world only by the intellect; we apprehend it just as much by feeling. Therefore, the judgment of the intellect is, at best, only the half of truth, and must, if it be honest, also come to an understanding of its inad-equacy."[8] Heinrich Zimmer also speaks to the limitations of the intellect in his description of the Irish folk hero Conn-eda, who, by virtue of the quality of his being and his innocence, is able to be guided on his mythic quest by more than reason: "The higher human faculties would have been inadequate to conduct and support Conn-eda through his trials which are of a character essentially incompatible with either the credence or the judgment powers of the conscious human intellect."[9] And again,

> Being an Irishman—and, moreover, one of the early period—he is spared the characteristic fault of modern man, the too exclusive reliance on intellect, rea-soning, and consciously directed willpower. As far as Conn-eda is concerned, the basis for the modern problem does not exist; he offers no resistance whatsoever to the guidance of the unconscious. Spontaneously and wholeheartedly, he sub-mits to all the inscrutable commands and outlandish agents that steer him on.[10]

When thinking is a problem, it's usually a problem in one of four ways.[11] Thinking can be a problem when we're thinking and it's not necessary to think. Second, thinking is a problem by its absence, when we need to think and we don't. It's also, obviously, a problem when we need to think and are thinking, but the thinking is distorted in some way. Buddha taught that what and how we think leads to either suffering or happiness. In the verse named "Twins," or "Pairs," in the Dhammapada,[12] his early teachings, he said,

> Mind is the forerunner of all actions.All deeds are led by mind, created by mind.
> If one speaks or acts with a corrupt mind, suffering follows,
> As the wheel follows the hoof of an ox pulling a cart.
> Mind is the forerunner of all actions.
> All deeds are led by mind, created by mind.
> If one speaks or acts with a serene mind, happiness follows,
> As surely as one's shadow.

The fourth way that thinking can be a problem is when we believe our thoughts that are not true or take our thoughts to be the reality they repre-sent. In Buddhism, believing what isn't true is the fundamental problem, particularly in the belief that things, including and especially "this thing" (as

Harada Roshi would say) called my ego-self, have a permanent, inherent self; whereas the reality is that everything is temporarily made up of other things.

One of the problems with an overdependence on thinking is that we may continue to turn to thinking when thinking doesn't solve our problems. It's like repeatedly using the wrong key to try to open a door. Koya Kibose[13] illustrates this with the traditional Japanese story of the horsefly Buddha. He describes how the fly keeps bouncing against the shoji screen, trying to get out, while all around there are openings that would allow his freedom. He might notice that, if only he would just stop banging his head against the screen.

You might ask, What value could there possibly be in not thinking? But by not thinking, I do not mean being thoughtless, as in being inconsiderate or careless. I mean not getting involved with thinking when thinking is not appropriate. We are so used to getting involved with our thinking that we are used by thinking rather than using thinking as the instrument it is. Our habitual involvement with thinking has led us to predicate our identity on our thinking: we become identified with our thoughts. But if you are aware of your thoughts, whether the thoughts are useful or troublesome, who is it that is aware of the thoughts? In exploring this question, it becomes clear that we are more than our thoughts. The Indian thinker Jiddu Krishnamurti makes a distinction between thinking that is appropriate and that which is not:

> Let us now go into the question of what is thinking, the significance of that thought which must be exercised with care, logic and sanity (for our daily work) and that which has no significance at all. Unless we know the two kinds, we cannot possibly understand something much deeper which thought cannot touch. So let us try to understand this whole complex structure of what is thinking, what is memory, how thought originates, how thought conditions all our actions; and in understanding all this we shall perhaps come across something which thought has never discovered, which thought cannot open the door to.[14]

Often we are lost in thought and don't even know that we are thinking. On the other hand, we become very aware of thinking when thinking is going on and we wish it weren't, such as when we're trying to fall asleep and we just can't turn it off. But even during the day, thinking can be a problem when we are thinking and we don't need to be thinking. Of course, from the perspective of thinking, it makes sense that we're thinking because thinking thinks it needs to think. That is a habit of thought. Similarly, unwanted thinking makes its presence known through its intrusive contents, or through the moods and emotions that it triggers. It's important to note that sometimes unwanted thinking, even disordered or intrusive thinking, can be a problem because we don't know what to do with it. However, using skillful means such as Jung's active imagination, Richard Schwartz's Internal Family Systems Therapy, and other psychodynamic and psychoanalytic approaches to inner work and the unconscious, the reluctant recipient of unwanted thoughts might learn that there is value in what is unwanted.[15] Additionally, what comes, unbidden, from the unconscious can be material for creative works.

A common and significant way that thinking is a problem is demonstrated by an overactive inner critic, what Freud termed the "super ego." This is that inner voice that is always evaluating our experience against a set of standards that were inherited long before we had a choice. Standards are indispensable in the appropriate context, but when those standards are used against ourselves, or projected onto others, we suffer. The inner critic can find fault with whatever it might lay its eyes on, anything we say or don't say, any part of our body, and so forth. It can also find fault with anything that has to do with our lives, resulting in the sense that there is always something missing, something that has to be done, some condition that has to be met before we can allow ourselves to be all okay. When the inner critic is active, there is never enough or we are not enough or too much, and in any case, contentment is forever elusive.[16]

The painful irony of the inner critic is in its origin, in part, as a means of guidance and protection. The toddler uses the introjected, disapproving, and protective parental voice, for example, to remind him to not run into the street or touch the stove. Once we can think for ourselves, however, the inner critic loses much of its value. A. H. Almas, in his foreword to *Soul without Shame*,[17] says,

> Depth psychology has demonstrated that we always develop a part of our selves to take the role of inner conscience, traditionally referred to as the superego. But this ego structure of conscience is built mostly through identification with the judging, critical, blaming, and punishing attitudes in the environment we grow up in. It becomes a harsh judge and a cruel source of punishment, instead of being the light of true conscience.[18]

Thinking is also a problem when I do not consider the implications or consequences of my actions or inaction. Helen Keller famously quipped, "People do not like to think. If one thinks, one must reach conclusions. Conclusions are not always pleasant."[19] At the collective level, history is replete with examples of the consequences of not thinking or, more accurately, not thinking of the consequences of what thought has wrought. Hannah Arendt asks,

> Could the activity of thinking as such, the habit of examining and reflecting upon whatever happens to come to pass, regardless of specific content and quite independent of results, could this activity be of such a nature that it "conditions"

men against evil-doing? (The very word conscience, at any rate, points in this direction insofar as it means "to know with and by myself," a kind of knowledge that is actualized in every thinking process.)[20]

And again, "Do the inability to think and a disastrous failure of what we commonly call conscience coincide?"[21]

One need only glance at the newspaper to see where the powers of thinking have led us. On the one hand, thinking has brought us improvements that enhance our lives, but on the other hand, thought has led us to the brink of disaster. We live at a time when there are any number of catastrophes that threaten us without precedent. It's the other side of the coin, the side we don't want to look at. On one side is nuclear energy, on the other, nuclear war; there is the convenience of plastics and petroleum products, but there is pollution and poisoning; where there is industry and progress, there is also the threat of catastrophic climate change. The list goes on. Every accomplishment of the collective application of thought has brought with it consequences that we may struggle to control, or even acknowledge. The most recent example may be what's called the artificial intelligence (AI) alignment problem, that is, the lag between the abilities created in an AI system and moral values. In a recent broadcast of her program, Christiane Amanpour refers to the "godfather" of AI, Geoffrey Hinton, and says that he "joins a growing chorus of experts worrying that bad A.I. could conceivably even lead to the extinction of the human race."[22,23] It calls to mind the image of the sorcerer's apprentice who got hold of the sorcerer's magic wand and wielded powers he couldn't control. The Dalai Lama has written,

"It is all too evident that our moral thinking simply has not been able to keep pace with the speed of scientific advancement. Yet the ramifications of this progress are such that it is no longer adequate to say that the choice of what to do with this knowledge should be left in the hands of individuals."[24] Again, Jung, almost fifty years earlier:

It is not that present-day man is capable of greater evil than the man of antiquity or the primitive. He merely has incomparably more effective means with which to realize his propensity to evil. As his consciousness has broadened and differentiated, so his moral nature has lagged behind. That is the great problem before us today. *Reason alone no longer suffices.*[25]

The irony here is that Jung is appealing to reason. While reason, alone, is insufficient, its practice is an essential part of living. In one of the selections in this book, Harada Roshi writes of "Putting an End to the Discriminating Mind,"[26] but as you'll see, he is referring to the discriminating mind that makes it impossible "to see the flower as it is." Thinking, and its discriminations, are not a problem when they are called for. In fact, Buddha taught the right use of the discriminating mind to help us understand the thoughts, attitudes, and behaviors that perpetuate our suffering. Buddhism is known for the many lists of mental states and behaviors that serve to help us see, and wake up to, where we're at and what we're doing.[27] One of the effects that some of these discriminations have is to help free ourselves from our entanglement in the content of our thinking, the stories that we concoct that explain (and predict)[28] what I am and what is happening, by shifting our attention from the content to the state or activity itself. A practical example of this is that I may be angry, caught up in the story of some wrong, but if I am aware that I am angry, I can better take care of my anger and protect others from its expression. This is different than suppressing my anger. It's allowing the anger to be in the larger field of my awareness. Then I'm in a better position to act with care and, if necessary, "speak for the anger, rather than from it," as the popular phrase goes. Often it's enough to be present to what I'm feeling without acting on it. That is, the awareness acts on it, as noted in this well-known Tibetan phrase: "All defilements are self-liberating in the great space of awareness."

However, when the limitation of reason is seen, there is often an overcorrection, resulting in a devaluation of thinking, especially among those who have a meditation practice. As Seiso Paul Cooper notes, thinking gets a bad rap.[29] When, before, one might have lived a life immersed in thought, now one sees thinking as the root of all our problems. Suppressing thoughts and feelings may have its place, particularly when your focused attention is required, but as a way of life, it only creates more problems. And suppressing thoughts during meditation or Zen makes meditation a battle. It's our nature to think, but it's also our nature to be beyond thinking.

BEYOND THINKING

The first part of this book is about thinking and looks at thinking from several different perspectives to give a sense of the activity of thinking altogether and bring to light that which demands—or captivates—our attention. As stated earlier, the word "thinking" can mean different things. Arendt's use of the word "reflecting" in her description of thinking, from earlier, "the habit of examining and reflecting upon whatever happens to come to pass, regardless of specific content and quite independent of results," suggests giving one's care and attention to something with an attitude of receptivity, as opposed to the kind of thinking used in calculating or working out a problem. And it is similar to Jung's notion of "intuitive thinking":

Active thinking is an act of the will, passive thinking is a mere occurrence. In the former case, I submit the contents of ideation to a voluntary act of judgment; in the latter, conceptual connections establish themselves of their own accord, and judgments are formed that may even contradict my intention. . . . Active thinking, accordingly, would correspond to my concept of directed thinking. Passive thinking . . . I would call . . . intuitive thinking.[30]

Buddha likened the mind to water, the age-old symbol of reflection, suggesting that the mind's ability to clearly reflect reality is hindered by the presence of disturbing mental factors such as restlessness, ill will, and others. He says, for example, while one can clearly see his reflection in still water, the presence of anger is like trying to see one's reflection in boiling water, while the presence of restlessness or anxiety is like trying to see one's reflection in wind-swept water, and so forth.[31] Similarly, the Dalai Lama compared the mind to water:

The Mind is primordially pure. If we disturb the water of a lake, it will become muddy, but the nature of water itself is not muddied. We only have to let the waters grow calm again for the mud to settle at the bottom, and the water will regain its original purity. What can we do to restore our mind to its original purity? How can we eradicate the various factors in mental pollution? We cannot get rid of them through outside struggles, nor by ignoring them, but only by injecting powerful antidotes via the channel of meditation. If you are able to practice meditation a little every day, gathering your scattered mind by focusing on an internal object, that would be a great help. The stream of thoughts thinking of good things, bad things, and so on, will quieten down. You will find it's like taking a short vacation: finding yourself beyond your thoughts and resting there.[32]

The second section of the book considers what lies beyond thinking, again from several different perspectives. It's interesting to note, here, that the inability to think—or to go beyond thinking—is not a matter of one's intellect. Arendt states, "Inability to think is not stupidity, it can be found in highly intelligent people."[33] And as for one's ability to go beyond thinking, Dogen says, "intelligence or lack of it is not an issue, make no distinction between the dull and the sharp-witted. If you concentrate your effort single-mindedly, that in itself is wholeheartedly engaging the way."[34]

Thinking has its place, and yet what lies beyond thinking, beyond the knowledge, intention, and limitation of thought, is the immediacy of life, unfolding without—or beyond—knowing.

> The wild geese do not intend to cast their reflection;
> The water has no mind to receive their image.[35]

By definition, what is beyond our conceptualizing is not accessible to thought. Thought can bring light to darkness, but light cannot reveal the nature of darkness; as soon as darkness is touched by light, it becomes light. It's like using words to describe silence. You can talk about silence, and think about it, but what you have when you think of silence is thoughts about silence, not silence itself. Whatever is thought about brings about additional thought. Thought cannot conceive of what is beyond itself because of the limitations of thought, but then what of that which is beyond those limitations? For example, Joseph Campbell said, "God is a metaphor for a mystery that absolutely transcends all categories of human thought . . . it's as simple as that."[36]

While the fact of our life is mysterious and beyond our comprehension, thinking can make the fact of our lives subordinate to and defined by thought; but thinking can also lead to contemplation and wonder at the intelligence beyond our intellect. Krishnamurti has spoken of intelligence in distinction to our intellect:

> So what is intelligence? Intelligence is the capacity to see the truth that thought is limited. And how does that capacity come into being? . . . It can only come into being when there is the art of placing—when there is the placing of thought in its right place. . . . But thought thinks it can also perceive the whole—pretends, imagines, conceives—but it is not the whole. So we are saying, the perception of the whole is intelligence.[37]

Buddhist teachings, and Zen teachings in particular, make the distinction between thinking, not thinking, and nonthinking or beyond thinking. Furthermore, it makes sense to use thinking to talk about what is beyond thinking. For example, Dzongsar Jamyang Khyentse Rinpoche answers a questioner who asks, "If we ourselves are dualistic, can we ever understand emptiness, which is something beyond description?"

> Rinpoche: Buddhists are very slippery. You're right. You can never talk about absolute emptiness, but you can talk about an "image" of emptiness—something that you can evaluate and contemplate so that, in the end, you can get to the real emptiness. You may say, "Ah, that's just too easy; that's such crap." But to that the Buddhists say, "Too bad, that's how things work." If you need to meet someone whom you have never met, I can describe him to you or show you a photograph of him. And with the help of that photo image, you can go and find the real person.[38]

Many decades ago, when I was studying somatic therapies, the instructor came over to my table where I was working with a volunteer client. The instructor asked me, "How is your client doing?" I regarded him lying there, very still. I said, "He seems to be peaceful." The instructor asked, "Is he peaceful, or just quiet?" When I looked again, I could see that there was a lot going on that he was keeping a lid on. I had been so caught up in working on a particular area that I lost track of the person. In the same way, we can suppress our thoughts, but the seeming quiet is not the same as peace. John Daido Loori speaks to the distinction between abiding in nonthinking and not thinking, the result of using thinking to suppress thought, in this commentary on Dogen's 300 Koan Shobogenzo, Case 129: "Yoashan's Non-Thinking":

> **The Main Case:**
> When Priest Yaoshan was sitting in meditation a monk asked,
> "What do you think about, sitting in steadfast composure?"
> Yaoshan said, "I think not thinking."
> The monk said, "How do you think not thinking?"
> Yaoshan said, "Non-thinking."
> **The Commentary:**

Abide in neither thinking nor not thinking. Thinking is linear and sequential, a separation from the reality that is the subject of thought, and thus is an abstraction rather than the reality itself. Not thinking is suppressive. It cuts away thoughts the moment they arise, making the mind into a great impenetrable mountain-dead, unresponsive. Non-thinking has no such edges. It is the boundless mind of samadhi that neither holds on to, nor lets go of, thoughts. It is the manifestation of the buddha mind, in which the dualism of self and other, thinking and not thinking, dissolves. This is the dharma of thusness that is the right thought of all the buddhas in the ten directions.[39]

Finally, here is another contemporary Zen teacher, Norman Fischer, speaking on Dogen's *Shobo Genzo* fascicle, "Space." He makes the point that thinking has its place, and is, itself, a manifestation of the larger reality. Reading a passage from Dogen, he then comments on it.

Dogen: In this way, Buddha ancestors all expound sutras. What expounds sutras is empty space. Without being empty space, no one can expound even one single sutra. Expounding the Heart Sutra and expounding the body sutra are both done with empty space. With empty space thinking is actualized and beyond thinking is actualized.

Fischer comments: So now this is a point that Dogen uniquely makes over and over again, because Zen would seem to be against thinking you know, against ideas; Dogen is not against thinking and ideas. He's not against studying the Buddhist teachings and understanding the concepts of Buddhism. He just wants us to remember that when we're doing that it's empty space that is doing that, and he wants us to remember that when we're doing that, concepts are concepts, language is language, ideas are ideas. They are valuable, but let's not forget what they are. So, we need thinking, and we need beyond thinking. We need to balance these two. We need to honor them both.[40]

NOTES

1. Uchiyama Kosho, *Opening the Hand of Thought: Approach to Zen*, trans. Shohaku Okumura and Tom Wright (New York: Penguin Books, 1993).

2. Grace Schireson, *Naked in the Zendo* (Boulder, CO: Shambala, 2019).

3. Whereas Arendt refers to common sense as the sixth sense, Buddhists regard thinking as the sixth sense. Conventionally, ESP is referred to as the sixth sense. [C.E.]

4. Hannah Arendt, "Thinking and Moral Considerations," *Social Research* 38, no. 3 (Autumn 1971), 417, 425. © 2000 Bell & Howell Information and Learning Co., © New School for Social Research.

5. Yunmen Wenyan was an early Chinese Buddhist master (d. 949 CE).

6. Zenkei Blanche Hartman, *Seeds for a Boundless Life: Zen Teachings from the Heart* (Boston: Shambala, 2015).

7. © Daryl Sharp, *Personality Types, Jung's Model of Typology* (Toronto, ON, Canada: Inner City Books, 1987).

8. C. G. Jung, *Psychological Types, the Collected Works*, Vol. 6, ed. Sir Herbert Read, Michael Fordham, MD, Gerhard Adler, PhD, a Revision by R. F. C. Hull of the translation by H. G. Baynes (London: Routledge, 1991).

9. Heinrich Zimmer, *The Kind and the Corpse*, ed. Joseph Campbell (New York: First Princeton/Bollingen Paperback Edition, 1971), 38.

10. Zimmer, *The Kind and the Corpse*, 41.

11. See Shohaku Okumura's chapter for another perspective on four ways that thinking can be a problem. [C.E.]

12. Ven. Balangoda Ananda Maitreya, trans., and Rose Kumar, ed., *The Dhammapada* (Novato, CA: Omni Foundation, 1988).

13. Koya Kubose, Change Your Mind Day, presented by Volusia Buddhist Fellowship, YouTube, 2013. https://www.youtube.com/watch?v=NUea8iVIgbI.

14. Jiddu Krishnamurti, *Freedom from the Known*, © 1969 Krishnamurti Foundation Trust (New York: Harper Collins).

15. For more discussion of this, see my book *Inner Dialogue in Daily Life* (London/Paris: Jessica Kingsley/Hachette, 2014).

16. Some resources for exploring this aspect of the psyche include books by Richard C. Schwartz, Byron Brown, Hal Stone, and Byron Katie. [C.E.]

17. Byron Brown, *Soul without Shame* (Boston: Shambala, 1999).

18. Brown, *Soul without Shame*, ix.

19. Simran Khurana, "Helen Keller Quotes," ThoughtCo, September 3, 2021, thoughtco.com/helen-keller-quotes-2832699.

20. Arendt, "Thinking and Moral Considerations," 418.

21. Arendt, "Thinking and Moral Considerations," 418.

22. *Amanpour and Company*, PBS, May 3, 2023.

23. In the same broadcast, Amanpour interviews Connor Leahy, AI researcher and CEO, Conjecture. Amanpour: "In some of the reading I've done, it appears that what's kind of scary is that the amount of resources put into the capability of this A.I. far outstrips—and the graph is getting wider—the resources put into the safety aspect

of it, what they call the moral alignment to make sure it's not bad and destructive. Can you see that continuing like that?"

Leahy: "It seems completely unsustainable to me. Billions of dollars, and you know, thousands, tens of thousands of our brightest engineers and scientists are working day in and day out to create, you know, ever more powerful systems. Well, the number of people who work full-time on like the alignment problem is probably less than 200 people, if I had to guess."

24. Tenzin Gyatso, the fourteenth Dalai Lama, op-ed, "Our Faith in Science," *New York Times*, November 12, 2005.

25. C. G. Jung, *The Undiscovered Self* (Princeton, NJ: Princeton University Press, 1990), 54.

26. Sekki Harada, *The Essence of Zen, the Teachings of Sekki Harada*, trans. and ed. Daigaku Rumme (Boston: Wisdom, 2008).

27. For example, see the Four Foundations of Mindfulness, the Five Hindrances, the Six Realms, and so forth. [C.E.]

28. A recent book on neuropsychology suggests that, as a survival mechanism, the brain has developed a dominant function as an instrument of threat assessment and prediction. See Anil Seth, *Being You: A New Science of Consciousness* (New York: Dutton, 2021). [C.E.]

29. Seiso Paul Cooper, "Thinking's Bad Rap," in *Psychoanalysis and Zen Buddhism* (New York: Routledge, 2023).

30. Sharp, *Personality Types*.

31. See the Five Hindrances. [C.E.]

32. H. H. Dalai Lama, *The Spirit of Peace*, trans. Fredderique Hatier (Paris: Le Pre aux Cleres, 1996), 124.

33. Dalai Lama, *The Spirit of Peace*, 423.

34. From Dogen's Fukan Zazengi.

35. Zenrin-Kushu (Collection of Sayings from the Zen Forest), an anthology of Chinese wisdom, from Ch'an, Confucian, and Taoist sources, compiled by Ijūshi, 1688. *The Concise Oxford Dictionary of World Religions*.

36. Joseph Campbell, "Conversation with Joseph Campbell/On Mythology," with Garry Abrams, *New York Times*, May 27, 1987.

37. Public Discussion 4, Ojai, California, USA, April 14, 1977.

38. This article is based on a talk titled "What Buddhism Is, and Is Not," given in Sydney, Australia, in April 1999.

39. © Dharma Communications, Inc., Reprinted from *Mountain Record: The Zen Practitioner's Journal*, Summer 2000, by permission of Dharma Communications, Inc.

40. Norman Fischer, talk for Upaya (www.upaya.org), March 5, 2023, "How the World Is Made," (minute 59), speaking on Dogen's Shobo Genzo fascicle, "Space," Quoting Kazuaki Tanahashi's translation, *Treasury of the True Dharma Eye: Zen Master Dogen's Shobo Genzo* (Boulder, CO: Shambhala Publications, 2013).

Part I

ABOUT THINKING

Chapter 1

Every Kind of Seed[1]

Thich Nhát Hanh

THE SECOND VERSE:

In us are infinite varieties of seeds—
seeds of samsara, Nirvana, delusion, and enlightenment,
seeds of suffering and happiness, seeds of perceptions, names, and words.

Our store consciousness contains every kind of seed. Some seeds are weak, some strong, some large, some small, but all are there—the seeds of both samsara and nirvana, of suffering and happiness. If a seed of delusion is watered in us, our ignorance will grow. If we water the seed of enlightenment, it will grow and our wisdom will flourish.

Samsara is the cycle of suffering, our dwelling place when we live in ignorance. It is difficult to remove ourselves from this cycle. Our parents suffered and they transmitted the negative seeds of this suffering to us. If we don't recognize and transform the unwholesome seeds in our consciousness, we will surely in turn pass them on to our children. This constant transmission of fear and suffering drives the cycle of samsara. At the same time, our parents also transmitted seeds of happiness to us. Through the practice of mindfulness, we can recognize the wholesome seeds within ourselves and then in others and water them every day.

Nirvana means stability, freedom, and the cessation of the cycle of suffering. Enlightenment does not come from outside; it is not something we are given, even by a Buddha. The seed of enlightenment is already within our consciousness. This is our Buddha nature—the inherent quality of enlightened mind that we all possess, and which needs only to be nurtured.

In order to transform samsara into Nirvana, we need to learn to look deeply and see clearly that both are manifestations of our own consciousness. The seeds of samsara, suffering, happiness, and nirvana are already in our store consciousness. We need only to water the seeds of happiness and avoid watering the seeds of suffering. When we love someone, we try to recognize the positive seeds within them and water those wholesome seeds with our kind words and deeds. The seeds of happiness grow stronger when they are watered, while the seeds of suffering diminish in strength because we are not watering them with unkind words and deeds.

Our store consciousness also contains seeds generated from our perceptions. We perceive many things, and the objects of these perceptions are then stored in our store consciousness. When we perceive an object, we see its "sign" (lakshana). The Sanskrit word like "lakshana" also means "mark," "designation," or "appearance." The sign of a thing is the image that is created by our perception (samja) of it. Suppose we see a wooden platform supported by four legs. That image becomes a seed within our consciousness. The name we assigned to this image, "table," is another seed. "Table" is the object of our perception. We, the perceiver, are the subject. The two are linked every time we perceive the object we have named as a "table," or even when we simply hear the word "table," our image of a table manifests in our mind consciousness.

Buddhism identifies three pairs of signs of phenomena. The first pair is the universal and the particular sign of something. When we look at a house, the sign, or image, "house" is initially universal. The universal sign "house" is like its generic label. Now, you can buy generic food in some supermarkets. Instead of color images and brand names, the label on a can of corn, for example, displays simply the word "corn" in black type on a plain white wrapping. The universal sign of an object is like that.

Using our discriminative mind, however, we soon perceive thousands of details about each house—the brick, wood, nails, and so on, that are specific to it. These specifics are the particular sign of a house. The house can be seen as a whole—its universal sign—or as a combination of its parts, its particular sign. Everything has both a universal and a particular nature.

Connected to this, the second pair of signs is unity and diversity. Our notion of house is an idea of unity. All houses are part of the designation "house," there is no difference between one house and another. But the universal notion of "house" does not show us any individual house, which is unique in its particulars. There are countless variations of houses, and that is the nature of diversity. When we look at any phenomena (dharma), we should be able to see unity in the diversity, and diversity in the unity. While the first sign distinguishes between a universal house and a particular house, the second sign is about how we distinguish between different particular houses.

The third pair of signs is formation and disintegration. A house may be in the process of being built, but at the same time it is also in the process of disintegrating. Even though the wood is new, and the house is not yet completely built, already the moisture or dryness of the air is beginning to weather it. Looking at something that is beginning to take form, we should already be able to see that it is also in the process of disintegrating as well.

Meditation training is designed to help us learn to see both aspects of each pair of signs. We see the whole when we are looking at the parts, and each part when we are looking at the whole. When a carpenter looks at a tree, he can already envision a house, because he has been trained in constructing a house from the material of the tree. He is seeing both universal and particular aspects of the tree. Through mindfulness we train ourselves to see all six signs—universal and particular, unity and diversity, formation and disintegration—whenever we perceive a single sign, a specific object. This is the teaching of interbeing.

We assign names and words, or "appellations," to the objects of our perception, such as "mountain," "river," "Buddha," "God," "father," "mother." Every name we've assigned to a phenomenon, every word we've learned, is stored as a seed within our consciousness. The seeds give rise to other seeds in us called "images." When we hear the name of something, an image arises in our consciousness, and we didn't take that image to be reality. As soon as we hear someone say the words "New York," for example, we immediately touch the seeds of the image of New York we have in our store consciousness. We picture the Manhattan skyline or the faces of people we know there. These images may differ from the current reality of New York, however. They may be entirely creations of our imagination, but we cannot see the boundary between reality and our erroneous perceptions.

We use words to point to something—an object or a concept—but they may or may not correspond to the "truth" of that thing, which can only be known through a direct perception of its reality. In our daily life we rarely have a direct perception. We invent, imagine, and create perceptions based on the seeds of the images that we have in our store consciousness. When we fall in love, the image of our beloved that we hold in our minds may be quite different from the actual person. You might say that we end up marrying our false perception rather than the person herself.

Erroneous perceptions bring about much suffering. We feel certain that our perceptions are correct and complete, yet often they are not. I know a man who suspected that his son was not his own but was the child of a neighbor who had visited his wife often. The father was too proud and ashamed to tell his wife or anyone else about his suspicion. Then one day a visiting friend remark how much the boy looked like his father. At that moment, the man realized that the boy was indeed his own son. Because he had held onto this wrong perception, the family endured much pain for many years. Not only these three people but everyone around them also suffered because of this wrong perception.

It is very easy to confuse our mental image, our sign of something, with its reality. The process of mistaking our perceptions for reality is so subtle that it is very difficult to know that it is going on, but we must try not to do this. The way to avoid this is mindfulness. We practice meditation to train the mind in direct perception, in correct perception. When we meditate, we look deeply into our perceptions in order to find out their nature and to discover the elements that are correct and the elements that are incorrect.

If you are not mindful, you will believe that your perceptions, which are based on prejudices that have developed from the seeds of past experiences in your store consciousness, are correct. When we have a wrong perception and continue to maintain it, we hurt ourselves and others. In fact, people kill one another over their different perceptions of the same reality.

We live in a universe filled with false images and delusions, yet we believe that we are truly in touch with the world. We may have a deep respect for the Buddha and believe that if we were to meet him in person, we would bow before him and attend all of his teachings. But in reality, we may have already met the Buddha in our own town and not have the slightest wish to even go near him, because he didn't conform to our image of what a Buddha is supposed to look like. We are certain that a Buddha appears with a halo, wearing beautiful robes. So when we meet a Buddha in ordinary clothes, we do not recognize him or her. How could a Buddha wear a sport shirt? How could a Buddha be without a halo?

There are so many seeds of wrong perception in our consciousness. Yet we are quite sure that our perception of reality is correct. "That person hates me. He will not look at me. He wants to harm me." This may be nothing more than a creation of our mind. Believing that our perceptions are reality, we may then act out of that belief. This is very dangerous. A wrong perception can create countless problems. In fact, all our suffering arises from our failure to recognize things as they are. We should always ask ourselves, humbly, "Am I sure?" and then allow space and time for our perceptions to grow deeper, clearer, and more stable. In medical practice these days, physicians and caregivers are reminded by each other to not be too sure of anything. "Even if you think you are certain, check it again," they urge each other.

NOTE

1. This chapter is Nhát Hanh's commentary on the second verse of the great fifth-century Buddhist master Vasubandhu's fifty verses on the nature of consciousness. Thich Nhát Hanh, *Understanding Our Mind* (Berkeley, CA: Parallax Press, 2006). Used with permission of the publisher.

Chapter 2

Thinking Problems and
Jung's Typology

Frederick R. Gustafson

Recently, I saw a friend of mine wearing a T-shirt upon which was written the following statement: "I never made one of my decisions through the process of rational thinking." That was from Albert Einstein.[1] My first reaction was "really?!" Here was probably the greatest mind of the twentieth century seemingly sidelining his incredible thinking ability. But then I remembered how some time ago I had heard that many of the initial discoveries in physics did not occur through rational thought but through intuition (more commonly known as the hunch or speculation). Such an experience "comes" to a person. It is not consciously created. It is a leap into an unknown possibility that could lead to a truism or a dead end. But because of the uncertainty of this initial platform of vague wondering, the task of thinking is required to give substance and rational concrete validity to any intuitive possibility.

It was the late Swiss psychologist Carl Gustav Jung that gave the world what is so popularly known today as typology of consciousness, of which thinking and intuition are a part. Of all his voluminous writings, typology of personality remains one of the most understood, practical, and utilized discoveries today. Typology of consciousness is Jung's description of how we consciously move through our daily lives with a predictable ease. It is our manner of dealing with the world in the most natural way given specifically to each individual.

What Jung gave were four types: thinking and its opposite, feelings, along with intuition and its opposite, sensation. To make this easier to understand, consider two roads intersecting each other, one coming vertically and the other horizontally. At the top of the vertical road is the thinking function and at the bottom its opposite, feelings. They are oppositional only because it is difficult for a person to interface with both at the same time. A person may reason his way through life, thinking with the reason of logic and feeling with

7

the reason of evaluation of pleasant or unpleasant. Both thinking logic and feeling evaluations might be right on in accuracy or completely misguided. But both must eventually deal with the other.

At one end of the horizontal road is the typology of intuition, and at the other is sensation. These are considered irrational, but not in any pejorative sense of the word. They are irrational because neither of them requires reasoning. Intuition, for example, just happens to a person. Here would be the hunch, a flash of insight, a possibility. But if intuition can go from a to z in a moment, sensation makes an accounting for a, b, c, d, e, f, g, and all the way to z. Sensation ability just is, no reasoning is required, just respect for the details. Again, both sensation and intuition have their gifts, and one would benefit by both, but both are hard to attain. Further, if sensate people can get lost in details, an intuitive person might be 50 percent right or 50 percent wrong flying from a to z. The bottom line is that all four functions need the qualifying ability of each other. The ideal place for any person to achieve over time is in the middle of the intersection where the roads meet.

These four types of relating to the world also have both an introverted and extroverted side (which Jung referred to as attitudes). In other words, one person would be more naturally extroverted in their thinking while another would be introverted in their thinking. Thus, counting the other three types, Jung developed eight possibilities of how we consciously and quite naturally face and deal with the world. Additionally, his typological understanding was grounded in research and experience, an empirical ground still respected today in the world of psychology. Yet it had its limits in that it lacked flexibility. It was too concise; one was either this or that without any particular type being able to stretch its arm to include the other types. If Jung were alive today, I am sure he would agree that his research was just the beginning and subject to future refinement.

That refinement came when a woman by the name of Katharine Briggs came upon Jung's typological model. She had done her own research on the similarities and differences of individuals around the time of World War I. Her research and acceptance of Jung's typology later intrigued her daughter, Isabel, who graduated first in her class at Swarthmore College in 1919, married Clarence Myers in her junior year, and after World War II developed what later became known as the Myers-Briggs Type Indicator or MBTI, which further developed Jung's initial work.

Simply stated, the MBTI includes an auxiliary function type (a helper if you will) for the dominant function. Again, using the thinking as the dominant type, its auxiliary (helper) function would be either intuition or sensation. The feeling function would be the hardest to access for the thinker. This does not imply that that person is devoid of feelings or cannot express them, it is just that it is usually not his or her first response consciously.

From the Myers-Briggs perspective, the thinking type has four possible expressions instead of two: the introverted thinking type with either
extroverted sensation or intuition as the auxiliary, or the extroverted thinking
type as the dominant with an introverted sensation or intuition as the auxiliary
helper. It should be noted here that the auxiliary takes on the opposite attitude
from the dominant type. If one is predominantly extroverted, the auxiliary
function is introverted (or vice versa). Including the other three types, this
results in sixteen different type indicators for the MBTI, which makes the
typology flexible and attuned to personality differences.

It is very important that any type indicator must not be used to lock people
into rigid categories but must be used to get a very general understanding
of the differences between individuals that can make or break relationships.
Also, any perspective given by typology must be qualified by the family
background, personal characteristics, and cultural context in which a person
lives. For example, the United States has historically been predominantly an
extroverted/thinking/sensate culture. Someone who is introverted and more
feeling/intuitive might, out of a felt need to adapt to the dominant culture,
adapt a persona that is extroverted/thinking/sensate, rather than their natural
type, simply because they have been conditioned to live in that arena. This
can also happen in families where a child just does not "fit in" with the rest
of the family. A child who is introverted in an outgoing extroverted family might be seen as withdrawn; or, in an introverted family an outgoing
extroverted child might be experienced as "acting out." In the end, a solid
understanding of these typological differences has the potential for alleviating
a host of relationship issues.

Many years ago, a young couple came into my office because of a specific
marital problem that kept getting in the way of their relationship. Over several sessions, it became apparent to me that the husband was firmly stuck in
a thinking/sensate way of relating. He was quite logical in approaching his
wife. What he did not see was that his logic had little effect in nourishing
the relationship with his wife. He was in no way mean spirited or crude; he
just was missing her on the feeling level, a function in which she was quite
skilled. Exacerbating the problem, he would accuse her of always being
"emotional," while she would accuse him of being distant and cold.

Rarely do I speak in Jungian terms in my work, but in this case, I made an
exception. I began to share some of the typological dynamics that were being
played out in their relationship. They were just beginning to get the concept
when one session the wife was not able to come because it was around
Christmas time and there were matters to attend to at home. Near the end of
my session with her husband, he said he would be going home immediately
after our time together. I spontaneously asked him what she would be doing
when he got home. He replied that she would be baking cookies. It came to

me to ask him how he felt about this. Because it was a simple question about a simple subject, he was able to say that he really likes her doing that, as well as loving the smell of the cookies. Again, I rarely give advice, but suggested that when he got home, he might try practicing his rarely expressed feeling function by putting his arms around her and telling her how much he appreciated her doing all that great cooking, and that he loved her. It was a simple feeling gesture on his part that had the potential of being a model for a more sensitive relationship. It also would aid her to be careful not to assume, when conflicts arose, that he is just a cold, unfeeling husband.

This somewhat lengthy explanation of typology was necessary to better understand the topic of this writing; namely, thinking, along with all the various nuances that go with it. It is especially important in this country because, as stated earlier, we live in a dominant extroverted thinking culture. Perhaps a more focused and pertinent question here would be: When does thinking become a problem in itself? A short answer would be that any of the four basic functions named by Jung can become a problem in themselves if they are not balanced by the other functions and understood in the sociocultural context in which they are lived.

Thinking becomes a problem, creating a tyrannical imbalance, when it stands alone, without qualifiers like sensation or intuition or even some dim awareness of accompanying feelings. Then the conviction forms that "I am right in my logic and everyone else is wrong" or "the evidence I have is all I need." Thinking that has become frozen and dominant will produce an unconscious reactive inferior feeling function, which can create an emotional reaction. In other words, the specific feeling of anger becomes a diffuse emotional rage; happiness becomes undifferentiated goodwill toward everybody and everything whether it is good for you or not; grief becomes undifferentiated hopelessness and despair; and so forth. Unfortunately, as a result the more unconscious inferior feeling function joins along with the conscious logical conviction to give it the fuel it needs. This does not create a specific feeling response, but rather an oceanic emotion that will drive the ill-thought-through logic to absurd and often horrific ends. This is the dynamic behind any holocaust, any of the mass shootings that we see so often these days, any form of prejudice, any kind of oppressive dictatorship. We see this played out in politics, religion, and science when the logic of these often opposing fields locks into certainty. I have come to believe that certainty is a dangerous word, because every certain position we take has a shadow side. Inflexible certainty stops the evolution of thought, a process that has continued for millennia.

There was a time, for example, when the world thought the sun circled the earth. That fact gave people a center for their lives. They were certain of it. It was a fact. But then along came Copernicus who defied that certainty and declared that the earth, in fact, goes around the sun. We can smile today at such an obvious truth. But to the world of Copernicus's day, it violated the security of their known world, because now the earth was no longer the center of the universe. It was experienced as such a threat to that security that Copernicus was made to recant his discovery by the Church of his day. Though he recanted, I am sure he knew he was right. In the end, his discovery won out. The logical certainty of his day broke down.

However, lest we think we are beyond such a limited perspective, consider what is happening today in the field of astrophysics. Now, not only does the earth and its companion planets orbit the sun, but our solar system is just a very small part of a greater Milky Way galaxy. Further, thanks to the Hubble space telescope, our Milky Way galaxy is now observed to be one of billions that exist. What does that do to our certainty as inhabitants of planet earth, which has been our center from the beginning? To be open to new discoveries, even if they seem absurd, keeps the logic behind thinking always open to new considerations.

By contrast, thinking that has frozen logic into an unmovable doctrine, dogma, or theorem, stops, or at best slows, the evolution of human thought. On an individual level, a person will then end his or her life with the same worldview, supported by the same logic he or she had at age twenty. This is in contrast to a political or religious belief that has a foundation of basic principles which are modified by a lifetime of maturation. For example, one may have a basic belief in God or a basic position of being a political conservative or liberal yet evolve in their belief to a position of maturity reflected in inclusivity and openness to new perspectives.

As I previously stated, our dominant function in this Western culture is thinking/(sensation). Unfortunately, what happens is that when our thinking becomes so dominant that it is not modified by other functions, it becomes frozen. We think that we are thinking but are really recycling the same logic ending in the same logical conclusions. It is the stuff of extreme fundamentalism, which is found not only in the world of religion (which is the popular view), but is found also in politics and science. Religious beliefs are held, political positions are taken, scientific theorems are discovered, and that's the end of it. Sadly, what really happens is that religion, politics, and science have betrayed their vocational calling to always keep their thinking processes open and dare to walk the edges of what the existing worldviews might call heresy. When the evolution of thought stops, the worst forms of fundamentalism emerge. This is a frightening reality in our present times.

There is another unfortunate loss when thinking has gone too far and focuses too narrowly. It destroys the moment of beauty. Not too long ago, a dear friend of my wife developed cancer. The two of them had just had an enjoyable and meaningful weekend together with some other women friends. It seemed that hardly a moment had passed before my wife's friend lay in a hospice bed waiting for death to come. Near the end, we visited her and her husband, who stood by her throughout the entire ordeal. Then I saw it. My wife and her friend became quiet. Their faces drew very close together, while not a word was spoken. They shared a smile that transcended any other kind of smile, a knowing smile, beyond words, beyond cancer, beyond dying. Souls connected. I turned to her husband who was standing next to me and said: "There is a beauty moment!" I wasn't even trying to come up with that statement. I now believe that in that moment looking at them touched both her husband and me beyond any thoughts, beyond any logic, beyond anything explainable. It was an experience of beauty beyond concepts or words.

As important as logical thinking is, it can get in the way. It reminds me of a scientific report I heard several years ago of a young scientist who could explain the chemical changes in leaves that made them change colors in the fall. As factual as that may be scientifically, what does that have to do with beauty, with the rhythms of seasonal changes, with the hibernating moment of nature coming to rest, and with the anticipation of winter? Can scientific fact make room for beauty? A young water quality scientist recently told me that when he is testing streams and sees the beauty of the natural surroundings, he cannot mention that in his scientific report. Though I understood that, I wanted him to know that in those moments he was having a religious experience by worshipping or worth-shipping what he saw. If the logic of scientific thinking can respect that difference, then the logic of both science and religion can live side by side. In recent history they have been enemies; witness, again, the opposition to Copernicus.

When one beholds beauty in whatever form it comes to us, it is time to quiet the mind. Hold the moment and savor it. Let it nourish the soul. It is the stuff of poetry, music, and deeply inspired art. It is that which can raise up any thought process to the level of true integrity and value.

Quieting the mind. What an interesting and envied thought. But there I go, thinking about quieting the mind. Impossible, or so I thought! But it is different than emptying the mind—which I have for so long thought the Buddhist tradition expected. Who can empty their mind? But quiet it; even the thought is calming. It seems like so much work, though, to find the time and place to quiet the mind in this overly demanding culture with so many expectations and evaluative scales as to what a successful person is. I have come to believe these are all excuses. After all, it seems so un-American to quiet the mind.

About five years ago, I was invited to spend a week with some guy friends on a fishing trip in northern Wisconsin. It was a great time, as we say, "to get away from it all." The day before we were to leave, however, it happened. It was a quiet sunny afternoon. Since the other guys were either resting or otherwise occupied, I decided to go fishing by myself. So, there I was in a rowboat alone in a lily pond area. I threw my line in and saw the bobber resting among the lilies. All there was now was the boat, the fishing pole, and the bobber among the lilies. A rest came over me and it was as if time stopped or at least also rested. I have no idea how long clock time had passed but suddenly I became aware that my mind had quieted. It, too, became a beauty moment. I was like a child having discovered something. I actually thought of calling my wife and telling her but fortunately had no cell phone. It would have broken the moment. It is not as though these kinds of things have not happened to me before. Nor do I believe I am the only one to experience such moments. The real issue is intentionally making the place and time to be reminded of our own inner center and the sense of unity internally with myself and externally with the world.

It is hard in our culture to quiet the mind. The last thing we need is to feel guilty about not being mindful to create time and place. We are not taught this early on in our lives, nor is its value recognized enough even in the world of religion which has had a long history of contemplation and meditation. Let's face it, thinking dominates. It even interferes with our sleep. So many people wake in the middle of the night and cannot stop thinking of the previous day or the upcoming one and what was done or needing to be done, how to do it, when to get at it, can it be done, etc. Lying awake at night trying to stop thinking but then, in frustration, knowing that thinking about not thinking creates an endless cycle. I have heard it said the Hopi Indians have a saying: "All house cats at nighttime become mountain lions." How very true this is. In the middle of the night, thoughts take on sometimes monstrous proportions only to find the next day the nighttime issues, in most cases, were quite doable.

Regardless of such experiences and those that parallel them, thinking is a very valuable function as Jung and so many others have made clear. We know this from our own experience. Without clear thinking on a personal and collective level we would all be in serious trouble. If the logic of thinking can see that it makes sense to be aware of the fact and data, or simply, the gifts of the sensate function, it would have detailed information to back up any given thought. Then, also, if the logic of thinking were to make room for the intuitive function, it might have imagination and hunches that would act as doors for expanding further thinking. Again, remember Einstein's words. But then the tough one, the feeling function, and the one that is in the fuzzy zone of unawareness, of unconsciousness. It is not impossible, though, for the thinking person to access the feelings behind any thinking logic. It is just that this awareness comes after the fact if at all. But if it does come, it will tend to humanize any logic whether to more deeply validate it or qualify it.

In the end, the ability to think is a great achievement in human evolution. Our caution is that it can be used for good or evil and justify any act or opinion. I have frequently said that the words "religion" and "politics" have been in the linguistic trash can. They do not carry the original meanings of these two great words. Now the word "thinking" is dangerously close to joining them, for where else is thinking used so much if not in the world of religion and politics, which has seen the best and the worse of human endeavors—all of which comes down to how and about what we think. In the final analysis, we must truly consciously think and not just think that we are thinking which is an unconscious act. The difference will make or break us personally and collectively.

NOTE

1. Often attributed to Einstein, but its attribution is uncertain. [C.E.]

Chapter 3

How My Mind Works and Visualizes the World

Temple Grandin

When I was in my twenties, I assumed that everybody's mind worked the same way my mind worked. Over the years, I have become increasingly aware that my way of thinking is radically different than the mind of a person who thinks in words.

My first insight that my thought process was really different occurred during a discussion with a woman at a conference. We discussed how thoughts occurred in her head and in my head. When I think about an object, such as a church steeple, I see many different specific examples. My concept of what a church steeple is is based on many different ones I have seen in the past. The images flash into my imagination like a series of PowerPoint slides. I was shocked when the lady told me that the only image that came into her mind was a vague "pointy thing." Her image of a steeple was vague lines, and my thoughts were photographs of steeples I had seen in the past. In previous writings in my book *Thinking in Pictures*, I describe how I see pictures of different individual church steeples. You may wonder why I chose church steeples. It is something most people don't own, but everybody sees them. I discovered that if I ask about something a person is really familiar with, such as their own house or dog, they will see it. They are more likely to see a vague image if I ask about something they do not own.

SEEING VISUAL DETAIL

In my animal behavior work in the early 1970s, it was obvious to me that I should get into the cattle handling system and see what the cows were seeing. I learned that visual distractions that many people fail to notice will attract the animal's attention and cause it to stop moving through the chute. Cattle may refuse to move when they see a shadow, a reflection on shiny metal, a coat on a fence, a person walking by, or a sunbeam. If visual distractions are removed, the animals will move more easily. Over the years, I have written extensively about cattle handling, and I have provided checklists of all the distractions that may impede animal movement. Even when people have my instructions, they often fail to see the visual distractions that are slowing down cattle movement. This may give me job security as a cattle handling consultant, but I find it frustrating that people do not see it.

Recently, I visited two places that were having cattle handling problems and I immediately saw their problems. At the first location, approaching cattle could see motion of people through holes in a door. A few pieces of tape fixed the problem. At the second place, the motion of moving people was visible through cracks around a door. When I point it out, they often scratch their heads and wonder why they failed to see it. At a third place, cattle stopped and refused to approach a gate that was jiggling. Stopping the jiggling immediately improved movement.

Why is this important? Understanding how I think differently can help me learn how to work better with the more verbal thinkers. Verbal thinkers have to have the overall concept first. This is top-down thinking. Top-down thinkers tend to overgeneralize because the concept is verbal. People ask me all the time to help them solve animal behavior problems. A dog owner might say something vague such as, "What do I do about my crazy dog?" I actually get these kinds of questions all the time. They expect me to provide an immediate answer. The first thing I need to find out is: Is the dog crazy happy, jumping on people, or crazy nasty and biting? Correcting these two different problems requires different methods of training. To answer the question and provide answers that may help the dog owner, I have to get additional information. Some of the additional information I will need is when and where does the dog perform the behavior, and whom it is directed at.

ARTIFICIAL INTELLIGENCE

About two years ago, I started reading about how computers solve problems. I was shocked to learn that artificial intelligence (AI) systems are bottom-up thinkers. AI thinks the same way I do. Specific examples are put into categories to form concepts. In my book *The Autistic Brain* and other writings, I discuss bottom-up thinking. When I was three years old, I was severely autistic with no speech. Fortunately, intensive therapy got me talking. Over the last twenty years, people have told me that I have become less autistic. At the age of seventy, I became a better communicator compared to age fifty. The reason for this is due to adding additional data to my database. I can create smaller and smaller, more nuanced categories filled with additional specific information. This is also how an AI system works. It has to be trained with a huge amount of data. There are AI systems that can read lung X-rays and diagnose melanoma. The program is trained by showing it hundreds of specific examples of melanomas and other skin lesions.

It was a mind-blowing experience for me to learn that my mind works like an AI system. It turns out that the computer programmers are creating the autistic brain with electronic circuits. When I read about AI systems in various science magazines, it was weird to learn that the programmers do not fully understand how they work. When circuits are assembled in an architecture that resembles the brain, they are too complex to fully understand. One thing these systems need is a really good nonelectronic mechanical off switch. It should instantly disconnect the AI system from its power supply. I want to have the ability to shut off the system if something goes wrong.

Visual thinkers see risks. Many important systems are increasingly being run by computers. I can see vulnerabilities that others may not see. I have learned that the mathematically minded engineers may not see vulnerabilities that I can see in pictures. In my TED talk and in *The Autistic Brain* book, I discuss a third thinking style. It is the pattern thinking mind of the mathematician. They think in patterns instead of words or pictures.

A prime example of a visual thinking failure is the meltdown of the Fukushima nuclear power plant. A visual thinking mistake was made that was so obvious to me that I could not believe they made it. It is a really bad idea when a reactor is located near the sea to put the super important electrically operated emergency cooling pump in a nonwaterproof basement. If they had installed watertight doors, the accident would not have happened. The engineers did not "see" water filling the basement. Instead they attempted to calculate risk with mathematics. I can see water filling the basement, and electrical equipment does not work underwater. I cannot possibly design a nuclear reactor, but they need me to visualize serious things that could go wrong. I could see the flooding risk and tell them that they must install watertight doors.

Chapter 4

SEEKING Thinking

Greed and Need in Affective Neuroscience

Lucy Biven

What gives us zest for life yet makes us restless and dissatisfied? Why do we become addicted? Why can we think rationally but also harbor crazy irrational ideas? Why do we dream? The answer in all cases lies in an emotional system that is the topic of this article.

In the 1990s, Jaak Panksepp identified seven basic emotional systems that evolved long ago and have been retained throughout mammalian evolution. All mammalian brains contain these seven ancient emotional systems. In contrast, the more recently evolved cortex differs dramatically from one species to another, which is why mammals have different perceptual acuities and levels of intelligence. Emotionally, however, we are all cousins (Panksepp, 1998; Damasio, 1999).

Panksepp used simple words to describe these systems, but he wrote the words in capital letters to highlight the fact that emotional systems are physical entities rather than metaphorical descriptions. Each system consists of specific brain structures, and each is fueled by specific chemicals. Briefly, these systems are SEEKING (enthused curiosity), FEAR (typically of physical danger or death, but you can also be afraid of any threat, like a tax audit), RAGE (in the face of threat or frustration), LUST (the sexual urge), GRIEF (a system that has a positive and negative side; the negative side generates misery in the face of social isolation and the positive side generates contented comfort when in the company of friends and family), CARE (the urge to nurture, which is typically, but not exclusively, maternal), and PLAY (joyful friendly competition) (Panksepp, 1998). Some of these systems are also found in vertebrate brains; birds, for example, have GRIEF systems, and baby birds cry in distress when separated from their mothers (Panksepp & Biven, 2012).

Each emotional system causes two things to happen. First are physical responses. These included reactions inside the body, like the influx of stress chemicals that cause pupil dilation, elevated blood pressure, sweating, churning stomach, and so on. Emotional reactions also include behaviors like smiling, frowning, approaching, or running away. When neuroscientists speak of *emotion*, they refer to these purely physical responses and behaviors. The second response caused by emotional arousal is emotional feeling or *affect*. Affects include feelings like curiosity, fear, rage, lust, sorrow, contentment, tenderness, and joy.

Much of Panksepp's research was carried out on animals, and you might ask how we can know that animals experience affects because they cannot tell us how they feel. The answer lies in a series of experiments, the first of which was carried out in the middle of the last century. Two researchers, Giuseppi Moruzzi and Horace W. Magoun, destroyed a cat's cortex but left the brainstem intact. Even in the absence of a cortex, the cats remained awake. The reverse, however, did not hold true. When a cat's brainstem was destroyed and the cortex was left intact, the cat fell into a permanently comatose state (Moruzzi & Magoun, 1949).

Embedded in the brainstem is a loosely knit conglomeration of cell bodies and neuronal fibers known as the extended reticular thalamic activating system (ERTAS). Moruzzi and Magoun discovered that the ERTAS generates wakefulness in the absence of the cortex (Watt & Pincus, 2004). Even when the cortex is intact, it cannot wake up—we cannot think or perceive—without input from the ERTAS (Yeo et al., 2013). This result was a great surprise. Before Moruzzi and Magoun's experiments, almost everyone believed that the cortex was the part of the brain that created consciousness (Solms, 2013). Nobody thought that the brainstem had anything to do with conscious mental functions (Solms, 2000).

These results were replicated in human beings. The surgical removal of parts of the human cortex removed aspects of consciousness such as sight or hearing but did not disrupt consciousness itself (Penfield & Jasper, 1954). However, people who suffer pervasive ERTAS damage as a result of injury or illness also become irrevocably comatose (Cochrane & Williams, 2015).

Other experiments destroyed increasingly deeper layers of the brain. The lower the level of destruction, the more completely was motivated, purposeful behavior obliterated (Panksepp, 1998; Watt & Pinkus, 2004; Merker, 2007; Panksepp & Trevarthen, 2009). When the brainstem was destroyed, all motivated behavior was extinguished, and the animal became comatose (Solms, 2018). It seemed that deep brain structures, especially those in and around the brainstem, generated not just wakefulness but motivation, which appeared to be a cardinal feature of consciousness.

Most of us believe that we are motivated by thoughts. I send my sister flowers for her birthday because I know she will be touched that I remembered. However, deep subcortical brain structures cannot generate ideas. What kind of motivation is provided by deep brain structures?

A clue is found in research about pleasure and pain. Painful stimuli are processed along two neural pathways. The *sensory discriminative* pathway encodes the nature of pain: whether it is sharp, dull, throbbing, or scratchy; its location in or on the body; as well as how intense it is. This pathway is located quite high in the brain, coursing through the somatosensory thalamus, as well as the primary and secondary somatosensory cortices. In spite of the fact that the sensory/discriminative pathway provides detailed information about pain, it does not include any suffering (Auvray et al., 2010).

The second pain pathway involves deeper structures like the medial thalamus and the amygdala (a small almond-shaped structure located in the temporal lobe) (Auvray et al., 2010), as well as structures in the brainstem. It is called the *affective/motivational* pathway, and it generates the ouch factor—the experience of physical pain and suffering (Melzack & Casey, 1968; Auvray et al., 2010).

Suppose that I slammed my hand in a car door. The sensory/discriminative pathway in my brain would register that the pain was in my hand, that it was due to pressure, and that it was intense, but this information would not cause me any distress. The deeper affective/motivational pathway would generate my miserable experience of physical pain.

Subsequent research about empathy demonstrated that many of the brain structures that cause physical pain and suffering overlap with brain structures that generate empathy with other people who are in physical pain. These overlapping structures include subcortical structures in and around the brainstem (Decety et al., 2008).

If you saw me slam my hand in the car door, you might wince or even rub your hand although it did not hurt. You would do this because many of the brain structures that cause you to empathize with me are the same structures that are active in my brain when I experience physical pain. Empathy is an affective response. When you empathize with my physical pain, you are in affective pain. This research indicated physical and affective pain emerge from many of the same subcortical/brainstem regions.

Research about physical and affective pleasure presents a similar picture. Studies on the pleasure of sweet tastes reveal that the pleasure in sweetness must be generated by an affective *hedonic gloss*, as well as by purely sensory systems in the brain. Many of these sensory and hedonic substrates are subcortical and they include the brainstem (Berridge & Kringelbach, 2011; Berridge & Dayan, 2021).

This evidence indicates that the brainstem and surrounding structures in the human brain generate motivating feelings of pleasure and pain that include affective feelings. Subcortical mammalian brains are virtually identical (Panksepp, 1998). Therefore it is reasonable to believe that the same subcortical structures in the brains of other mammals also generate affective pleasure and pain. This is why Panksepp believed that other animals are affective creatures. When they exhibit emotional behaviors, we can believe that they experience corresponding affects.

This evidence also poses a hypothesis that has far-reaching implications about the nature of consciousness. There are many neural connections between all emotional systems and the ERTAS. The thinking cortex cannot function without prompting by the ERTAS. If emotional systems and the ERTAS work together, this suggests that the cortex cannot function without affective arousal. Affects are aroused by particular things and situations. When the cortex is aroused, it thinks about those things and situations. If this line of thinking is on the right track, it indicates that affects guide our thoughts (Watt, 2001; Panksepp & Biven, 2012).

THE PRIMACY OF THE SEEKING SYSTEM

Panksepp's SEEKING system provides answers to the questions posed at the beginning of this discussion. It explains why we have a zest for life but why we are apt to be dissatisfied. It explains addiction. It explains why we think rationally and why we have crazy thoughts. It also explains why we dream.

The SEEKING system holds a special place in Panksepp's taxonomy because it energizes all the other systems. A pregnant cat will look for a quiet, secluded spot to give birth, rearranging bedding and kneading blankets to make them soft. Her CARE system motivates this nurturant behavior, but the SEEKING system gives her the energy and drive to carry it out. Even when danger arouses our FEAR systems, our SEEKING system prompts us to find a way to escape. In the wild, the SEEKING system prompts hungry and thirsty animals to find food and water. Without this system, other emotional systems fail to function. If it is damaged, animals are lethargic and appear depressed. They do not bother to eat available food and they usually die unless they are carefully nursed (Panksepp, 1998).

SEEKING ORIGINS

Discovery of the SEEKING system began in the middle of the last century when two Canadian researchers, James Olds and Peter Milner, discovered that animals would vigorously *self-stimulate* particular subcortical brain structures. Self-stimulation occurs when an electrode is placed in a part of an animal's brain. The animal then learns to work—to perform a task like pressing a lever—in order to electrically stimulate that brain region. In this case, the electrode was placed in the *lateral hypothalamus* and in the *medial forebrain bundle* (LH/MFB). The medial forebrain bundle is a collection of neural fibers that pass through the lateral hypothalamus (Olds, 1977).

Animals work in order to obtain rewards or avoid punishments (Cherry, 2019), and this brain stimulation appeared to be extremely rewarding because animals would press levers frantically, to the point of exhaustion and even death, in order to achieve electrical stimulation of the LH/MFB (Panksepp, 1998).

Neuroscientists now know that the LH/MFB is part of a system known as the *mesolimbic pathway*, which is fueled by the brain chemical *dopamine*. All laboratory animals ever tested become readily addicted to drugs like cocaine and methamphetamine, which prolong dopamine activity at synapses along the mesolimbic pathway and keep it in an active state. When animals take these drugs, they exhibit the same enthused frenetic behavior that Olds and Milner observed when they applied electrical stimulation (Panksepp, 1998).

At first, researchers thought that the mesolimbic pathway was rewarding because it signaled feelings that hungry or thirsty animals have when they consume a good meal or a long drink. However, experiments by Kent Berridge demonstrated that the mesolimbic pathway lights up before eating and drinking and closes down when animals start to eat or drink. In other words, the mesolimbic pathway is a signal indicating that hungry or thirsty animals want to eat or drink (Berridge, 2007). But Berridge's research did not explain why mesolimbic stimulation is rewarding. After all, it occurs typically when animals are hungry or thirsty, which are unpleasant states. Years earlier Panksepp proposed that arousal of the mesolimbic pathway is rewarding because it generates positive affects characterized by euphoric anticipation, curiosity about novel things, confident feelings of personal agency, and a willingness to take risks (Panksepp & Biven, 2012). Other researchers agree that the mesolimbic dopamine system is rewarding because it provides the happiness of pursuit rather than the happiness of reaching a goal (Sapolsky, 2023).

Subjective experience supports Panksepp's view. When the mesolimbic pathway is electrically stimulated in the human brain or when people take cocaine or meth, they do not describe the relaxed sense of satisfaction and contentment after a good meal, a deep drink on a hot day, or the glow following sexual consummation. Rather they report a high-hearted sense of antici-pation when they are looking forward to those rewards (Panksepp, 1998).

Panksepp renamed this rewarding dopamine/mesolimbic pathway the SEEKING system because when animals are given free arousal of the mesolimbic pathway—when they do not have to work in order to obtain electrical stimulation—they immediately explore their environments, examining nooks and crannies with purpose and enthusiasm. Rats sniff vigorously, which they typically do when they are looking for something—when they are seeking (Panksepp, 1998).

THINKING

What does all this have to do with thinking? Everything. There are numerous neural connections between all emotional systems, including the SEEKING system and the cognitive cortex. The SEEKING system plays a role in all appetitive behavior. When it is aroused, we think about the things we want and we devise cognitive strategies to get them (Panksepp & Biven, 2012).

You are probably reading this book because your SEEKING system prompted you to learn more about the nature of thinking. You imagined that after reading it, you would be wiser, or at least more informed than you were. You took the time to find the book and spent your money to obtain it. If you plan a dinner party, you think about your friends sitting happily about your table. You plan the meal, poring through cookbooks and taking care to provide favorite foods and avoid any allergies. If you are keen on getting a job at a particular firm, you think about the money you will make and about the prestige of your desired position. You learn about the firm, its personnel, its latest achievements and drawbacks, and how your particular talents and personality will fit in. If you are interested in dating a woman, you ponder how great it will be to have her as your girlfriend and even muse on the possibility of marriage. You get to know her friends and find out about her likes, dislikes, and habits. You might devise ways of meeting up with her apparently on accident.

TWO STRANGE FEATURES OF THE SEEKING SYSTEM

The SEEKING system generates two peculiar behavioral phenomena. The first are *adjunctive* ritualistic behaviors. B. F. Skinner (who had no interest in emotion) noted that hungry pigeons would engage in a predictable wing-flapping, strutting dance between receiving small morsels of food (Panksepp, 1998). Extreme hunger unconditionally arouses the SEEKING system (Ceunen et al., 2016), indicating that the system drives this dancing behavior. One sees similar behaviors in other animals, including our own species. A hungry rat might run at its spinning wheel or shred paper. We too tend to pace or fidget when we are hungry. These behaviors do nothing to relieve distress, which is why they are seen as adjunctive.

Adjunctive behaviors do, however, have an adaptive function because they generate repetitive actions. Most skills require repetition in order to be properly honed. Think back to when you learned to ride a bike. No doubt you got some instruction, but after a while you developed your own individual pattern. Perhaps you sat on the seat, steadying yourself with your right foot, while placing your left foot on the pedal. You pushed off with your right foot as you pressed down on your left, leaning your torso forward at a particular angle that felt comfortable and right. This became your habitual and efficient way of starting off.

One sees rituals of this sort all the time. Some are adaptive and some are not. When men shave, they usually begin with one part of the face before going on to other parts. They will typically move their mouths over to one cheek, down to the chin, and move the lower lip over their bottom teeth in order to shave the hairs around the mouth. These ritualistic habits help them to shave more efficiently. Tennis players typically bounce the ball a set number of times, or adjust different parts of their shirts, before serving. This does not help with their game, at least not in any direct way. But they hold the racket in a particular grip and throw the ball in the air with a typical amount of force. All these habits contribute to the accuracy of their serves.

The second strange phenomenon associated with SEEKING arousal is *autoshaping*, which appears to be a cause-and-effect behavior. In the laboratory, autoshaping emerges when a very hungry animal (whose SEEKING system aroused) is exposed to a short extraneous stimulus. In one experiment with pigeons, a key above the pigeon's food tray is lit just before the delivery of food. Soon the pigeon will begin to interact with the key, usually by pecking on it. Indeed, pigeons will continue pecking at the lit key long after food delivery has ceased. To our intelligent brains, it might seem that the pigeon has reasoned that the lit key causes the food to appear. The same sort of behavior happens with rats, although the rat usually sniffs about the lit key. To us it seems that the rat thinks there is a causal connection between the lit key and food. It is unlikely, however, that either the pigeon or the rat is capable of reasoning about cause and effect. Their prefrontal cortex, the part of the brain that is capable of reasoning, is very small, as are their cognitive capacities. Instead it appears that autoshaping is directly generated by SEEKING arousal (Panksepp & Biven, 2012).

In these kinds of laboratory experiments, the lit key bears no causal relationship to food delivery, but in the real world, extraneous stimuli often provide adaptive cues. Consider a hungry bird of prey flying above a lake when it sees a silver flash in the water. This silver flash, like the lit key in the laboratory experiment, is a novel extraneous stimulus that arouses the bird's

SEEKING system, and it dives down to see it at closer range. It turns out that the silver color was caused by a fish on the surface. The bird catches the fish, and from then on the flash of silver reliably indicates a good meal.

Unlike other animals, we humans possess a large cortex that is capable of discerning cause and effect. A deer hunter follows fresh droppings in the woods because he knows it means that the deer is not far off. Gathering clouds predict a rain shower and we go indoors. Of course, cause-and-effect reasoning is fallible. It might seem reasonable to believe that by lowering taxes on business, the government will have less money. But this is not always the case. When businesses do not pay as much in taxes, they have more money to grow and hire more employees who themselves pay taxes, thereby increasing overall government revenue.

You can imagine that in the case of the bird of prey, adjunctive behavior and autoshaping work in tandem. Autoshaping causes the bird to notice the silver flash in the water, and over time adjunctive behaviors hone an efficient way of swooping down and catching the fish. The same can be said of any skill. When you saw your big brother riding a bike, it sparked your interest, much like the lit key. Even though you probably fell over a few times, scraping your knees and elbows, you did not lose your ambition to ride as well as your brother. In time, you developed good skills and you too became a bike-riding expert.

SUPERSTITIONS AND RELIGIOUS BELIEFS

Autoshaping and adjunctive behaviors play a role in superstition. Gamblers are notorious in believing that particular actions or objects will affect the outcome of the game or race on which they place bets. They develop rituals like blowing on dice, knocking on wood, crossing their fingers, and rubbing a talisman to bring them luck.

Autoshaping and adjunctive behaviors may also play a role in religious rituals. Consider tribal people enduring a drought. In a moment of frustration, one of them might kick at the ground. If rain followed, they might believe that this action had caused the rain. In time, this manner of kicking the ground might turn into a ritualized dance that was designed to bring on rain (Panksepp & Biven, 2012).

Adjunctive behaviors and autoshaping might also play a role in the development of religious symbols. Suppose that during the drought, a tribesman absentmindedly whittled a piece of wood, which turned out to resemble a wolf. When the rains came, this piece of wood might attract the attention of the village elders, who might think that wolves had supernatural powers to bring on rain. From then on, they would perform religious rituals involving wolf icons (Panksepp & Biven, 2012).

ADDICTION

Although the dopamine/SEEKING system is essential in living a productive life, it has a downside in the creation of addictions. The matter of dopamine and addiction is tricky because one can become addicted to dopamine itself, which is what happens to cocaine and meth addicts. They crave the enthused state of hyperarousal that attends dopamine secretion. But dopamine plays a role even when you are addicted to a different kind of sensation (Diana, 2011). Opiates like heroin or morphine produce a sense of relaxing pleasure, which is in many ways the opposite of a dopamine rush. Nevertheless, dopamine plays a role in opiate addictions because addicts look forward to taking the drug. For a heroin addict, obtaining the drug, setting up the paraphernalia, heating it, and so on are attended by dopamine secretion. Alcoholics crave a fuzzy sense of oblivion, but they are enthused by dopamine when they choose a bottle, open it, and pour out the drink. Tobacco smokers crave a nicotine hit, but dopamine causes them to be enthused when they open a new pack, tap down the tobacco in the cigarette, and spark up their lighters. In sex addiction the search for a sexual partner is exciting, though different than the gratification of the sex act. Weed smokers are animated when they deftly encase marijuana in cigarette paper. Gambling, overeating, and any other kind of addiction you can think of are partially fueled by dopamine (Panksepp, 1998).

Because the SEEKING system responds to novelty, it is easy to become addicted to novelty itself. Walking down the street, you regularly see people addicted to their phones, checking the Internet and social media to learn something—anything—new. Nowadays these activities are known as "dopamine hits," which is exactly what they are. In Panksepp's terms, they are SEEKING addictions (Panksepp & Biven, 2012).

Although all laboratory animals become readily addicted to dopamine-enhancing drugs, it is not so easy to create drug addicts in the wild. A lab rat leads a boring life with few distractions to arouse its dopamine SEEKING system, so when you give meth or cocaine to the rat, it will enjoy the enthused affects that dopamine provides. In the wild, however, there are a multitude of interesting stimuli, such as family, interactions with society at large, foraging for food, fights for turf, pursuing a mate, avoidance of predators, and so on. These normal life stimuli arouse the animal's SEEKING system, giving it a multitude of dopamine hits. These animals do not need drugs to enjoy the affective rewards of dopamine, which is why they do not easily become addicted to artificial stimulation (Peterson & Sapolsky, 2023).

RISK TAKING

The SEEKING system generates a sense of personal agency that encourages us to take risks. If we are reckless, risk taking can have bad consequences, but considered risk taking is a ubiquitous feature of life. We take risks when we choose a career, get married, have children, buy a house, engage in sports, or cross the street.

Considered risk taking is a sign of good mental health. Life is interesting and exciting when we take risks. When a risk has a good outcome, we become more confident. If risk results in failure, it gives us an opportunity to correct our mistakes (Derrow, 2019). Risk taking is also essential for social progress. In Mark Zuckerberg's view, the most egregious risk in business is the refusal to take risks (Zuckerberg, 2017).

The Wright brothers, for example, were not daredevils. Because they knew the dangers involved, they rarely flew together. Yet they repeatedly risked their lives because of their burning desire—a manifestation of their SEEK-ING systems—to conquer flight. Their efforts were beset by many disappointments, each of which they addressed with dogged perseverance. For example, in the early days, they flew gliders. A drawback of the glider was that it flew in a straight line. Only when the pilot shifted his weight would the direction and altitude change. But weight shifting was hazardous and imprecise. The brothers wanted to find a way for the pilot to control direction by means of mechanical manipulation. They achieved this by testing over a hundred wing designs before inventing what they called "wing warping," a method of inducing a helical twist of the wings. By lifting one wing and decreasing the other, the pilot could cause the glider to climb, dive, and bank to the left or right. The brothers tested these new gliders nearly a thousand times (Crouch, 2024).

The Wright brothers were not reckless, but they were fearless. In 1908, Orville's plane crashed from an altitude of 125 feet, killing his passenger and causing a hip injury that led to medical complications for the rest of his life (Akpan, 2015). When Orville was recovering from his injuries, a friend asked if he had lost his nerve. Orville replied, "Oh, do you mean will I be *afraid* to fly again? The only thing I'm afraid of is that I can't get well soon enough to finish those tests next year" (Kelly, 1989).

Why were they not afraid as most of us would be? An answer is found in an examination of extreme sports like sky diving, rock climbing, skiing, hang gliding, and the like. When people engage in extreme sports, they continually confront and overcome new challenges that cause a dopamine surge. This is why they find these sports so thrilling. Extreme sportsmen become embroiled in repeating tides of dopamine. The Wright brothers were not addicted to danger, but they were addicted to the challenge of conquering flight. Like the SEEKING systems of extreme athletes, their systems were operating in overdrive, and probably this ongoing dopamine rush obliterated their fear.

GREED AND NEED

SEEKING arousal is essential for a productive life. Without it, animals would not look for food, water, or a mate. Individual animals would die as would the species. We humans would be devoid of ambition and would achieve nothing. However, a curious aspect of SEEKING arousal is that it makes us want more. The thing that satisfies us today is tomorrow's disappointment. The comedian Bill Burr once said that when a joke got a big laugh, he wanted to tell another that got a bigger laugh. We all want more.

Robert Sapolsky explains that the dopamine SEEKING system resets after each reward, which means we habituate to a reward, and it no longer provides the same excitement. We always want to recapture that excitement in another reward (Peterson & Sapolsky, 2023). Suppose that you have a bite of an exquisite cake. The unique flavor and texture fill you with delight. If you have the same cake tomorrow, it will still be delicious, but it will not provide the same surprised pleasure. The day after that, you will be craving the thrill of your first bite, and you will be searching for a new and even more delicious cake.

This wish for more has both productive and tragic consequences. The consequences are productive because the SEEKING system prompts us to create and discover new and interesting things. All the arts and sciences, all individual achievement, civilization itself, would grind to a halt if we were not constantly searching for something better. Comedians want to tell a better joke, artists want to create a better painting, engineers want to make a better machine, doctors want to find better treatments, and everyone seems to want a better and fitter body. The consequences are tragic because we are never satisfied with what we have. One dopamine hit raises our expectations, but we soon habituate, and we are always looking for a bigger and better hit (Peterson & Sapolsky, 2023).

SEEKING PATHOLOGY

Psychotic disorders like schizophrenia and mania result from a surfeit of dopamine activity in the SEEKING mesolimbic pathway. Similarly, when people take large quantities of drugs like meth or cocaine for long periods of time, their SEEKING systems become overactive, and they develop psychotic delusions. Normally, the SEEKING system induces us to think in terms of cause and effect and we feel an enhanced sense of personal agency. When this system is overstimulated, these features go into overdrive. A psychotic person may see cause and effect in irrationally extravagant ways. For example, if a psychotic person has accidentally broken a mirror, she might believe that this accident caused someone else to become ill or die. Psychotics also are apt to suffer from delusions of grandeur, wildly overestimating their beauty, talents, or intelligence. This kind of thinking is an exaggeration of the confidence that attends normal SEEKING arousal. It is no surprise that neuroleptic medications are effective antipsychotics because they inhibit dopamine activity along the SEEKING mesolimbic pathway (Ameer et al., 2024).

DEPRESSION

On the other end of the scale is an underactive dopamine system. When dopamine is underactive, the SEEKING system is sluggish and the anticipation of good outcomes wanes. Life becomes empty, without hope of happiness or fulfillment. SEEKING underarousal can occur when someone has suffered a crushing disappointment or loss. Such unfortunate people do not think productively but rather tend to perseverate on unhappy ruminations (Panksepp & Watt, 2011).

DREAMS

Dreams, like psychosis, are characterized by delusional thoughts. Neuroscientists discovered a brain mechanism known as rapid eye movement (REM) that occurs about every ninety minutes during sleep. It is during REM episodes that most dreaming occurs. REM is generated by the *pons*, a structure that lies deep in the brainstem. The pons is incapable of generating the mental activity that is present in dreams. This led neuroscientists to conclude that REM activity in the pons randomly activates the cortex when we dream. In their view, dreams are nothing more than haphazard, meaningless hallucinations. This view discredited Freud's theory that dreams were psychologically meaningful (Solms, 2023).

Research by Mark Solms demonstrated that the REM/dream equation was incorrect. Solms worked with patients who had suffered brain damage and discovered that REM and dreaming are independent of each other. Damage to REM-generating pons does not cause dreams to cease. Instead dreaming relies on two other brain areas. The first is the part of the cortex responsible for visual and spatial perception and for cognition. This accounts for the vivid sensory content and ideation of dreams. The second area on which dreaming depends is the SEEKING system, the part of the brain that wants things. Solms concluded that dreams are hallucinations about the things that we want. Thus, Solms rehabilitated Freud's theory that dreams are hallucinatory wish fulfillments (Solms, 2000).[1]

The theory of dreams as wish fulfillment has difficulty explaining why we have nightmares, which feel like the opposite of wish fulfillment. According to Freudian theory, dreams are powered by an urge to gratify brazen sexual and aggressive wishes that are either socially unacceptable, morally repugnant, or both. In dreams, the rational part of the mind, which Freud called the *ego*, transforms these unacceptable impulses, rendering them more palatable. For example, the wish to kill may be transformed into a dream about winning a competitive game. Nightmares occur when this ameliorating ego transformation fails. If you dreamt about actually killing a rival, your ego would react with anxiety, which is why the dream would be a nightmare (Brenner, 1955).

Neuroscience offers an alternative explanation for nightmares. Emotional systems can be sensitized by experience. *If a rat is repeatedly* exposed to a cat, the exposure creates new neural connections within the structures that constitute the rat's FEAR system (Adamec et al., 2009). Thereafter the rat becomes generally anxious and fearful. GRIEF systems in young animals can also be sensitized by poor maternal care or by prolonged separations from mother. If rat pups are separated from their mothers and kept in isolation, the number of *opioid* receptors in their brains decreases (Bernardi et al., 1986). Opioids are brain chemicals that create a sense of emotional comfort that young animals enjoy when under the care of an attentive and affectionate mother. Damage to the GRIEF system appears to be permanent and these neglected youngsters continue to be anxious into adulthood (Daniels et al., 2004).

If a negative emotional system like FEAR or GRIEF is sensitized, it can generate negative affects and corresponding ideation in dreams. These dreams are not wishes. They are the painful expression of a sensitized system. A person who has endured this kind of sensitization will be more likely to have bad dreams, as well as an unhappy waking life (Biven, 2022).

SUMMARY

This article began by explaining a hypothesis held by Panksepp and a number of his colleagues—namely, that affects are the most fundamental form of consciousness and that we think about the things that arouse our affects. The SEEKING system generates affects of enthusiasm, curiosity, and confidence. It causes the cortex to generate thoughts about the things we want and how to get them. When the SEEKING system is working well, we think rationally in terms of cause and effect, and we have the will, energy, and daring to achieve our goals. However, it can go awry, inducing addiction, superstition, and, at worst, insanity. Despite its pitfalls, the SEEKING system is a blessing that nature has given us. It provides a wellspring of personal happiness when we strive for our goals. By striving and attaining these, we create a better life.

NOTE

1. Current psychodynamic practice, including analytical psychology, has shown that dreams, and the unconscious in general, also serve to "correct the conscious attitude," according to Jung, and reveal our blind spots. [C.E.]

REFERENCES

Adamec, R., Berton, O., & Razek, W. A. (2009). Viral vector induction of CREB expression in the periaqueductal gray induces a predator stress-like pattern of changes in pCREB expression, neuroplasticity, and anxiety in rodents. *Neural Plasticity,* 2009. https://www.ncbi.nlm.nih.gov/pmc/articles/PMC2664642/.

Akpan, N. (2015). 8 things you didn't know about Orville Wright. *Science.* https://www.pbs.org/newshour/science/8-things-didnt-know-orville-wright.

Ameer, M. A., Patel, P., & Saadabadi, A. 2024. Neuroleptic medications. National Library of Medicine. https://www.ncbi.nlm.nih.gov/books/NBK459150/#:~:text=Neuroleptics%2C%20also%20known%20as%20antipsychotic,generation%20or%20%22atypical%22%20antipsychotics.

Auvray, M., Myin, E., & Spence, C. (2010). The sensory-discriminative and affective-motivational aspects of pain. *Neuroscience and Biobehavioral Reviews,* 34: 214–223 http://www.nstu.net/malika-auvray/files/malika-auvray-auvray-myin_spence_nbr_2010.pdf

Bernardi, M., Genedani, S., Tagliavini, S., & Bertolini, A. (1986). Effects on long-term sensitivity to pain and morphine of stress induced in the newborn rat by pain or manipulation. *Physiology & Behavior, 37,* 827–31.

Berridge, K. C. (2003). Pleasures of the brain. *Brain and Cognition, 52*(1), 106–28.

Berridge, K. (2007). The debate over dopamine's role in reward: the case for incentive salience. *Psychopharmacology,* 191: 391–431. http://citeseerx.ist.psu.edu/viewdoc/download?doi=10.1.1.122.4519&rep=rep1&type=pdf

Berridge, K., & Kringelbach, M. L. (2011). Building a neuroscience of pleasure and well-being. *SpringerOpen.* https://psywb.springeropen.com/articles/10.1186/2211-1522-1-3.

Berridge, K. C., & Kringelbach, M. L. (2015). Pleasure systems in the brain. *Neuron, 86.* https://lsa.umich.edu/psych/research&labs/berridge/publications/2015%20Berridge%20&%20Kringelbach%20Pleasure%20systems%20in%20the%20%20brain%20-%20Neuron.pdf.

Berridge, Kent C., & Dayan, P. (2021). Liking. *Current Biology,* 31.24: R1555–R1557.

Biven, L. (2022). *A Short-Cut to Understanding Affective Neuroscience.* Meadville, PA: Fulton Books.

Brenner, C. (1955). *An elementary textbook of psychoanalysis.* New York: International Universities Press, Inc.

Ceunen, E., Vlaeyen, J. W. S., & Van Diest, I. (2016). On the origin of interoception. *Frontiers in Psychology, 7,* 743. https://www.ncbi.nlm.nih.gov/pmc/articles/PMC4876111/.

Cherry, K. (2019). What Is Operant Conditioning and How Does It Work? How Reinforcement and Punishment Modify Behavior. https://www.verywellmind.com/operant-conditioning-a2-2794863

Cochrane, T. I. & Williams, M. A. (2015). "Disorders of Consciousness: Brain Death, Coma, Vegetative and Minimally Conscious States." *Dana Foundation.* https://dana.org/article/disorders-of-consciousness-brain-death-coma-and-the-vegetative-and-minimally-conscious-states/

Crouch, T. (2024). The Wright brothers: American aviators. Britannica. https://www
.britannica.com/biography/Wright-brothers.

Damasio, A. R. (1999). *The feeling of what happens: Body and emotion in the making
of consciousness*. New York: Harcourt Brace.

Daniels, W. M., Pieetersen, C. Y., Carstens, M. E., & Stein, D. J. (2004). Maternal
separation in rats leads to anxiety-like behavior and a blunted ACTH response and
altered neurotransmitter levels in response to a subsequent stressor. *Metab. Brain
Dis.*, 19(1–2): 3–14. https://www.ncbi.nlm.nih.gov/pubmed/15214501

Decety, J., Michalska, K., Kalina, J., Akitsuki, Y., & Lahey, B. B. (2008). Atypical
empathic responses in adolescents with aggressive conduct disorder: A functional
MRI investigation. *Biological Psychology*, 1–9.

Derrow, C. (2019). Why taking risks can be good for your mental health. *Entre-
preneurship Life*. https://www.entrepreneurshiplife.com/why-taking-risks-can-be
-good-for-your-mental-health/.

Diana, M. (2011). The dopamine hypothesis of drug addiction and its potential therapeutic value. *Frontiers in Psychology, 22*(64). https://www.ncbi.nlm.nih.gov/pmc
/articles/PMC3225760/.

Guyton, A. C., & Hall, J. E. (2006). *Textbook of medical physiology*. Philadelphia,
PA: Saunders Elsevier.

Kelley, A., & Berridge, K. C. (2002). The neuroscience of natural rewards: Relevance
to addictive drugs. *Journal of Neuroscience, 22*(9), 3306–11. https://www.jneuro-
sci.org/content/22/9/3306.

Kelly, F. C. (1989). *The Wright brothers: A biography*. New York: Dover Publications.

Kringelbach, M. L. (2010). The neuroscience of happiness and pleasure. *Social
Research, 77*(2), 659–78. https://www.ncbi.nlm.nih.gov/pmc/articles/PMC3008658.

Melzack, R. & Casey, K. L. (1968). Sensory, Motivational and Central Control of
Determinants of Pain. In The Skin Senses: Proceedings of the First International
Symposium on the Skin Senses Held at The Florida State University at Tallahas-
see, Florida. (Dan R. Shalo PhD. Ed.). Charles C. Thomas: Springfield, Ill. Chapter
20, pp. 423–439. http://www.researchgate.net/profile/Kenneth_Casey/publication
/233801589_Sensory_Motivational_and_Central_Control_Determinants_of_Pain/
links/0912f50ba3ff1ca8e9000000.pdf

Merker, B. (2007). Consciousness without a cerebral cortex: A challenge for neuroscience and medicine. *Behavioral and Brain Sciences* 30: 63–134. http://www
.willamette.edu/~levenick/cs448/Merker.pdf

Morgenson, G. J., & Kucharczyk, J. (1978). Central neural pathways for angiotensin-
induced thirst. *Federation Proceedings, 37*(13), 2683–88. https://pubmed.ncbi.nlm
.nih.gov/213317/.

Moruzzi, G. & Magoun, H. W. (1949). Brain stem reticular formation and activation
of the EEG. *Electroencephalography and Clinical Neurophysiology* 1: 455–73.
http://www.ncbi.nlm.nih.gov/pubmed/18421835

Olds, J. (1977). *Drives and Reinforcement*. New York: Raven.

Panksepp, J. (1998). *Affective neuroscience: The foundations of human and animal
emotions*. New York: Oxford University Press.

Panksepp, J., & Trevarthen, C. (2009). Psychobiology of music: Motive impulses
and emotions in expressions of musicality and in sympathetic emotional response

to music. In S. Malloch and C. Trevarthen (Eds.), *Communicative Musicality* (pp. 105–146). Cambridge, UK: Cambridge University Press.

Panksepp, J., & Watt, D. (2011). What is basic about basic emotions? Lasting lessons from affective neuroscience. *Emotion Review, 3*(4).

Panksepp, J., & Biven, L. (2012). *The archaeology of the mind: Neuroevolutionary origins of human emotions*. New York: Norton.

Penfield, W. & Jasper, H. H. (1954). *Epilepsy and the Functional Anatomy of the Human Brain*. Little, Brown, & Co.

Peterson, J., & Sapolsky, J. (2023). Of baboons and men. YouTube. https://www.youtube.com/watch?v=3Pup-XSH98o&ab_channel=JordanBPeterson.

Solms, M. (2000). Freudian dream theory today. *The Psychologist, 13*(12). https://faculty.fortlewis.edu/burke_b/personality/Readings/Dreams%20-%20Solms.pdf.

Solms, M. (2013). The Conscious Id. *Neuropsychoanalysis*, 15(1): 5–19. http://www.tandfonline.com/doi/pdf/10.1080/15294145.2013.10773711

Solms, M. (2018). The Hard Problem of Consciousness and the Free Energy Principle. *Front. Psychol.*, 29 January 2019. Sec. Psychoanalysis and Neuropsychoanalysis, volume 9. https://www.frontiersin.org/journals/psychology/articles/10.3389/fpsyg.2018.02714/full

Solms, M. (2023). Freud & the neuroscience of dreams. YouTube. https://www.youtube.com/watch?v=K2nr4vxMyv0&ab_channel=TheWeekendUniversity.

Stuber, G. D., & Wise, R. A. (2016). Lateral hypothalamic circuits for feeding and reward. *Nature Neuroscience, 19*(2), 198–205. https://www.ncbi.nlm.nih.gov/pmc/articles/PMC4927193/.

Watt, D. (2001). Affective neuroscience and extended reticular thalamic activating system (ertas) theories of consciousness. In Alfred Kaszniak (Ed.). *Series on Biophysics and Biocybernetics: Volume 10: Emotions, Qualia, and Consciousness*.

Watt, D. F. & Pincus, D. I. (2004). Neural substrates of consciousness: Implications for clinical psychiatry. In *Textbook of Biological Psychiatry*, J. Panksepp (ed.). Hoboken, NJ: Wiley.

Yeo, S. S., Chang, P. H., & Jang, S. H. (2013). The Ascending Reticular Activating System from Pontine Reticular Formation to the Thalamus in the Human Brain. *Front. Hum. Neurosci.*, 7: 416. https://www.ncbi.nlm.nih.gov/pmc/articles/PMC3722571/

Young, P. T. 1959. The role of affective processes in learning and motivation. *Psychological Review, 66*(2), 104–25.

Zuckerberg, M. (2017). Mark Zuckerberg on taking risks and finding talented people. YouTube. https://www.youtube.com/watch?v=VAUt2j6juHU.

Chapter 5

Thinking about Thinking[1]

Raymond Tallis

Philosophers spend much of their time thinking. Sometimes they think about thinking itself; but thinking about thought is a strange business. It should be impossible—like trying to navigate a stream in a boat made out of water.

We most often characterize thinking as "inner" (of which more presently) speech. "Speech" because, as Bryan Magee says in his *Confessions of a Philosopher*, we "cannot express in language what thought is like before it is translated into language." And so, as we cock our inner ears, we hear a voice "in our head"—the head being an ill-defined location closer to the intracranial darkness behind our eyes rather than, say, to our feet or indeed the rest of the universe.

It is tempting to think that this imaginary sound is necessary so that we can inform ourselves as to what we are thinking. This hardly holds up: it would suggest that we require our thoughts to be fully formed *before* we tell ourselves what they are. We would end up having to have our thoughts before we know what thoughts we are having. At this point vertigo beckons. Let us temporarily retreat from philosophy to psychology.

Psychologists have pointed out that our silent soliloquy, footnoting our wakefulness from early childhood to our final days, serves many functions. As well as assisting us to plan, control, and direct our actions, thoughts also propose alternative realities. All in all, thinking to ourselves seems an instance of something that Wittgenstein said was impossible: the right hand giving the left hand a gift. Talking to ourselves is a part of the process of registering and making sense of what is going on in and around us. Articulated, that sense becomes "we" sense, an internalization of dialogue. As Charles Fernyhough put it in his excellent *The Voices Within: The History and Science of How We Talk to Ourselves*, "A solitary mind is actually a chorus."

Our heads are echo chambers. And it is no surprise that our thoughts come in a variety of styles, with tones of voice, as if they were meant to be spoken out loud. We are not always so considerate of our imaginary audience: our muttering is fragmentary and frequently condensed or elliptic. Many things are left unsaid, and the dots left unjoined. After all, we do not have to explain everything to ourselves. *I* know what I am on about.

Some people report that their thinking is not only decorated but dominated by images. A flow of images would seem to be an appropriate alternative to one's native language, given the tangle of connections between cognition and sight. Vision is the most epistemic, or knowledge-like, of our senses. Advances in understanding are often regarded as in*sights* and their cumulative effects as "en*light*enment"; the activity that drives them is "reflection," while the final breakthrough to higher consciousness is seen as a revelation that may present itself as a "vision."

The most fundamental connection between vision and thought lies perhaps in their shared property of clear separation from their objects. Unlike sensations such as pains that, so long as they are not interpreted as intransitive, vision is transitive: the aboutness of vision holds open a distance between the seer and the seen, between the seeing subject and the seen object. Thought is even more clearly separate from its object, given that it reaches into a boundless "out there" from a place that is the very center of "here." My thoughts about the Big Bang effortlessly glance backward through the entire history of the universe.

Nevertheless, for most people, thought is overwhelmingly in words rather than images. We have already observed that thought is often a rehearsal of one's contribution to an anticipated conversation. There is another reason: words are not tied to any one of the five senses. How words look or sound is largely irrelevant to their meaning. They are therefore able to integrate information from different senses, helping us to piece the world together, to weave together different currents in the stream of consciousness.

Thinking about thinking gives us an excuse to visit the most famous moment in Western philosophy: the Cartesian revelation "I think therefore I am." Any reassurance that I exist must presuppose that the thoughts originate from me. And so we come up against one of the great puzzles of psychology: our ability to identify ourselves as the source of events, of happenings that we have *done*. This might be anticipated to be tricky because there are no external cues—no physical effort with visible movements and audible grunts and groans—to give thoughts the stamp of ownership. It is hardly surprising that people with schizophrenia sometimes suffer terribly from the experience of "thought insertion." They hear their thoughts as voices that they ascribe to an outside source, believing them to have been implanted by alien, often malevolent agents.

Ownership of thoughts, however, seems rather more plausible than owner-ship of perceptions. There is no equivalent even in transitive perception to intellectual property: what I perceive over there seems to belong to the world; whereas what I think about it seems to belong to me. Nevertheless, while we are more likely to be responsible for our thoughts than our experiences, this is not always the case: we frequently seek out experiences while thoughts may just occur to us, as if we were their recipients.

And there are, of course, different degrees of activity and passivity in thought. An unceasing flow of ideas, images, and bits of chatter spontane-ously wells up in the cognitive spaces. There is idle recollection and fantasiz-ing. And there is possession by thoughts that circle around the same miserable place, anchoring the thinker to obsessive guilt and fear: thought as "mind-forg'd manacles" rather than an expression of freedom. Against this, there is effortful thought, driven by a determination to think, to examine, to solve, to explain. The effort may not be most richly rewarded when our brows are most furrowed. As is often remarked, happy accidents occur only to the prepared mind, and the mind's self-preparation may be a matter of months, even years. The "Eureka!" moment may be the result of earlier mental effort, honored as we seize and build on it.

One of the most astonishing of our cognitive capacities is our ability to *re*trace the journey that led up to a thought we are puzzled to find ourselves thinking. How did we get here? Why did last year's holiday "pop" into my mind? The backward glance, looking for the engine that set a train of thought in motion, is an extraordinary act of inner attention and cognitive will, of our capacity to inspect our own connectedness.

Back to philosophy. Since Gilbert Ryle's assault on Cartesian dualism in *The Concept of Mind*, philosophers have been reluctant to think of thoughts as ghostly goings on in the head. And yet it is difficult not to think of the thoughts I am having now as being "inside" but not in the same space that the letters appearing on the computer screen as I type them out are located as "outside." My thoughts seem to be nearer to me even than the sensations that arise from my body, such as an itch.

Which brings us to another mysterious aspect of my thoughts: their dual character. It is worth pausing on this for a while, because it helps us to define the distinctive roles of psychology and philosophy in investigating thought.

Token thoughts—for example, my thought at a particular time that "Stock-port is in Greater Manchester"—are personal, taking their place in my internal soliloquy. They are perhaps suitable for psychological investigation. The type-thought to which "Stockport is in greater Manchester" belongs is impersonal. It is thinkable by and intelligible to any number of people, and its referent is a part of the world that belongs to everyone and no one. It is a suitable topic for philosophy. While our token thoughts are embedded in me-here-now, they instantiate type-thoughts whose objects are disconnected from any here: they are about permanent, general possibilities, whose realization would not be confined to, or even in part captured by, a sensory field, a discrete part of space-time. It is not without reason that we say of someone lost in thought that they are "miles away," but those are not the miles that separate physical locations.

The daunting challenge—and the excitement—of thinking about thought is what we noted at the beginning: the requirement to inspect thoughts by means of other thoughts. Those other thoughts have somehow to rise above their fellows to count as vantage points on thought-in-general, or as a means of arriving at the essence of thought.

It is hardly surprising therefore that, while nothing could be nearer to us than our thought, it remains elusive. Employing introspection to catch thought in action is, as William James remarked, "like trying to turn the gas up quickly enough to see how the dark looks." Or, to change the metaphor, endeavoring to take hold of tassels of fog with tweezers made of mist. To develop a *theory* of (all) thought is like attempting to grasp with our hand the sum total of its grasps.

Perhaps things are not quite so challenging for the philosopher as they are for the psychologist. While in thinking about thought, philosophers have to utilize some instruments of thought—strategic recall, assembling reminders, and logic—they do not have to catch themselves catching themselves. That this seems possible—and that thinking can transcend itself to think about "Thought"—is extraordinary. It is even more of a feat than standing outside of our own body. This alone should enable us to resist the temptation to seek an account of thought that draws on one of the late, sophisticated products of thought: objective science and, in particular, neuroscience.

Our capacity to think about thought is one of a family of enigmas arising out of a fundamental mystery: our ability to encompass ourselves—as when we talk about "matter" or "human beings" or "the self"; or try to get our head around (as the saying goes) the totality of things as when we talk about "the universe" or, indeed, about "the totality of things." It is the most developed expression of our capacity to make what is explicit and to assert *that* it is.

We may argue over the logic of "I think therefore I am" and how much "am" it delivers, but we must concede that to think about one's own thoughts, to chase after this thought that I am thinking, is to place the astonishing joy-filled sense of our own being, the *that I am*, in italics.

NOTE

1. Raymond Tallis, FRCP, "Thinking about Thinking," *Philosophy Now*, no. 147 (2021). Used with permission of the author and publisher.

Chapter 6

Introduction to Thinking at the Edge[1]

Eugene T. Gendlin

"THINKING AT THE EDGE" (in German: "WO NOCH WORTE FEHLEN")
is a systematic way to articulate in new terms something which needs to be
said but is at first only an inchoate "bodily sense". "TAE" stems from my
course called "Theory Construction" which I taught for many years at the
University of Chicago. Students came to it from many fields. The course
consisted half of philosophy and logic, half of the difficult task of getting
students to attend to what they implicitly knew but could not say and never
considered trying to say. It took weeks to explain that the usual criteria were
reversed in my course. Whereas everywhere else in the University only what
was clear counted at all, here we cared only about what was as yet unclear.
If it was clear, I said "We don't need you for this; we have it in the library
already." Our students were not used to the process we call "FOCUSING,"
spending time with an observation or impression which is directly and physically sensed, but unclear. All educated people "know" such things in their
field of study. Sometimes such a thing can feel deeply important, but typically
people assume that it "makes no sense" and cannot be said or thought into.
"Oh," one student exclaimed when he grasped what I was looking for, "you
mean something about which we have to do hemming and hawing." Yes, that
was just what I meant. Another asked: "Do you mean that crawly thing?"

HOW IT IS POSSIBLE THAT SOMETHING NEW AND
VALUABLE CAN BE IMPLICIT IN A FELT SENSE

Of course, I know that it is a very questionable project to think from what is
unclear and only a bodily sense. A rational person, and especially a philosopher, will immediately wonder: Why should such a sense be more than mere

confusion? And if there were something valuable in it (say an organismic experiencing of something important in one's field), how would speech come from it? And if it sometimes can, how would one know whether what is said comes from it, rather than from reading something into it? Should one just believe whatever one said from such an unclarity, or would some statements be preferable to others? These questions do not have single answers. They require entering a whole field of considerations. They require certain philosophical strategies about which I have written at length. Since summaries of this kind of philosophical work are not possible, I can only refer to the works that lie behind what I will say here.

An internally intricate sense leads to a series of statements with certain recognizable characteristics. Statements that *speak-from* the felt sense can be recognized by the fact that they have an effect on the felt sense. It moves, opens, and develops. The relation between sensing and statements is not identity, representation, or description. An implicitly intricate bodily sense is *never* the same thing as a statement. There are many possible relationships between the body and statements, and we have developed some precise ways to employ these relationships.

Every topic and situation is more intricate than the existing concepts. *Every living organism is a bodily interaction with an intricate situation and with the universe.* When a human being who is experienced in some field senses something, there is always something. It could turn out to be quite different than it seemed at first, but it cannot be nothing.

Here I would like to give an example: Suppose you are about to fly to another city in a small plane, and your experienced pilot says "I can't explain it. The weather people say all clear, but the look of it gives me some odd sense of doubt." In such a case you would not tell the pilot to ignore this sense just because it is not clear. I have stacked this example. Of course, an *experienced* pilot's unclarity has already taken account of all the clear knowledge that the profession uses, so that what is unclear is something more. We need not be certain that this "sense" is in fact due to the weather; it is enough that it may be. You decide to stay safely at home. But if the weather does become dangerous, then it is important to all of us to find out what it was that the pilot sensed, which escaped the weather people. The federal aviation people and the whole society would want that pilot to articulate just what was in the look of the weather which the unclear sense picked up. Adding this to the knowledge of the Weather Service would make us all safer when we are in the air. And so it is also with any person who is experienced in any field. But such a sense will seem to be beyond words.

We are all imbued with the classical Western unit model. We can hardly think in any other way. What we call "thinking" seems to require unitized things which are assumed to be either cleanly identical or cleanly separate, which can be next to each other but cannot interpenetrate, let alone have some more complex pattern. If, for example, there are two things which also seem to be one in some intricate way, rather than try to lay out this intricate pattern in detail, thinking tends to stop right there. We consider the sense of such a thing as if it were a private trouble. It seems that something must be wrong with us because "it doesn't make sense." And yet we keep on having this stubborn sense which does not fit in with what is already articulated in our field. It probably stems from a genuine observation which does not fit the unit model.

HOW IT IS POSSIBLE FOR THE SAME OLD WORDS IN THE DICTIONARY TO SAY SOMETHING NEW

The unit model is regularly the reason why some new insights cannot be said. But to reject the unit model in general is not possible, because it inheres in our language, in our machines, and in all our detailed concepts. We fall back into it the moment we want to speak further. The new insight cannot be said in terms of the old concepts and phrases. In class I used Heidegger, McKeon, and my own philosophy, three critiques of the unit model, but as it turns out, the capacity for breaking out of the unit model cannot be imparted in this way. Critique does not prevent us from falling into the old model. Some say that it will take three hundred years for the assumptions that inhere in our language to change. To a philosopher it seems unlikely that people can think beyond the pervasive assumptions. Therefore, TAE can seem improbable.

On the other hand, Wittgenstein showed that the capacity of language far exceeds the conceptual patterns that inhere in it. He demonstrated convincingly that what words can say is quite beyond the control of any concept, pre-existing rule, or theory of language. He could give some twenty or more examples of new meanings that one word could acquire through different uses.[2] Building on this, we have developed in TAE a new use of language that can be shown to most anyone who senses something that cannot yet be said. This new way of speaking is the key to this seemingly impossible venture.

In my philosophy I have developed a new use of bodily-sourced language with which we can speak directly from the body about many things—especially about the body and language. Language is deeply rooted in the human body in a way that is not commonly understood. Language does not consist just of the words. The situations in which we find ourselves, the body, and the language form a single system together. Language is implicit in the human process of living. The words we need to say arrive directly from the body. I have a bodily sense of what I am about to say. If I lose hold of that, I can't say it. If I have the sense of what I want to say, then all I do is open my mouth and rely on the words that will come. Language is deeply rooted in the way we physically exist in our interactive situations.

The common situations in a culture each have their appropriate phrases, a cluster of possible sayings that one might need. The words mean the effect they have when they are used in a situation. Our language and the common situations constitute a single system together. However, this bodily link between words and situations applies no less when the situation is uncommon and what needs to be said has no established words and phrases.

All living bodies create and imply their own next steps. That is what living is, the creating of next steps. The body knows to exhale after inhaling, and to search for food when hungry. And, in a new situation new next steps come from the body. Even an ant on a fuzzy rug crawls in an odd way in which it has never crawled before. When we sense something that doesn't fit the common repertory and nevertheless wants to be said, the body is implying new actions and new phrases.

TAE EMPOWERS PEOPLE TO THINK AND SPEAK

We find that when people forgo the usual big vague words and common phrases, then—from their bodily sense—quite fresh colorful new phrases come. These phrases form in such a way that they say what is new from the bodily sense. There is no way to say "all" of it, no sentence that will be simply equal, no sentence which will simply "represent" what is sensed. But what can happen is better than a perfect copy. One strand emerges from the bodily sense, and then another and another. What needs to be said expands! What we say doesn't represent the bodily sense. Rather it carries the body forward.

First it must be recognized that no *established* word or phrase will ever be able to say what needs to be said. The person can be freed from trying to "translate" the felt sense into regular sayings. Yet what a person wanted a word to mean can be expressed but only in one or more whole sentences that use words in a fresh and creative way. In certain kinds of sentences a word can go beyond its usual meaning, so that it speaks from the felt sense. When one has tried several words and found that each of them fails to say what needs to be said, fresh sentences can say what one wished the word to mean. Now it turns out that each of the rejected words gives rise to very different fresh sentences. Each pulls out something different from the felt sense. In this way, with some further developments, what was one single fuzzy sense can engender six or seven terms. These terms bring their own interrelations, usually a quite new patterning. This constitutes a whole new territory where previously there was only a single implicit meaning. One can move in the field created by these terms. Now one can enter further into the experiential sense of each strand and generate even more precise terms. People find that never again are they just unable to speak from this felt sense.

Up to this point TAE enables fresh language to emerge. The last five steps concern logic, a very different power. But there is also an inherent connection between a felt sense and how we make logic. (See *A Process Model*, VIIA, VIIBa and VIII.)

The new terms and their patterning can be given logical relations, in a series of theoretical propositions. Now it becomes possible to substitute logically linked terms for each other. Thereby many new sentences (some surprising and powerful) can be derived. Expanding this can constitute a theory, a logically interlocked cluster of terms.

At every point in the process we can see that explicating a felt sense is not at all arbitrary. Although it involves creating new terms rather than merely copying or representing what is already given, its implicit meanings are very precise. The various relations between sensing and speaking have not been well studied until now, because only representation was looked for. By using these very relations between sensing and speaking in order to study them, I have initiated this field of study and developed it in some depth. Here I only want to say that once one experiences this "speaking-from," the way it carries the body forward becomes utterly recognizable. Then, although one might be able to say many things and make many new distinctions, one prefers being stuck and silent until phrases come that do carry the felt sense forward.

TAE was envisioned and created by Mary Hendricks. The idea of making it into an available practice seemed impossible to me. TAE requires a familiarity with Focusing. The participants in our first TAE were experienced Focusing people. This took care of the most difficult part of my university course. Nevertheless, I expected it to fail, and I certainly experienced that it did fail. Some people did not even get as far as using logic, and most created no theory. Yet there was great satisfaction and even excitement. A great thing seemed to have happened, so I was grateful that I was saved any embarrassment. For some reason they did not feel cheated.

Later I understood. During the ensuing year many people wrote to us. They reported that they found themselves able to speak from what they could not say before, and that they were now talking about it all the time. And some of them also explained another excitement. Some individuals had discovered that they could think! What "thinking" had previously meant to many of them involved putting oneself aside and rearranging remembered concepts. For some the fact that they could create and derive ideas was the fulfillment of a need which they had despaired of long ago.

Now after five American and four German TAE meetings I am very aware of the deep political significance of all this. People, especially intellectuals, believe that they cannot think! They are trained to say what fits into a pre-existing public discourse. They remain numb about what could arise from themselves in response to the literature and the world. People live through a great deal which cannot be said. They are forced to remain inarticulate about it because it cannot be said in the common phrases. People are silenced! TAE can empower them to speak from what they are living through.

People can be empowered to think and speak. We have come to recognize that, along with Focusing, TAE is a practice for people generally. They do not all need to build a theory with formal logically linked terms. Thinking and articulating is a socially vital practice. In ancient times philosophy always included practices, and now philosophy does so again. One need not necessarily grasp all of the philosophy from which the practices have come. I have accepted the fact that without the philosophical work no description of TAE (as in this *Folio*) can be adequate.

I need to make clear that with TAE we are not saying that thinking or any other serious human activity can be reduced to standard steps of a fixed method. When people said they discovered that they could think, they certainly did not mean these little steps which I myself couldn't remember exactly, at first. The steps help break what I might call the "public language barrier" so that the source of one's own thinking is found and spoken from. After that nobody needs steps. Precise steps are always for precise teaching so a new way can be shown and found. Then it soon becomes utterly various.

Steps 4 and 5 of TAE reveal a more-than-logical creativity inherent in the nature of language, which has remained largely unrecognized until now. Language is not the deadly trap it is often said to be. Language is often blamed when something exciting becomes limited and lifeless. Philosophers of many sorts hold that anything will fall into old categories by being said. This might be true when one uses only common phrases, but in the case of fresh phrasing it is quite false. *New phrasing is possible because language is always implicit in human experiencing and deeply inherent in what experiencing is. Far from reducing and limiting what one implicitly lives and wants to say, a fresh statement is physically a further development of what one senses and means to say.* Then, to write down and read back what is said can engender still further living. What one physically senses in one's situation is not some fixed, already determined entity, but a further implying that expands and develops in response to what is said. Rather than "falling into" the constraints of the said, we find that the effects of the said can open ways of living and saying still further.[3]

Many current philosophers deny that the individual can think anything that does not come from the culture, from the group, from interaction. This view is an overreaction to a previous philosophy which treated the individual as the universal source. But both views are simplifications. Culture and individuality constitute an intricate cluster. Each exceeds the other in certain respects.

We have a language brain and we live in interactional situations. But language is not an imposition upon a blank. Even plants are quite complex, and animals live complex lives with each other without language. When the living body becomes able to carry itself forward by symbolizing itself, it acts and speaks from a vast intricacy. Of course, we get the language from culture and interaction. But we have seen that language is not just a store of fixed common meanings. Humans don't happen without culture and language, but with and after language the body's next steps are always freshly here again, and always implicitly more intricate than the common routines. You can instantly check this by becoming aware of your bodily aliveness, freshly there and implicitly much more intricate than the words you are reading.

From the start, I had the students in my class meet in listening partnerships during the week. They divided two hours, taking turns purely listening. "Just listen. Only say when you don't follow," I instructed them. "If your partner is working on a paper, don't tell about how *you* would write the paper." They always laughed because they knew the problem. Nobody is ever willing to keep us company where we are stuck with our unfinished paper, so that we can think our way through. But in a Focusing partnership we do just that. We attend entirely just to one person at a time. This mutually sustaining pattern was always a main reason why students praised the course.

TAE has a *social* purpose. We build our inter-human world further. It is not true that merely developing as individuals will somehow change the patterns in which we must live. We need to build new social patterns and new patterns of thought and science. This will be a mutual product no single person can create. On the other hand, if we work jointly too soon, we lose what can only come through the individual in a focusing type of process. Nobody else lives the world from your angle. No other organism can sense exactly "the more" that you sense. In TAE for the first three days, one is constantly warned to "protect" one's as yet inchoate sense. We interrupt anyone who says, "mine is like yours," or "yours made me think of..." or any sentence that begins with "We...". *We* may have uttered the very same sentence, but the intricacy that is implicit for you turns out to be utterly different from mine. These two intricacies are much more significant than what would come from this spot, if we articulate it together. There is an interplay which happens too soon and stops the articulation of what is so fuzzy and hard to enter. Because we are inherently interactional creatures, our implicit intricacy opens more deeply when we are speaking to another person who actually wants to hear us. But if that person adds anything in, our contact with the inward sense is almost always lost or narrowed. In TAE we provide the needed interaction without any imposition, by taking turns in what we call a "Focusing partnership." In half the time I respond *only* to you. I follow you silently with my bodily understanding, and I tell you when I cannot follow. I speak from this understanding now and then but only to check if I follow. In TAE I write down all your exact words as they emerge (because otherwise they might be gone a moment later) and I read anything back to you when you want it. Then in the other half of the time you do *only* this for me.

Once the individual's sense of something has become articulated and differentiated enough, then what happens is something we call "crossing." Other people's insights enrich ours by becoming implicit in our own terms. If one first develops and keeps one's own terms, one can then cross them with others. Keeping one's own terms means keeping their intricate precision. Crossing enriches their implicit intricacy and power. At that point collaborative interaction can create a new social product right here in the room. This is of course the intent of the current emphasis on "dialogue" and Shotter's (2003) important work on "joint action" since we humans live fundamentally in an inter-human interactional space.[4] But we need the individual's unique implicit store of world–interaction, and this requires articulating the individual's bodily felt sense first.

When many TAE theories cross, they need not constitute one consistent logical system. There is a different way in which they go together. They cross. Crossing makes the other theory implicit in the felt sense under one's own logically connected terms. Then we find that we can say more from our own felt sense, using the other theory and its connected terms. Implicit intricacy connects all the TAE theories in advance. Each theory opens an intricate location in the public world and in philosophy and science. It enables the implicit intricacy to be entered at that location. A TAE theory relates to many other locations not only through its felt sense but also through logical connections to other things.

LOGIC AND SPACE-TIME SCIENCE EXIST ONLY WITHIN EXPERIENTIAL EXPLICATION

Pure logical inference is retained in TAE, but we *also* find a certain "odd logic" in articulating a felt sense. We find, for example, that a small detail which would usually be subsumed *under* wider categories, can instead overarch them and build its more intricate patterning into them. Another example of the odd logic. We find that when more requirements are imposed, degrees of freedom are not lessened; more requirements open more possibilities. There is an odd logic of experiential explication.[5] Next we must consider regular logic.

In order to understand our reductive sciences within a wider experiential science, we must first appreciate the power of the unit logic. I need to laud what I call "graph paper," the units that logic requires. The little logical units are familiar to everyone from mathematics (1+1=2+170=172). The units of which numbers are composed are external to each other, next to or after each other. With Newton they became characteristic of space and time and therefore of anything that exists in space and time. If you imagine everything external gone, there still seems to be a space and time which is empty but still quantitative in this unit measured way. The reality which Science represents is constructed in this space and time. Science turns what it studies into nice clean logical units that can be used with mathematics. By calling this space and time "graph paper" I want to bring home that physics, chemistry, organic chemistry, biology, microbiology—every scientific specialty—is an elaborate construction of little units on this kind of screen, such as molecules, cells, genes, neurons. The unit model is not the only possible model for science. Of course, nature doesn't really come in little units, but we can project it onto such a screen of units. We also enlarge it very greatly so that the units capture what cannot normally be seen. Then we can institute very specific operations with these units. We can test the results of these operations, and eventually create things that have never existed before. Among other things we also map ourselves onto these screens of units when we study ourselves. No, of course we are not these screens. It is a bad mistake to think that we consist just of these little units on all the screens. We are the ones who live and look at screens that we make. When I was young we were all supposed to be chemical. Then biochemistry and microbiology expanded vastly. Then, later, we were supposed to be neurology. Obviously, there are many sciences; what they say changes every few years, and new kinds of screens are constantly being added. We are not little units on a screen, not the sum of all the current and future screens. But let us not pretend that we could do without the wonderful things that have been constructed from such units—for example, medicine, electric lights, and even this computer on which I am typing. Once we make a screen of units, logical reasoning and inference are very powerful and can lead us to places nothing else can find.

On the other hand, logic is not what creates the units. Only we create the units, and we keep on creating them. The solution of long-standing problems usually requires creating new units. Even Euclid proves a theorem about triangles only by extending one of the lines, or by dropping a new line from the apex to the base—in other words, only by creating some new unit.

When one is using a well-defined concept, if one enters the felt sense at that juncture, one can find exactly how that concept is working at that juncture, its precise effect in that context. This will be a much more precise pattern than the definition one had for that concept. A felt sense is a source of much greater precision and can enable one to generate new units.

The "Complexity" theorists who make analog computer models still assume that the starting set of units must last through to the end. So their results are disappointing.

Logical analysis is being widely rejected even in Analytic Philosophy today, but giving up on logical analysis is a great mistake. It is true that logic depends on premises it cannot examine. Logic is helpless to determine its own starting position. But TAE shows that new logical inferences can be instituted at significant junctures with new units that are first arrived at by Focusing and TAE. The possibilities are greatly enhanced, when we can give logical analysis an articulated way to determine new starting locations and to generate new units there.

From new experiences and new phrases that come, we can fashion new units for logical inferences. In this way we can build something in the world with articulated strands and terms. Then it is a new logic with new units. Then logical inference applies again, and leads again to new places, new insights and new questions at which one cannot arrive in any other way.

What comes from a bodily felt sense is often of an odd sort that doesn't lend itself to the little boxes of graph paper. And, this "illogical" character is often the most important aspect of what we need to say. We can develop logically connected terms nevertheless. With TAE we have a way to let the "illogical crux" redefine all the terms, so that logical inference then lends them its power without losing an intricate new pattern or violating the life that the theory articulates.

When terms articulate a felt sense and also acquire logical connections, this duality enables us to move in two ways from any statement: once we have logically linked terms, logic generates powerful inferences far beyond what can be found directly from experiencing. On the other side, by pursuing the experiential implications, we can arrive where logic would never lead. We need both.

For example, my *A Process Model* (Gendlin, 1997) employs both. In Focusing, new and realistic steps arise from the body, but this seems illogical. Focusing is possible, since we do it. But to conceive of a world in which Focusing is possible leads to a cluster of logically interlocking terms in which *the living body is an interactive process with its environment and situation.* This is the case for plants. Animals require understanding how "behavior" is a special case of such interaction, and human language again a special case of behavior.

In this way I have developed a conceptual model for physics and biology, which can connect to the usual concepts and data (as we must be able to do), but with conceptual patterns which are modeled on and continuous with living and symbolizing. This kind of concept can connect with the usual units, but also embodies what cannot be reduced. This model can let one reconfigure any concept. With such concepts, one can think about all physical bodies in such a way that some can be living, and about all living bodies in a way that some can be human bodies.[6]

I can only indicate the philosophy behind the above. This philosophy is original with me, but of course I could not have arrived at it if I didn't know the history of philosophy and Dilthey, Husserl, Heidegger, Merleau-Ponty, Wittgenstein, Whitehead, McKeon, and many others.

My new way was to put the ancient concepts, strategies, and issues into a direct relation with implicitly intricate experiencing. I found that each philosophical approach can open avenues in the implicit experiencing, instead of canceling the others out.

Every major philosophy changes the meaning of the basic terms such as what "basic" means, what "is" or "exists" means, as well as "true," "understand," "explain," and all other such words. Each philosophy gets its changed meanings by entering into that bigger realm at the edge of thinking which is more organized than any system of concepts. But then the philosophy tells a story, its own story in its own terms about how it got its terms. It gives us only a conceptualized report about its entry and return. It doesn't enable us to do this. My philosophy lets us enter and return. It studies and uses what happens to language, and also (differently) what happens to logical terms when we enter and return.

There are ancient sophisticated conceptual strategies to think about how human beings live in reality in such a way that we can know something. It is after knowing many of these strategies and their pitfalls, that I say: we don't just have interactions; we *are* interaction with the environment—other people, the world, the universe, and that we can sense ourselves as such.

What we sense from there is never nothing.[7]

NOTES

1. Eugene Gendlin, *The Folio* 19, no. 1 (Nyack, NY: The Focusing Institute, 2004), 2. Used with permission of the publisher.

2. E. T. Gendlin, "What Happens When Wittgenstein Asks 'What Happens When . . . ?'" *The Philosophical Forum* XXVIII, no. 3 (Winter–Spring 1997). See also E. T. Gendlin, "Thinking beyond Patterns: Body, Language and Situations," in *The Presence of Feeling in Thought*, ed. B. den Ouden and M. Moen (New York: Peter Lang, 1991), Chapter A-1, section 6.

3. See my reply to Nicholson in E. T. Gendlin, "How Philosophy Cannot Appeal to Experience, and How It Can," in *Language beyond Postmodernism: Thinking and Speaking in Gendlin's Philosophy*, ed. D. M. Levin (Evanston: Northwestern University Press, 1997).

4. J. Shotter, "'Real Presences': Meaning as Living Movement in a Participatory World," *Theory & Psychology* 13 (2003).

5. E. T. Gendlin, *Experiencing and the Creation of Meaning*, IVB (Evanston: Northwestern University Press, 1997).

6. E. T. Gendlin, *A Process Model* (Nyack, NY: The Focusing Institute, 1997).

7. E. T. Gendlin, "Crossing and Dipping: Some Terms for Approaching the Interface between Natural Understanding and Logical Formation," in *Subjectivity and the Debate over Computational Cognitive Science*, ed. M. Galbraith and W. J. Rapaport (Buffalo: State University of New York, 1991), 37–59.

Chapter 7

Mental Health and Normality

Toward a New Process-Oriented Perspective

Pierre Morin

Psychological normality and pathology, and mental health and sickness, are processes that intersect with biological, social, cultural, and spiritual factors. If we perceive them as static conditions, we marginalize the fluidity and dynamic diversity that lies beneath what we commonly see as normal or abnormal thinking and behaving. Conventional thoughts about disordered or psychologically normal thinking reinforce individual psychopathology. Cultural and medical definitions of what is normal or abnormal, pathological, a mental disorder, or mental health influence our values, beliefs, thoughts, and behaviors and create a chasm between the so-called normal and the sick. They stigmatize and marginalize vulnerable individuals and contribute to health disparities and reduced life expectancy. They have what I call a *nocebo* effect. In this chapter I propose a new process-oriented perspective that integrates conventional views with an attitude or therapeutic art that believes in the client's own current experience and sees it not only as symptomatic but meaningful.

PSYCHOLOGICAL NORMALITY, MENTAL HEALTH, AND REALITY

What is normal brain functioning and thinking?

What is health or mental health?

What is abnormal, pathological, or a mental disorder?

What is and who defines normality?

Can normality be used as a standard for mental health?

51

Today, most scientists subscribe to a materialistic view of the world and think that if we were to understand the complete physics of neurons, we would be able to elucidate the mind. Nevertheless, the working relationship between physical matter (brain) and subjective experience (mind) is far from being solved. While we know that our mind depends on the integrity of neurons, neurons are not themselves thinking. We occupy two worlds: the world of the body and physical reality, with its material and mechanistic properties, and the world of the mind, with its cognitive properties and subjective experiences. How they interrelate is still a mystery.

Imagine a child who finds a radio with its batteries loose. She plays with the radio and batteries, and when she puts the batteries into their right place, the radio starts to play music. By figuring out that the batteries help the radio operate, she still doesn't understand how the radio is able to transmit the music that is being played from somewhere in the distance, nor what makes music so beautiful to her.

In addition, body, mind, and world are entangled and connected in numerous ways that escape our full knowledge. Our brains and conscious minds are only the tip of the iceberg. There is a much bigger mountain and world under the surface of the water. Our identities expand beyond the boundaries of the brain into subconscious communications with our own endocrine and immune systems as well as the world around us. The submerged mountain and the surrounding water link us with all other mountains and connect us with the common ground of the unconscious wholeness or Spirit, God, the Tao that can't be said, etc.

Our brains experience the world through the lenses of multiple parallel neuronal networks (for example, emotional, rational systems, right/left brain, and two different memory systems). The various networks construct parallel simultaneous realities, some of which remain closed to language-based awareness or consciousness. From a neuroscience perspective, this verbally mediated consciousness is the CEO of our brain. On the other hand, most of our brain processes happen unconsciously, without our being aware of them. There are not only verbal but also physical (hormonal, neuronal) levels of awareness. There is a dream consciousness and a consciousness of physical symptoms that need to be translated into the language of our "CEO."

Our brains produce a useful and coherent narrative of the world that is unique to each of us. But this perceptual and experiential reality is, for the most part, limited to the tip of the iceberg. The submerged mountain and the surrounding water are the bigger reality and field that escapes our normal conscious senses and ability to understand. To function as a community, we come together and negotiate some agreement about the joint world of experiences that we then call reality. Mindell (2000, p. 27) calls the consented upon so-called objective or conscious realities of the tips of the icebergs *consensus reality* (CR), and the subjective and submerged aspects of our individual worlds and the surrounding world outside of our commonsense perception *nonconsensus reality* (NCR).

Throughout history, humans have engaged in many practices to connect with the NCR or surrounding world. Meditation and prayer are examples of such practices. The reality that can be described in terms of the tip of the iceberg marginalizes other nonconsensual imaginal worlds and deep-seated sentient experiences. We engage in these practices to unite with an essential ground, the surrounding water, or what others have called Mother Nature, Yahweh, God, the Great Spirit, the Universe, etc. Some forms of so-called psychopathology express unified and godlike experiences and may remind us of our own need to rekindle our spiritual lives.

Individually, we struggle with multiple parallel experiences, and within our communities we work hard to create some sort of coherent world. We grapple with competing experiences within and between us. To survive in this multitude of possible experiences, our CEO steps in and creates some unity, and as a group we create a hierarchy of experiences or a consensus reality and a hierarchy of values we call normality. In so doing we marginalize other experiences and relegate some to the realm of difference or abnormality. By giving precedence to identity, the tip of the iceberg, a CEO, or central values, we bolster some experiences and undermine others.

Andrew Solomon, in *Far from the Tree*, writes about different ways of thinking about identity. He describes two forms of identity: vertical and horizontal. Our ancestors, families, and parents imbue us with a sense of belonging to a lineage and family tree, our vertical identity. But then some of us also grow up with challenges that we don't share with our parents. A disability, a sexual orientation, or a mental illness separates us from our parental lineage and throws us into the fangs of a new marginal horizontal identity and culture. Being blind, deaf, little, autistic, gay, or mentally ill are illnesses and challenges as well as an identity that we horizontally share with all the blind, deaf, little, autistic, gay, and mentally ill people.

These culturally diverse ways of being are pervasive. They color every experience, sensation, emotion, and thought of the person, every aspect of their existence. These identities are often alien to our parents, but they are meaningful and form diverse cultures. They are also alien to mainstream cultures and the medical and other professionals that treat them.

HEALTH AND NORMALITY

In common-sense language, we take the meaning of the word "health" for granted. We speak about health and assume a tacit understanding and consensus that, for example, a muscular body is healthy or that smoking is, in general, bad for your health. Disease and health are culturally and socially defined concepts that are used to describe what are thought to be objective and real conditions of a person. This is the consented upon objective, pragmatic, or goal-oriented aspect of reality that Mindell termed consensus reality (CR).

Health and normality delineate a certain state or situation whose absence implies an illness or deviance. Historically, individual health was perceived as the accident-free functioning of organs and physiological processes comparable to the smooth functioning of a well-oiled machine. Since then, the more details and information we gathered about the human machine, the more complex became the understanding of its healthy working. In the last century, statistics allowed researchers to study the distribution of illnesses. To define health, researchers used reference groups of healthy people and laboratory reference values of so-called normal physiological processes. They identified states that were statistically associated with "normal" functioning and demarcated the boundaries of health or absence of disease. This process required that they differentiate between what counts as normal (that is, order) and what counts as abnormal (that is, disorder). Now, some say this classification is strictly neutral and without any personal or social values. But for others, it *depends upon* personal and social values.

In conventional medical terms normal has several meanings. At the individual organic or "machine" level, disease is either present or absent, a cell is either normal or cancerous, you have a fever or you don't. At the community level, statistics define normality for a specific condition by comparing it to a healthy reference group. Then society defines normality by its values and cultural moral codes.[1]

The word "health" derives from the Old German root word "heilag" or "whole, holy." "To heal" then stands for "to make whole" and "healing" figuratively encompasses the restoration of wholeness. Healing and health are related to the concept of wholeness: physical, emotional, and spiritual. Implicitly, as health care providers and "patients," we are supposed to aim toward a state of wholeness. The resulting virtue of holistic health contrasts with the fact that we are never completely whole, despite our desperate efforts to achieve wholeness by leading healthy lifestyles, eating well, exercising, and engaging in therapies of all kinds. Physical and emotional symptoms are always part of our lives. Whole, unimpaired health is an illusion; symptoms are a basic aspect of our lives.

This is the reason why CR definitions of health are incomplete. The concept of health is, as Hannah Arendt (1971, p. 431) said, "something like a frozen thought which thinking must unfreeze." The physical and mental health picture is obviously a more complex one. Biological, environmental, psychological, relational, and social factors intertwine to create a process with uncertain outcomes. Classical state-oriented medical theories separate the examining doctor from her patient, the healthy or so-called normal from the diseased and abnormal, as if they are separable from each other. They also marginalize the subjective, dreamlike illness experiences and the cultural systems in which they are embedded. The phenomenon health is so complex and elusive that some authors talk about the mirage of health (Dubos, 1959). Others are even critical about thinking of health as a positive goal. Medieval metaphysicians spoke of the *sanitas perniciosa* or *dangerous health* because good health was considered a moral risk. Health would lead to arrogance and indifference and the losing sight of the most important human endeavor, which was to seek the salvation of the soul. Today some speak of health as a privilege that comes with responsibilities. When Hanna Arendt speaks of health as a frozen thought that needs unfreezing, I think of health as a process that involves many levels of thought and experience. I believe that a new system and process-oriented thinking and methodology are required to handle the complexity of all the factors contributing to health and disease.

The World Health Organization (WHO) defines mental health as "a state of well-being in which the individual realizes his or her own potential, can cope with the normal stresses of life, can work productively and fruitfully, and is able to make a contribution to his or her community."[2]

Bartlett (2011, 233) defines mental health as "the set of typical and socially approved characteristics of affective, cognitive, and behavioral functioning, a set of characteristics derived from the reference group consisting of the majority in a society's population, and relative to which clinicians understand 'deviations from normality' and hence 'mental disorder.'" However, people perceived to be psychologically healthy and normal do a lot of bad or evil things, such as killing people in wars, destroying the environment, and abusing power and rank. The classical experiments that Milgram and Zimbardo conducted in 1960 demonstrated that, provided the right context or environment, regular students were able to engage in abusive behavior. These psychologically normal students sought social conformity and validation and were vulnerable to do bad things.

The new DSM V defines mental disorder as

a syndrome characterized by clinically significant disturbance in an individual's cognition, emotion regulation, or behavior that reflects a dysfunction in the psychological, biological, or developmental processes underlying mental functioning. Mental disorders are usually associated with significant distress in social, occupational, or other important activities.[3]

This classification and diagnosis of a mental disorder has clinical utility: it helps clinicians determine prognosis, treatment plans, and potential treatment outcomes for their patients. It also reinforces a discriminatory attitude toward experiences that are outside of our conventional understanding, comfort, and acceptance. It limits the spectrum of diversity we allow ourselves to experience internally as well as externally.

In his treatise about health and normality, Canguilhem (1989) says that being in good health means being able to fall sick and recover. Health is a process that includes sickness and recovery. Health is a feeling of assurance and resilience in life, a way of tackling existence, and feeling that one is not only the owner of health but also the creator of meaning and the holder of values. To be healthy is to feel secure in the present and assured for the future. Health is about the possibility of transcending the conventional normal and the possibility of tolerating infractions of the habitual norm (that is, falling sick) as well as establishing new norms in new situations.

For Canguilhem, health is an attitude and reaction with regard to the possibility of disease. It is not an objective state or fact but an experience. Health as a collective norm does not truly exist. Today he might say it is a process that cannot be separated from disease or illness. It is an experience that includes disease.

Canguilhem postulates there is no completely normal state, no perfect health. There exist only sick people; we are always moving back and forth on a continuum between health and sickness. Health is an individual value or a vision to which we aspire and that helps us modify our behaviors as we are sick and want to get better. Health is not a state but a norm whose function and value is to stimulate awareness and change if threatened. As such, health is a process that includes continuous normative activity and adaptation. Canguilhem refers back to Greek medicine, in which nature, both inside man as well as outside, was considered harmony and equilibrium. To ancient Greeks the disturbance of this harmony or equilibrium was thought of as disease. On the other hand, disease was perceived as an effort on the part of nature to re-create a new equilibrium. For the Greeks, the organism develops a disease in order to get well; disease is part of the healing process to restore balance, and it is part of the solution.

We usually examine experiences from a point of view of a bell curve with a certain range of the curve defining what is normal and pathologizing everything that lies outside the normal range. Our mood is normal and well adjusted when it remains between the confines of a middle range with some acceptable variance between feeling slightly depressed on one side and excited on the other end of the scale. If it crosses a certain boundary on each side, we step into the land of mental illness. Another way of looking at experiences across the whole spectrum is to see them as meaningful processes that want to inform us about our own diversity. As a mental health practitioner, I sometimes feel burned out, fatigued, or depressed. Most of the time, I fight the feelings and push myself to overcome them and continue living my life. Sometimes, I remember to allow myself to go through the fatigue, to let it slow me down and reconnect with a deeper ground that is my inspiration for my work. The fatigue or illness becomes the messenger of my vision and deeper health.

Identities and experiences outside the center of the bell curve are not only alien or different, they also challenge the well-being of the community. They force us to explore areas beyond our collective comfort zone. Mindell coined them as *City Shadows*, shared marginalized experiences that are hard to confront and learn from. With this concept Mindell aims at depathologizing experiences in mental health. Together with R. D. Laing's existential approach in psychiatry and Stan Grof's understanding of extreme states as spiritual emergencies, Mindell's City Shadow concept moves away from a deficit-oriented view of what is normal and questions the very concept of mental illness. Today peer support and advocacy groups such as the Icarus Project, Mad Pride, and the MindFreedom movements reclaim the experiences of "mental illness" as "mad gifts needing cultivation and care, rather than diseases or disorders."[4]

In human nature difference is a challenge, but in nature diversity is a sign of good health. When health, normality, and conformity become an enemy of difference, it is a problem. But people outside the bell curve help us become aware and conscious. Without difference we would remain unaware of our own uniqueness and commonality. Extreme aspects of difference such as a schizophrenic's delusions and paranoia have a meaning for the community. They, for example, represent expressions of fears that are relevant to all of us. Many psychotic individuals experience the persecution by authorities such as the FBI, CIA, etc. They will think that their apartments and phones are bugged, that agents of the governments are spying on them. Edward Snowden's leak of hundreds of pages of secret government information showed that the US National Security Agency was spying on its own citizens. And governments have always done so with more or less integrity. The delusions are real, maybe not in an individual case, but for the community. The delusions are maybe an aspect of the community discourse about privacy, the need for secrets or transparency and openness. In that sense they are coherent and meaningful.

Normality and psychological health are defined as an individual state in comparison to a reference value and norm and or group. I am normal, healthy, or sick in comparison to the rest of the group or community and outside of the health of the community. This perspective ignores the interdependence of and chain reactions that exist in a network of individual systems. Mental health and normality are embedded and dependent on multiple systems; some are biological in nature and others are social, cultural, and experiential. Studies of trauma and adverse childhood events (ACE) show that these have a huge impact on mental and physical health. Social disparities affect health and health outcomes significantly. Values and expectations shape the course of a disease and the chances for recovery. Biology and human experience are inseparable and require a new kind of knowledge and science that can bridge the gap between the world of objects and facts and the world of subjective and social processes, the world of physics and chemistry and the world of ethics, psychology, and sociology.

Psychological health and normality are outdated concepts. We need a new process understanding that goes beyond traditional views about normality and health. Normality and health as statistical averages, as adjustment and optimal functioning, as social desirability and conformity are limiting and restrictive concepts. They led to a generalized attitude of fighting a war against symptoms and to marginalizing individuals and groups who don't fit the standards and boundaries of health and normality. A new process-oriented perspective acknowledges all conventional levels of normality and includes interpersonal and social dynamics as an aspect of global or collective meaningful learning. Individual and collective shadow experiences transcend the division between normal and abnormal, psychological health and psychopathology. They are here to increase our awareness, to help us learn about diversity and create a deeper and more sustainable community.

THINKING VERSUS EXPERIENCING

Some psychotherapy methods are based on correcting our thinking patterns. Faulty thinking is thought to be at the base of symptoms and suffering and thus gets reframed to relieve the pain. Other schools of psychotherapy reach beyond the cognitive worlds. They are based on research that demonstrates that some therapeutic outcomes are based on what individuals do internally. They help successful individuals check inside themselves for lived experiences of their situation that expand beyond the tip of the iceberg. These therapies can be corralled under the umbrella of transpersonal psychotherapy. Their theories draw from the fields of humanism, existentialism, phenomenology, and anthropology. They include mindfulness-based therapies, focusing-oriented therapy (Gendlin, 1997), process-oriented therapy (Mindell, 2010), and others.

Through personal experience, both Gendlin and Mindell became interested in the connection between dreams and body experiences and the larger unifying forces. Gendlin, while tending to his duties aboard a ship in the Navy, realized he was pondering the "background feeling" that was left in his body from a dream he'd had the night before. He discovered that, as he continued to ponder this feeling, eventually, the whole dream came back to him. He believed the content of the dream was implicit, somehow, in the vague body sense that was left over. This inspired his inquiry into how we as human beings can discover or rediscover information by paying attention to the subtle, embodied *intuitive feel* of our life experiences.

Mindell, as a trainee at the Jung Institute in Zurich, asked his analyst Marie Louise von Franz, one of Jung's close collaborators, why she was not able to "see" his night dreams in his momentary behaviors. She retorted that ability might be his to discover. Soon after, Mindell consulted a man with advanced stomach cancer. He asked his client how the body experience of his cancer felt. The man said it was like an explosive force coming from within, wanting to explode outwardly. While exploring his experience, the man remembered a night dream he'd had of fireworks, and he also shared how he had always repressed more violent or explosive feelings. Mindell encouraged his client to express his passion, and the man went on to live beyond the time span his doctors had prognosticated. Both experiences transcend common-sense realities, scientific understandings of the physical world, and material cause and effect relationships.

One tenet of experience-focused therapies is that we are not just related to each other and nature through the way in which we think and relate to one another within the context of our own unique perceptual worlds. We are also inwardly related to one another by virtue of sharing an inner relation to the larger field of our surrounding world, the ocean on all sides of the icebergs

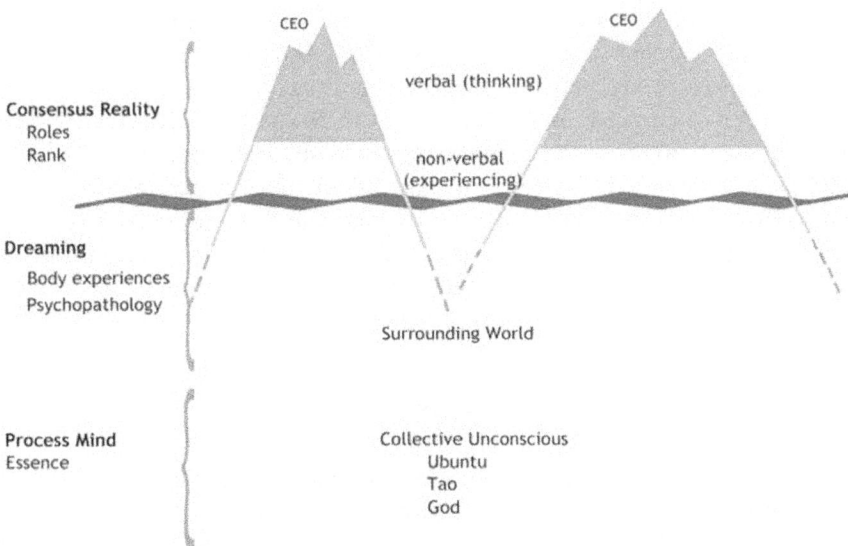

Figure 7.1   **Iceberg Metaphor of Awareness.** *Source*: Created by Pierre Morin.

that is our common ground. Drawing on phenomenology, subjective biology, quantum mechanics, process philosophy, and existentialism, that larger force field is defined as a more expansive field of awareness from and within which every life-form takes shape.

On a verbal or thinking level, Mindell's client was dealing with a serious health problem, a stomach cancer that was causing pain and threatening his survival. The medical point of view sees it as something pathological, a disease that needs treatment. On an experiential level, the symptom becomes an explosive force that is connected to marginalized passionate feelings. From a process or transpersonal perspective, the client's passion is an expression of a shared life force that seeks awareness and integration. His strong feelings are needed for us all to become more aware and grow. Amazingly, his symptom belongs to all of us. Our individual identities, roles, and ranks are a manifestation of individual processes as well as of the surrounding world diversifying itself and generating consciousness for the benefit of each and every one.

CONCLUSION

Cognitive concepts help us make sense of our world and give us some orientation about ways to understand pain and relieve suffering. Health, normality, mental illness, identity, etc. are helpful guideposts for grasping human experiences and developing treatments. They are also potentially harmful and contribute to the marginalization and discrimination of sensitive, creative, and wounded individuals who have experiences that go beyond the middle range of the bell curve. A new process-based approach values all the CR aspects of life (social determinants, power and rank, culture, diversity, identity, genetics, trauma, ACE, etc.) and recognizes their relevance in creating suffering and symptoms. In addition, this new approach examines the individual's and community's experience as a doorway into healing pathways. Symptoms and illnesses are not meant to be defeated and recovered from; they are experiences we tend to marginalize—but when unfolded, convey meaningful information that can lead to personal growth and community building.

NOTES

1. It is also important to remember that health and normality are not only related to the health care sector but also to security, justice, infrastructure, and employment.

2. World Health Organization, "Mental Health: Strengthening Our Response," Fact sheet no. 220 (Geneva: World Health Organization, 2022), http://www.who.int/mediacentre/factsheets/fs220/en/, retrieved March 29, 2014.

3. D. J. Stein et al., "What Is a Mental/Psychiatric Disorder? From DSM-IV to DSM-V," *Psychological Medicine* 40 (2010): 1759–65.

4. http://www.theicarusproject.net/.

REFERENCES

Arendt, H. (1971). "Thinking and Moral Considerations: A Lecture." *Social Research, 38*(3), 417–46.
Bartlett, S. J. (2011). *Normality Does Not Equal Mental Health: The Need to Look Elsewhere for Standards of Good Psychological Health.* New York: Praeger.
Canguilhem, G. (1989). *The Normal and the Pathological.* Cambridge: Zone Books.
Dubos, R. (1959). *Mirage of Health.* New York: Harper & Bros.
Gendlin, E. T. (1997). *Experiencing and the Creation of Meaning (Studies in Phenomenology and Existential Philosophy).* Evanston: Northwestern University Press.
Mindell, A. (2000). *Quantum Mind: The Edge between Physics and Psychology.* Portland: Lao Tse Press.
Mindell, A. (2010). *Processmind: A User's Guide to Connecting with the Mind of God.* New York: Quest Books.

Chapter 8

In Thought We Trust

A Podcast Conversation[1]

Gangaji with Hillary Larson

Intro by host, Hillary Larson: Thoughts come in the form of an endless stream of considerations and evaluations. They consist of our hopes, plans, dreams, fears, successes, and failures. I like my life. I don't like my life. I have enough. I need more. Some are exalted and some are painful. Either way, they are still just thoughts. But most of the time, they appear real. They appear to be the content of who we are.

(audio clip) Gangaji: *Just as an experiment, as an investigation, just right now, stop trusting your thoughts! Why not? (Gathering laughs.) Haven't they failed you over and over and over? (Gangaji joins in the laughter.) Yes! Yes, do you see, this is telling the truth then.* (end clip)

Hillary: With our thoughts being so convincing, how do we know what is truly reliable? What is the role of intuition? Doesn't that seem like something we can count on? And what is the solution for those who find themselves living in their heads? Where is freedom there? From getting caught in the thoughts that make up our daily lives—to asking the deepest question: Who am I? Where is it that we put our trust? And what if our thoughts ultimately are not true? I'm Hillary Larson and this is *A Conversation with Gangaji*.

H: I would like to call this the whole enchilada—because I was listening to someone the other day who is a mindfulness practitioner and she helps people deal with chronic pain issues and cancer and, you know, serious, serious things. And she was saying even when people spend weeks consistently observing their breath, observing their body sensations, it's still really, really difficult for them to consider that they can also observe thought. And also, even that they're telling themselves a story because it's like glue! And I have come to refer to thought as one continuous drunken bender.

Gangaji: Well, we are deeply, profoundly programmed to identify with thought; that's linked into our survival but it's also part of our culture, and it's part of the way that we have assumed so much power as a species. And, and it is powerful. And, and it is wondrous! The fact that we think—surely, other species think too—but that we think and have language. And then of course, the language, the spoken language, reinforces the internal dialogue and so that becomes reality. Thought becomes reality in our minds, in our thoughts.

H: You know, I wanted to actually start with really practical life stuff— which is what you and I do here anyway. So, I wanted to break down thought, if you don't mind. First of all, I think it's actually easier to start with a story—"I'm telling myself a story"—rather than thought itself because that goes deeper. The other day I was giving somebody an example of an email I'd sent to somebody, and I expected them to respond fairly quickly. I'm sure everybody has had this experience—at least, I hope they have. And, you know, the end of the day, no response. A couple days later and I was so full into some story of why they hadn't responded. And ultimately, why they hadn't responded had absolutely nothing to do with me, but even though I am vigilant about stopping, there was something so sticky about that. I couldn't just drop it once and for all. It was almost like I had to find out, ultimately, why their email, you know, came back late. And then, of course, there's the humbling of oh, like oh, oh right!

G: Well, we see how attached we are. And I think you hit on it when you said you figured out why in your mind, in your narrative, in your story, they hadn't answered. We give meaning to events with our narrative, our story. I just want to always say, I'm not saying that's wrong or a bad thing. It's just that it's limited. If we are just focused, or just believing our stories, our narratives, the same thing happens that you just described. We go off on tangents, drunken benders. And then maybe, later, we find out the truth that had nothing to do with what our narrative was. But in the meantime, we've suffered unnecessarily. And that's the power that our internal, personal narratives have. And it's huge! And we have to recognize that. That's the first point of actual inquiry: first recognize, what am I saying to myself? Don't change it. Just recognize it. I mean to change it you get too involved in it anyway. Then there's a whole narrative about "Am I changing it? Did it change?" But just recognize it. Don't change it. Recognize it. Let it roll! And recognize it. And then you see that there is consciousness that can disengage with this narrative. Then you are conscious of your narrative.

H: I wanted to break down thought more. Because there are thoughts that are harmless that we don't attach to. And then there are thoughts where we somehow merge with them. So, for example, I was taking a walk with a friend last month and I was thinking about this show. And I was like, how do we create something concrete that we can all relate to? And I was looking at this tree and it's like, well, when I look at the tree, it's the tree! You know, it's green, it doesn't have meaning to me. But then, let's just say, I start talking about the time I fell out of a tree and there was pain involved. And then all of a sudden, it's almost like a membrane. It passes from being out there—nothing to do with who I am and the world—and it crosses over into this is who I am.

G: Becomes personal.

H: Yes!

G: And that's what we do. That's part of our thinking mechanism. We make the world personal. We survive better. I mean in your story about the tree, you see trees and you know it's dangerous if you fall out of trees. So, it has this purpose and I keep coming back to this. There's a purpose or a deep purpose in thinking and in personalizing. But it's limited. That purpose is limited. If we can become conscious—just as you were relaying—of how we personalize, how we make it personal, then we actually have a choice. First, we have to see that we are doing it and then the choice can arise to actually stop. And even in the naming of the tree—because the naming is the beginning—we name things to separate from them. And we separate from things to have power over them. And we do that for survival. If we don't name tree and we don't name each other, we don't name male, we don't name female, we're already in some spaciousness. And it's scary, because we don't have the power over that thing then. And that scariness is the adventure of life. Many people hear the invitation to disengage from your thoughts or to stop thinking and assume that it will be a life of ignorance or a life of stupidity, or a kind of brainwashing. It's really the opposite. It opens up! I mean, then name the tree, you can name it, but you've had a moment where it's not named. And you recognize no name can ever touch reality. So, we may name, but the power of the name is revealed to be a mirage.

H: I want to play you a clip that just completely, coincidentally aligns with what you just said. (Laughter.) We're on a roll here. So let me play this. It was from a woman—she was so lovely—I just love the people that get up and speak with you. They're so sincere and they have such intelligent things to say, and their inquiry is so deep! This woman got up and spoke to you and she was talking about being betrayed by lots of people: "I don't trust people anymore because they've betrayed me." And what you were saying is, it's not the people that are the problem. It's your trust in the thought that they have betrayed you. So let me play this:

(audio clip) *SPEAKER: I mean it though.*

G: Yeah, so right now, give up any thought of what anything should be. You stop trusting any thought that you have of what anything should be. Yes, give that up. Give the trust in your thoughts up. Just right now as an experiment.

S: But what about the trust . . .

G: No, right now. As an experiment. (Laughter from the gathering.)

S: Okay, I'll just go to sleep!

G: Really? (Woman giggles.) Go to sleep then. (Pause, waiting.) Are you asleep?

S: No. (More laughter from the gathering.)

G: So, you were putting your trust in a thought. "Well, if I do that, then I will go to sleep."

S: I have no idea what'll happen.

G: Well, that's great. (Laughter.) That's a beginning. So in that, there's a little opening. "I had no idea what will happen." Excellent. Then, you can see, the habit of the ideas of what will happen or should happen or did happen. Don't trust those. Just as an experiment. Not as a religion. Not as a liturgy. Just as an experiment, as an investigation, just right now: stop trusting your thoughts! Just as—why not? (More laughter.) Haven't they failed you over and over and over? (Gangaji joins laughter.)

S: Yes.

G: Yes! Yes, you see this is telling the truth then.

S: (Sighs.) Well, then, I am utterly, I'm just—clueless.

G: Good! (Laughter.) Clueless—then that's a place of innocence. That's a place of innocence.

S: I'm a little afraid.

G: Yes, I understand. Often if innocence has not been met, fear arises because innocence has been abused in the past. Definitely, that's also part of the experience on this planet. But, right here, for this moment, you give yourself one second. One second—to be absolutely, completely clueless—to not know. And then tell the truth about the space of that. (end clip)

H: Wow.

G: Yeah, she was wonderful. To me really the spirit of inquiry is that we bring our knowing to a moment and we bring our self-betrayals, and other betrayals to a moment. But there was a willingness that was demonstrated in that clip—of maybe first . . .

H: Clinging.

G: . . . to the knowing. Clinging to the idea, to the thought, but a willingness to actually, just as investigation, in this moment, see what's here—what remains uncatchable by any thought, uncontrollable.

H: Hmmm. Just what you said to her when you said, just for a moment, give your trust in your thoughts up. When I look at that, I look at, the religion of trusting thought.

G: That's right.

H: It could be the deepest religion there is. In fact, I think that I've heard you say—crossing my fingers that I've heard you say that—that thought is really the ultimate addiction, but it just goes overlooked because there are so many other addictions that take up that are more obvious, like drug addiction, and . . .

G: Yes. So, I think I did say that, but I would like to clarify it. It's not the thought per se that's the addiction. It's our addiction to thought that's the addiction. Really that's the power of thought. Because when we think about something there's a way that we are managing reality. Even though it may be a miserable thought about something, and the reality that we come up with is an unhappy reality, there's some sense that we are in control of it because we can actually think about it. And so that's a hard one to give up. It's a willingness as it was in that clip for her to be clueless, to be vulnerable, to be exposed, and yet to be conscious! I mean, we fall asleep each night and we give up these thoughts. but to stay conscious in the waking state and let it all go, there's a great discovery! It cannot be thought (chuckles) beforehand, even if you've had a true experience of it. Whatever you've thought about your prior experience is useless in this moment.

H: I was thinking about the trap of that because if you say to somebody, "Just for this moment, let go of your thought," then, it becomes a doing-ness, so to speak. And there was another exchange you had with somebody that just is so. . . . It's something that I think comes up over and over again. This woman's predicament seems common to me and her problem was like, "I'm always stuck in my head." So I wanted to play this exchange you had with her:

(audio clip) *S: I live in my mind.*

G: Okay.

S: I admit that.

G: Great! So then this is an opportunity to see what maybe is deeper or closer than your mind. If for a moment, what you are trying to grasp you recognize you will never grasp. Does that evoke any emotion? (Silence.) What if certain failure is guaranteed in this grasping category. Is there any emotion that is evoked? In your gut?

S: Probably—a feeling of surrender.

G: Oh, really?

S: Yeah.

G: Probably?

S: Yeah. (Laughter.)

G: Like theoretically? (More laughter.)

S: I'm still in my mind.

G: Yeah, so in order to really answer this question, you have to drop out of your mind and just let your mind drop into your body and see if there's anything agitated in there—or anything that feeds the staying in the safety of theoretical discussion.

S: I have to confess that I live in my mind, and it drives me crazy when therapists and people tell me to drop into my body.

G: Okay, well, I'm here to drive you crazier than you have ever been driven.

S: Okay, I'll try. (Laughter.) Okay, I'll try. Okay, I'm working on it.

G: Yeah. (More laughter.) Because you don't just live in your mind. It's impossible. It's impossible.

S: I understood what you said: what you are here to invite us to is not something that is able to be expressed in words.

G: Mm. Oh, beautiful!

S: I understood that.

G: Yes, and that understanding is deeper than your mind. Because in that understanding there's a resolution of paradox—and opposites—and that's more than the mind can handle. So maybe what you're calling the mind is actually more inclusive of the depths of being. Maybe it's like the Buddhist mind, Big Mind, which includes every phenomenon, every appearance, every disappearance, every thought, every emotion. Then there's no problem with mind. But this mind still lives in you. You don't live in it. (end clip)

H: I want to tack on a listener question that pertains to what you were saying to this woman. This person says: "Dear Gangaji, I hear you talk about how untrustworthy thought is, but what about intuition? How do you trust that?"

G: Well, I don't suggest that you do trust intuition. Finally, of course, intuition—a sense of this is what I should do, a sense of this is going on—is unformed thought. Then it gets translated into thought and sometimes it's correct and sometimes it's wrong. You know we have thoughts that are intuitive and creative. And we have thoughts that are correct sometimes and sometimes they're incorrect. If we're speaking of trustworthiness, what's trustworthy is what does not appear and disappear. It's what's always here. Intuitive flashes appear and disappear. Sometimes they're right, sometimes they're wrong. Thoughts appear and disappear. Emotions appear and disappear. Phenomena of all kind appear and disappear. It's not that they're wrong or right. It's just that they're not ultimately trustworthy—as reality. People would ask Papaji, "What is reality?" And he would say, "Reality is what doesn't come and go." And so that's our assignment, as thinking creatures, to recognize that the things we have based our hopes on, our thoughts, are unreal. They come and go. They change. They change according to what our digestion is, or when somebody looks like our mother, or talks to us in a strange tone of voice. I mean they're very fickle! They're expressions. They're manifestations, but they aren't trustworthy as reality. And that's the point. We have the opportunity, not to grasp reality, but to take a moment and open to reality. Thought, the mechanism of thinking is a mechanism of grasping. It's very intelligent, very powerful. But reality is too big! It's bigger than can be thought. You know the Zen Buddhists talk about the unborn face. I used to really ponder that: What could the unborn face be? It's what's here.

H: That's an interesting way of putting it, isn't it? I know you're not fond of comparisons, (laughs) but I found it really useful in certain surprising ways, because I was thinking about the example I gave of the email—and tell me if I'm wrong on this but—I still think you're unique. I think that your awakening created a sustained awareness of what is Real. And so that my idea is that if *you* send somebody an email and you don't hear back, you actually don't give it much thought. Or is that true?

G: This is your narrative. And this is why comparison is useless. You know, I may or may not. There's not a formula. I don't hold myself to a formula: I should or I should not give it meaning. I tell stories. I think. I'm right or I'm wrong. I'm unique, just as you're unique—but, our storytelling is not that unique. It's based on past experiences and the interpretation of those experiences and the management of present experiences based on those past experiences. When you're invited to just be here, just be present, to stop, it's an opportunity to recognize that in the deepest sense the slate is already cleared. That we're just thinking on top of this spaciousness and this clarity. If you don't tell yourself that story about what I would do with an email coming in, then what you did with the email coming in is more meaningless. (Chuckles.) It was just a story that was generated. You may even have a laugh at it.

H: I did. (Laughs.)

G: Good.

H: Well . . .

G: That's the opportunity, really.

H: Yeah, I just really love this conversation and unfortunately we only have three or four minutes left. I want to get this last clip that is actually really about what the ultimate function of the mind is outside of survival. You know when I look at the question I just asked you about, you know how you experience an unanswered email compared to me, I look at the function of the mind and that is protection. So, this is the continuation of this conversation that you had with the woman who said, you know, that she lives in her head.

(audio clip) G: In general, when one lives in thought, it's an avoidance of something that is big and uncontrollable—called Life—or Self, or Truth—or Death.

S: *So, how do you get there?*

G: Uh-huh, well, you don't get there.

S: *But . . .*

G: That very question, I can appreciate it, and, it's natural and it's appropriate. It's already here.

S: *Okay.*

G: It's like saying, how do I get to Life? Life is already here. You're in Life—or Life is in you—or both. You don't have to do anything to get there.

What is useful is to see how you are avoiding being where you are—and you've already seen that. You came up here saying that about your thoughts or your intellect.

S: Mm-mm.

G: Nothing wrong with thoughts—nothing wrong with intellect—both exquisite powers—but regarding Reality or the Continuum of Being—in this meeting, at least, useless. So, you can never grasp who you are—because to grasp it you would have to be separate from it as a subject grasping an object. (Silence.) But you can be who you are—not who you think you are. Closer than that. (end clip)

H: You know, what you speak of often is the wanting to avoid what's under the narrative—and that could just be the fear: fear of rejection, fear of being alone.

G: Fear of death.

H: Fear of death. Yeah!

G: Because that's what fear of rejection, fear of being alone is based on.

H: Yeah.

G: Loneliness would have no sting if it weren't for death, the fact we need each other. If we're alone, our loneliness is a survival drive to find another, so that we live.

H: I would love to wrap up this conversation talking about freedom. And I know I'm talking about relative freedom, but I was doing a little research on somebody who had been a racist for their whole life. They grew up that way. They were trained that way. And later on in life, they examined the thought of "this person is less than me." And in some miraculous way they were able to go, "that thought actually is not true." There was this freedom in just dropping that thought! And it may not be the ultimate freedom, but I think that's so valuable.

G: It's not separate from the ultimate Freedom. And in fact, it's a reflection of the ultimate Freedom, in that the hold that that thought had, had no power anymore. So, yes! That's the ultimate Freedom.

H: Well, I, I feel humbled again. As usual, I usually feel humbled at the end of our conversations. And I appreciate our conversations. But this one in particular that feels like it's the root of suffering in general. This conversation between you and me and all of us that are gathered as part of this conversation, it feels like the opening to true Freedom.

G: Yes. That's right.

H: If you can give me about a minute. I have one more clip of Gangaji talking about thought and the power of the mind. Thank you for joining us again—until next time.

(audio clip) *G:* Just the moment of simply being, without being anybody, without being anything, without getting it right, without missing it, without naming it, without knowing it, just being. This is the moment of awakening. And the truth is everyone has those moments every day! But it gets overlooked. Each moment gets overlooked because of our infatuation with this power of mind. And mind is not present in any of those moments. And then mind arises and we get on with the business or we get on with the definition of who's wronged us or who's righted us, or who we have to get or keep, or what we have to know. And then, all of a sudden, there's a moment: just being. Not needing anything. Not wanting anything. Not knowing anything, and yet, being known.

NOTE

1. Gangaji, *Podcast*, Episode 20, May 21, 2014, The Gangaji Foundation, Ashland, Oregon, www.gangaji.org. Used with permission of the author.

Chapter 9

Mind Only, beyond Thought

Ben Connelly

Here is a brief introduction to a way of looking at our relationship to thought and to the world, whose purpose is to help us realize our capacity to contribute to universal wellness. This way of looking at things is found in Yogacara Buddhist teachings, which are first millennium CE predecessors to what we now call psychology and phenomenology. It holds that each person's only opportunity to contribute to well-being is found in how they are viewing and thinking of the world at any particular moment. It holds that every bodily act, thought, or feeling affects everything else and is dependent on everything else. It holds that everything we believe to be a separate lasting thing is not what we think it is, and hence is beyond thought.

Yogacara Buddhism emphasizes that our experience always occurs as a process of consciousness. We can never experience or know anything that is not mediated by conditioned patterns of thought. Our sense of being a subject viewing objects, and all the objects we believe we are viewing are constructed by the tendencies of our consciousness. Every moment of experience is characterized by a massive array of conceptualizations that arise dependent on previous cognitive, behavioral, and emotional conditioning. Just consider the array of conditions necessary for you to interpret what you are seeing right now into meaning, you must have a sense that white and black are different, that a line is different from a curve, that an "l" is different from a "c," and that groupings of these things create meaning. All these thoughts, or imputations, happen far below the level of conscious awareness and are only a tiny part of the totality of what you are experiencing through imputation in this very moment. The Yogacara arguments for this view come from investigation of experience itself, but they resemble the worldview presented by twenty-first-century neuroscience. Brain science points to the fact that what we "experience" as an absolutely real world is a simulacrum, and that we can witness through scientific observation the conditioned processes in the brain and other aspects of the human body that produce our image of the world.

Yogacara teachings say that every moment of life is characterized by a cascade of *"cittas,"* which means thoughts and also means phenomena. Colors, shapes, emotions, letters, and the sense of being a subject that observes objects are all examples of cittas. Right now, a tiny part of my experience is the patch of grass off my porch and a cardinal hopping and chirping away in the greenery. The cittas present in this include all the many shades of green, the red, and black, the sense that the sound of the bird is a different kind of sensory experience from the colors, the idea that a bird is different from grass, that I am separate, over here, watching. All these are cittas, thoughts, imputations, phenomena. They arise from a vast well of cognitive habit; through eons of conditioning, consciousness has the tendency to think it is separate from the things it observes, that the senses are distinct, that the red is different from the green, and that birds are distinct from plants. I'm not saying these things are or are not actually different, I'm pointing out that the only way we can know their difference or sameness is through cittas, which we could also call thoughts, or imputations.

Our experience in any moment is of hundreds of thousands of cittas, that is to say phenomena, thoughts, or imputations. Cittas arise dependent on conditions. Yogacara takes a phenomenological view of these conditions based on early Buddhist teachings whose purpose is to emphasize the importance of our actions, to remind us that we have power. The conditions, also called karma, which produce cittas are the intentional, cognitive, or affective impulses that occur in any moment. When there is anger, it produces the conditions for more anger. When there is compassion, seeds of compassion are planted. When you ascribe meaning to a word, such as citta, you may in the future ascribe a similar meaning to this word. Seeds once planted will bear fruit. However, the system is not mechanistic, seeds produce similar fruit, not identical fruit. The main point here is that whatever feeling, thoughts, and perception you are putting into the world at any moment will have an effect. What you do always matters. This will hopefully encourage you to plant seeds of compassion, joy, altruism, humility, contentment, generosity, wisdom, and courage, to bring these qualities to each moment.

So our experience is a torrent of cittas, which are produced by conditions, but finally it is good to know that cittas are just that, imputations, thoughts, and they are not ultimately real things. Everything you think is an ultimately real thing is merely a concept, or as is sometimes said in Buddhist texts, mind only. Everything you think is a thing is already beyond thought. Whatever limitations or boundaries thought has put on it are not ultimately real, although they may have a great deal of utility. It is good to think about this beyond thought quality that is inherent to everything you experience. It can help break our fixations, our obsessions, our harmful habituated patterns.

I'll close with a simple example of why and how to apply this worldview. Imagine you are eating an apple. It tastes sweet and tart and has a satisfying crunch. If we recall that experience is constructed by habits of thought, we may remember that this very moment is an opportunity to plant beneficial seeds, to create beneficial conditions. We may recall that the quality of attention and intention we put into this moment of experience matters; it is our only opportunity to contribute something to the world. We may find ways to relate to eating the apple that are more beneficial, like bringing gratitude and mindfulness to the simple experience of eating.

We can also bring to mind the dependent nature of the cittas that are arising. We may draw to mind some of the near infinite conditions that produce this moment of experiencing a bite of apple: the ingenuity that led to the cultivation of apples; the love of family that motivates much farm labor, the sun, the rain, and the soil; the ignoring and denying of massive climate impacts that people do daily to keep our current food economy functioning; the beliefs that folks must uphold to accept living in a system where farm workers are often impoverished in a world with so much wealth. If we experience the eating of an apple in this way, it may change how we relate to eating apples, and to the rest of our lives and communities.

Finally, we may realize that whatever is happening is beyond thought, that though the patterns of our mind construct this experience, they are inherently limited and not ultimate truths. We may find some motivation to get a little closer to whatever this experience is by thinking about it less, and pouring our energy into seeing this experience just as it is, already beyond any ideas of it we could possibly have. Buddhist teachings invite us to give our attention to sensory experience: sunlight on a flower, birdsong at dawn, feet on the floor, the sensations of eating an apple. This subtly transforms consciousness so that we can shed gross layers of conceptual activity and get closer to what is. We can experience a profound humility and curiosity, a wonder, and a spacious sense of peace, when we realize even for a moment that everything is already beyond thought.

Part II

BEYOND THINKING

Chapter 10

Going beyond Thinking

*Thinking, Attachment, and
Interdependent Origination*[1]

Shohaku Okumura

INTRODUCTION: THINKING IS ALWAYS
A PROBLEM IN BUDDHISM

I've been practicing only Soto Zen based on the teachings of Japanese Zen Master Dogen for more than forty-five years, and therefore my knowledge of Buddhism is very limited. However, as far as I know, "thinking" is always a problem in "Buddhism" for at least four reasons. In this article, I use the word "thinking" in its broadest sense. It includes not only conceptual and logical ways of thinking but also the functions of our minds that make us discriminate about the things happening within ourselves and around us. As a Buddhist term, "thinking" here includes the function of the four (of five) aggregates: sensation, perception, formation, and consciousness.

The first reason: Subjective thinking, discrimination, and picking and choosing based on our desires make our lives go up and down through the six realms of samsara.[2] Traditionally in Buddhism, we and all living beings transmigrate within these realms according to the good or bad karma caused by our actions, but we are also transmigrating within this lifetime even moment by moment depending upon changes to the internal and external conditions of our lives.

The second reason: Even objective and rational thinking using words, concepts, and logic cannot reach the ultimate truth. Buddhist teachings found in written scriptures are not reality itself. Written teachings are considered merely the fingers that point to the moon of awakening. We need to free ourselves from our clinging to the fingers.

The third reason: Even though thinking can't reach the ultimate truth and can't replace actual practice, we human beings cannot live without thinking. To say "Thinking cannot reach the ultimate truth" or "Don't think, but do!" is still thinking. Therefore we need to study the nature of thinking to avoid falling into karmic habits formed by our experiences and the conditions of our lives. Depending upon the DNA we inherited from our parents, where we were born, how we are educated, and what we have experienced since our birth within certain conditions of society, our ways of thinking, making evaluations and judgments, and doing things are gradually formed by the time we begin to live as independent people. That's the karmic-self, the self formed by our particular causes and conditions, and it's the foundation of personality. It's necessary and useful to live as a member of society, but habitual ways of life can become a prison and we can lose our freedom because of our fixed ways of thinking and doing things. We can't live without thinking, and even Buddhist teaching must be expressed and shared among people using languages that are the products of thinking. Therefore we need to study the nature of thinking and how we can use it to see the reality beyond thinking and then practice based on that.

The fourth reason: Whether participating in formal activities in a temple or approaching our everyday activities as a means of awakening, actually doing things as practice in order to manifest the truth is more important than thinking about and discussing the truth or reality and constructing a system of philosophy.

I would like to consider these four points in the stream of Buddhist teachings. To do so, it's helpful to use Nagarjuna's comments on the "five eyes" mentioned in chapter 18 of the *Diamond Sutra*, which is considered one of the oldest scriptures within the group of the *Mahaprajnaparamita Sutras*. The five eyes are: physical eye, divine eye, prajna eye, dharma eye, and Buddha eye.[3] These eyes are how we see the absolute truth and the relative truths. In the *Diamond Sutra* there's no explanation about these five eyes, but Nagarjuna explains this in his *Mahaprajnaparamita Shastra*.

THE PHYSICAL EYE: THE FIRST REASON

Nagarjuna's comment: "The physical eye sees the near but not the far, the front but not the back, the outside but not the inside, the light but not the dark, the top but not the bottom. Because it is obstructed, a bodhisattva[4] seeks the divine eye."

The physical eye (literally "flesh eye") is our habitual subjective way of viewing things. This is the first reason why thinking is a problem in Buddhism. Shakyamuni Buddha taught that we are simply collections of five aggregates (*skandhas*), without any fixed permanent self (*atman*) that can exist without a dependent relationship with others or that can be considered the owner and operator of this collection. When each of our six sense organs, the first of the five aggregates, makes contact with its object, we receive some stimulation that is the second of the five aggregates, sensation. This sensation can be pleasant, unpleasant, or neutral. In our minds, we create some image of the object that is the third aggregate, perception. Then we evaluate this image and decide whether we like it or dislike it, whether we should get closer and make the object our possession or stay away, escape, or even fight against it. This is the fourth aggregate, formation. Then we name it, define it, and we think we understand its relationship to ourselves as the subjects. This is the fifth aggregate, consciousness.

We encounter the same kinds of objects again and again from our birth, and in our mind, using all of our education and past experiences, we create a certain picture of the world. We create a system of values in which some things are safe, positive, and valuable, and we chase after them. Other things are dangerous, negative, or valueless, and we want to stay away or escape from them. This is how our lives become divided into two or more separate parts, and we continue to move up and down within samsara.

Traditionally in Buddhism, it is said that living beings are transmigrating within the six realms of samsara life after life until we accomplish liberation. We run after things we think desirable and try to escape from things we don't like, and our lives become all about running. Sometimes we are successful and our desires are completely satisfied. We feel like heavenly beings. More often, we are not so successful, and we feel like we are hungry ghosts; the more we have, the more we desire. Sometimes we feel we are good and other people are bad, we need to fight against our enemies, and unless we eliminate them, we cannot be happy, or this world cannot be in good order. Then we are like the fighting spirits (*asura*). Sometimes, when we simply have our stomachs filled, we are satisfied like animals.

Sometimes we find ourselves in conflict with others and living without trust, hating and blaming each other and thinking we are each other's enemy. The extreme example is two nations at war, but the same kind of situation is possible even in family life. We have difficulties and troubles, and we fight and attack each other as if we are hell dwellers. No situation lasts forever; things are always changing, so we transmigrate within these realms of samsara. This transmigration is not necessarily life after life; we transmigrate moment by moment depending upon the situation around us. According to Buddhist teachings, this is the way we make everything in our lives into a cause of suffering.

With the physical eye, we can only see things near to us, so our views become self-centered. We cannot see the front side and the back side at the same time, and our view becomes one-sided. We see only the outside, and our view becomes stereotyped. We can see things only in the light, not in the dark, and our view becomes either pessimistic or optimistic. Our eyes can see only the surface and not the bottom, and our view becomes shallow. We feel we need to find a more unobstructed view and be free from limited ways of seeing things.

According to Yogacara[5] teaching, human consciousness has eight layers. The first five are the consciousnesses caused by the five sense organs when they encounter their objects. The sixth is our usual intellectual thinking mind. The seventh is called *manas* consciousness, which is translated into English as "ego consciousness." The eighth and deepest layer is called the *alaya* consciousness. The Sanskrit word *alaya* means "storehouse." All of our karmic experiences are stored in the *alaya* consciousness as seeds. The seventh layer, the ego consciousness, grasps the seeds stored in the storehouse as "I" and clings to them. Then this seventh consciousness influences and controls the first six consciousnesses. According to Yogacara, this is why our way of viewing things and behavior is always self-centered.

This is an explanation of how the five aggregates (*panca skandha*) become the five aggregates of attachment (*panca upadana skandha*) and our lives become endless transmigration, chasing after things we like and escaping from things we dislike.

THE DIVINE EYE: THE SECOND REASON (A)

Nagarjuna's comment:

> The divine eye sees both the near and the far, the front and the back, the outside and the inside, the light and the dark, the top and the bottom, all without obstruction. But the divine eye sees only those provisionally named things that result from the combination of causes and conditions and not their true appearance, not their emptiness or their formlessness, their non-existence, their birthlessness, or their deathlessness. The same holds for their past, their present, or their future. Hence, a bodhisattva seeks the prajna eye.

The divine eye (literally "heavenly eye") can be interpreted as the objective, rational way of viewing things. This is the second reason why thinking is a problem in Buddhism. Scientists don't see things in a self-centered way based on like and dislike but try to see things objectively. To see in this way ourselves, we try to collect as much information about the object of our study as possible, see it from all possible perspectives, and not evaluate it for our personal benefits or preferences. For example, with our physical eye, we can only see one side of the moon from the earth. By using the information from an artificial satellite, we can see the opposite side of the moon. We can't usually see inside of our bodies, but using various devices such as CT scanners, we can. Using the Internet, we can see all parts of the earth as if we were heavenly beings looking down on them from the sky. When we work on a problem of mathematics or philosophy, we think logically without being influenced by our individual desires, hopes, or self-centeredness. In the history of Buddhist philosophy, various systems of theories have been developed in this way.

After Shakyamuni Buddha had attained awakening while sitting under the bodhi tree, he enjoyed liberation by himself but hesitated to teach and share what he had discovered with others. He said to himself, "I have penetrated this truth, which is profound, difficult to perceive, difficult to understand, peaceful, sublime, beyond reasoning, subtle, intelligible only to the wise."[6]

He said that the truth he found is difficult to understand and that it is "beyond reasoning." When Shakyamuni made up his mind to teach the Dharma to five monks at Deer Park, he had to explain it using words to enable them to intellectually understand it, put the teaching into practice, and experience the same awakening and liberation. Both the truth or reality Shakyamuni found and his teaching about the truth are called *dharma*. Conventionally, the dharma as the truth is written with capital D ("the Dharma") and always singular, and his teachings are called "dharma" with lower case "d" and can be plural.

In Mahayana Teaching, for example, in *Mulamadhyamakakarika*, Nagarjuna discussed the two truths and said:

> The teaching of the Dharma by the various Buddhas is based on the two truths: namely, the relative (worldly) truth and the absolute (supreme) truth. Those who do not know the distinction between the two truths cannot understand the profound nature of the Buddha's teaching. Without relying on everyday common practice (i.e., relative truths) the absolute truth cannot be expressed. Without approaching the absolute truth, nirvana cannot be attained.[7]

The absolute truth refers to the Dharma to which Shakyamuni awakened when he attained enlightenment under the bodhi tree. This Truth is beyond the reach of neither subjective thinking nor rational thinking that is by nature dualistic. The relative (worldly or conventional) truth is the expression or explanation of the absolute truth using words, concepts, and logic as Shakyamuni taught using language. In the introductory verse of *Mulamadhyamakakarika*, Nagarjuna praised the Buddha, saying:

> I pay homage to the Fully Awakened One,
> The supreme teacher who has taught

The doctrine of relational origination,
The blissful cessation of all phenomenal thought constructions.

We can see that the reality beyond thinking is the way things really are within the network of interdependent origination (relational origination). "The network of interdependent origination" is an expression that comes from the image of Indra's net as it appears in the *Avatamsaka Sutra (Flower Ornament Sutra)*. All beings exist as knots in the beautiful decorative net hanging in the palace of the heavenly god Indra. There is a jewel in each knot and all of the jewels are reflecting each other. This shows that all things are connected and interpenetrating each other. In order to awaken to the ultimate truth, we need the prajna eye.

THE PRAJNA EYE: THE SECOND REASON (B)

Nagarjuna's comment:

> The prajna eye does not see beings, for all common and differentiating character-istics are extinguished. It is free of all attachments and immune to all dharmas, including prajna itself. But because it does not distinguish anything, the prajna eye cannot liberate other beings. Hence, a bodhisattva gives rise to the dharma eye.

The prajna eye is the way to see emptiness, oneness, or the equality of all things without any discrimination. This eye is not thinking, but rather the negation of our habitual way of thinking either subjectively or objectively. *Prajna* can mean wisdom in general—that is, a precise understanding of reality with a correct, analytical discrimination among things. In this case, *prajna* refers to the capacity to distinguish between the right and wrong, or good or bad qualities of what one encounters. However, within the *Prajna Paramita Sutras* "prajna" is used to refer to the wisdom that sees the reality that transcends ordinary comprehension based on the separation between subject and object and among objects. The physical eye and divine eye are discriminating thought. The prajna eye sees emptiness, oneness, or equality of all beings so that we can be liberated from the discrimination and picking and choosing that makes our lives into samsara.

In the *Vimalakirti Sutra*, another early Mahayana sutra, there is a famous story about entering into the dharma gate of nonduality. Nonduality means there is no separation, distinction, or discrimination, which are the functions of thinking using words and concepts.

In this story, Vimalakirti asked a group of bodhisattvas, "How do bodhisattvas enter the gate of nonduality?" One bodhisattva answered, "Arising and perishing form a duality. But since all dharmas are not born from the beginning, they do not perish. By grasping this truth of without arising and perishing, we are able to enter the gate of nonduality."[8]

One by one, more than twenty bodhisattvas went on to talk about various dichotomies and how to transcend them. Finally, they asked Manjushri how he entered the gate of nonduality. Manjushri said, "What you've said is all correct, but your sayings produce another duality. We can enter the gate of nonduality by saying nothing. We should not say even that we should stop speaking." Manjushri points that they had made a discrimination between discrimination and nondiscrimination, implying that discrimination is wrong or inferior and nondiscrimination is right or superior.

Finally, Manjushri asked Vimalakirti, "Now, it is your turn to speak. How does the bodhisattva enter the gate of nonduality?" At that time Vimalakirti kept silence without saying anything. Manjushri said, "Excellent! This is the way to enter the gate of nonduality where there is no word and letter."

This is one example of the prajna eye that goes beyond any duality. However, Nagarjuna said that to have the prajna eye is not the goal of bodhisattva practice, because nondiscriminating wisdom cannot help others who are suffering due to various causes and conditions. To understand the nature of each person's difficulty, a bodhisattva needs discriminating wisdom. Self-liberation is not the goal of bodhisattva practice. As the Buddha's children, we need both wisdom and compassion. To nurture our compassion, we need to remain in samsara and walk with all beings. That is the spirit of the first bodhisattva vow, "Beings are numberless; we vow to save them."

DHARMA EYE: THE THIRD REASON

Nagarjuna's comment:

> The dharma eye enables a bodhisattva to cultivate dharma and to realize a path as well as to know the expedient means by which other beings can do so. The dharma eye, however, is not omniscient in its awareness of the expedient means for liberating beings. Hence, a bodhisattva seeks the Buddha eye.

This passage concerns the third reason why thinking is a problem in Buddhism. We cannot eliminate thinking as long as we live as human beings. The dharma eye is again discriminating wisdom. This discriminative eye knows the emptiness and oneness of all beings, discriminating among things without attachment to them. Without being hooked by habitual discrimination, it seeks to understand each person's particular problem in order to offer help. A bodhisattva needs karmic consciousness (discriminating thinking) to understand others and live together with others. All Buddhist teachings need to be understood with this dharma eye instead of simply being understood by the divine eye with words and concepts.

BUDDHA EYE: THE FOURTH REASON

Nagarjuna's comment:

> There is nothing unknown to the Buddha eye. Though it might be completely obstructed, it can see everything. What to others is distant, to a buddha is near. What to others is dark, to a buddha is bright. What to others is confused, to a Buddha is distinct. What to others is fine, to a buddha is coarse. What to others is profound, to a buddha is shallow. There is nothing of which the Buddha eye does not learn, nothing it does not see, nothing it does not know, nothing that is difficult, and yet nothing that is perceived. The Buddha eye shines forever upon all dharmas.[9]

The Buddha eye isn't a human way of viewing things. It transcends the separation between subject and object but includes both of them. This is more like the dharma body (*dharmakaya*) of the Buddha, the reality of all beings itself that includes both subject and object and yet is beyond both of them. *Dharmakaya* is one of the three bodies of the Buddha developed in Mahayana Buddhism.[10] The Dharma, the way things are, is itself the body of the Buddha. This reality is itself the omniscient wisdom and also the perfect compassion of the Buddha.

As the *Diamond Sutra* says, the Buddha has all five eyes. As not-so-matured bodhisattvas we don't have the Buddha eye, we need to keep and nurture the first four eyes. According to Dogen, in our practice the Buddha's Dharma body manifests itself. In our practice we are a part of the Buddha eye. Though thinking and languages are only tools we can use to liberate ourselves and help others, instead of eliminating thinking we need to train ourselves to use our thinking ability to discern what is not reality in front of us.

According to the *Sutra of the Turning of the Wheel of the Dharma*, when Shakyamuni met with the five monks at the Deer Park after his own awakening, the first thing he taught them was that he had found the Middle Way (*majjhima patipada*) between the two extremes of self-indulgence and self-mortification. The Middle Way is the Eightfold Noble Path—that is, right understanding, right thought, right speech, right action, right livelihood, right effort, right mindfulness, and right concentration.[11]

According to the *Mahaparinibbana Sutta*, on the day Shakyamuni passed away, a person whose name was Subhadda wanted to ask him a question. Even though Ananda rejected his request because the Buddha was very sick and weary, the Buddha accepted and allowed him to ask his question.

Subhadda's question was about other famous religious teachers whose teachings were different from each other. He wanted to know whether they had all realized the truth as they all made out, or had none of them realized it, or had some realized it and some not? To this question, the Buddha said, "Never mind whether all, or none, or some of them have realized the truth or not." Then he said that the most important thing is whether or not the Eightfold Noble Path is found in their teachings. According to the Pali texts, the practice of the Eightfold Noble Path as the Middle Way is the first and the last teaching of the Buddha. That is, what the Buddha taught is not a fixed metaphysical theory that is the product of thinking but the practice of an actual way of healthy living free from self-indulgence and self-mortification. This story shows the fourth reason that thinking is always a problem in Buddhism.

CHINESE CHAN (ZEN)

Tathagata-garbha (Buddha-nature)

There are three important theories in Indian Mahayana Buddhism. The first two are the emptiness of Nagarjuna's Madhyamaka School and the consciousness-only of the Yogacara School.[12] The third is the theory of *tathagata-garbha* (buddha-nature). The oldest scripture about this theory is the *Tathagata-garbha Sutra*; its basic message is that although we are covered with all different kinds of defilements—greed, anger/hatred, ignorance, and so on—all of us have a *tathagata-garbha*, the womb or embryo of the tathagata, which is interpreted as buddha-nature, and which is never defiled and not different from the tathagata.[13]

In Chinese Buddhism, this theory became well known through *The Awakening of Faith in Mahayana*. This text is attributed to Asvaghosha and translated by Paramartha, but many scholars today think it might actually have been written in China rather than in India. The theory in this text is a kind of integration of Yogacara's consciousness-only and *tathagata-garbha*. "One Mind" has two aspects. One is the aspect of Mind in terms of the Absolute (*tathata*, suchness) and the other is the aspect of Mind in terms of phenomena (*samsara*, birth and death). Each of these two aspects embraces all states of existence. These two aspects are mutually inclusive.[14]

One Mind in terms of the Absolute is like a completely peaceful ocean without any wind or waves. In the aspect of One Mind in terms of phenomena, the Mind is influenced by the wind of ignorance and waves occur. These waves are discriminative thinking. In this phenomenal aspect, the Mind is the *alaya* (storehouse) consciousness, and it again has two aspects: one is the aspect of enlightenment, and the other is the aspect of nonenlightenment.

When the wind of ignorance starts to blow, the consciousness is called karmic consciousness (*gosshiki*, activating mind). Karmic consciousness also
has two aspects: one is the turning consciousness (*tenshiki*, evolving mind)
that appears as the subject, the other is manifesting consciousness (*genshiki*,
reproducing mind) that appears as objects. These two aspects function as
subjects and objects and make our lives into samsara, as it is said in early
Buddhist teachings.

The practice based on this theory is to restore the original One Mind by
stopping the function of the *alaya* consciousness by cutting off the wind
of ignorance. In short, that means to stop thinking based on the separation
between subject and object and to return to the reality (suchness) beyond
thinking.

Beyond Thinking in Chinese Zen

In Chinese Zen koan literature[15] there are many stories about pointing to or
expressing original reality through silence, probably inspired by the story of
the thunderous silence of Vimalakirti.

Dharma Transmission from Shakyamuni Buddha to Mahakasyapa

> A long time ago when the World-Honored One was at the assembly on Mount
> Grdhrakuta, he held up a flower and showed it to the people. At the time, every-
> one remained silent. Only Venerable Kasyapa broke into a smile. The World-
> Honored One said, "I have the true Dharma eye treasury, the wondrous mind of
> Nirvana, the gate of the subtle Dharma in which the true form is no-form. It does
> not rely on words and letters and is separately transmitted outside the teachings.
> I now entrust it to Mahakasyapa."[16]

This story appears in Case 6 of the *Gateless Barrier (Mumonkan)*. This story
was created in the Chinese Zen tradition, probably in the early Song Dynasty
(eleventh to twelfth century). Zen people divided all of Buddhism into two
parts. They insisted that all other Chinese Buddhist schools were based on
the Buddha's words as they appeared in the huge collection of sutras and
commentaries, but that Zen was based on the heart-to-heart transmission
of the Dharma (Truth) itself without relying on Buddha's verbal teachings.
This story is said to depict how that happened. In the story, when people in
the assembly expected that the Buddha would give some dharma discourse,
he took his seat but did not speak even one word. Instead he just picked
up a flower. The assembly did not understand what the Buddha was doing.
Only Mahakasyapa smiled, expressing his understanding without saying

anything. The Dharma was transmitted heart to heart, face to face, without any words. There was no thinking using words and concepts at all in this transmission.

The Buddha's words at the end of this story are a declaration of the superiority of the Zen tradition, transmitted heart to heart without using words and letters, to the teachings that were collections of the Buddha's words. However, we need to pay attention to the fact that this story needed those final comments to make its point about the superiority of Zen. The story is itself presented using language. Those who made up this story were "thinking" that transmission without language is superior than philosophical, conceptual discussion about the Buddha's teachings. This is the same as Manjushri's statement in the story of the thunderous silence of Vimalakirti.

Mahakasyapa, Ananda, and the Flagpole

> The Second ancestor Ananda asked Mahakasyapa, "Senior brother, beside the Buddha's golden brocade robe, what else have you transmitted?" Mahakasyapa called out, "Ananda!" Ananda responded, "Yes." Mahakasyapa said, "Pull down the flagpole in front of the gate." Ananda had a great realization.[17]

This story appears in Case 169 of *the Shinji Shobogenzo* and Case 22 of the *Gateless Barrier*. Ananda was the longtime personal attendant of Shakyamuni Buddha. He heard all of the Buddha's discourses and memorized everything. However, when the Buddha passed away, he had not yet attained arhathood, the highest rank of enlightenment in early Buddhism, and therefore he was not qualified to attend the first conference of five hundred elders. Right before the conference, Ananda asked Mahakasyapa what the Dharma (Truth) was that the Buddha had transmitted to him alone. Ananda was the very person who had memorized all of the Buddha's teachings and he knew all of them very well; still, he was not yet enlightened. What did he lack? Mahakasyapa called Ananda's name and Ananda responded. This meant that the Dharma was not some kind of "external thing" that Ananda could receive from someone else; the Dharma was found in his own practice. Then he asked Ananda to pull down the flagpole. At Buddhist monasteries, when they had dharma discourse or debate, it was customary to fly a banner at the top of a pole. To pull down the flagpole means to stop thinking about the Dharma using language. In the case of Ananda, it was an instruction to stop thinking about what he heard from the Buddha. The Dharma is not within the realm of memorizing, thinking, and discussing.

Dharma Transmission from Bodhidharma to Huike

The twenty-eighth ancestor said to his disciples, "The time [for me to return India] is coming. Why don't you say what you have attained?"

Then the disciple Daofu (Dofuku) said, "What I see now is neither clinging to words and letters nor being apart from words and letters, I carry out the function of the Way."

The Ancestor said, "You have attained my skin."

The nun Zongchi (Soji) said, "What I understand now is like Ananda seeing the land of Akshobhya-Buddha. He saw it only once and never saw it again."

The Ancestor said, "You have attained my flesh."

The disciple Daoyu (Do-iku) said, "The four great elements are originally empty. The five aggregates are not 'existence.' What I see is that there is no single dharma to be attained."

The Ancestor said, "You have attained my bones."

Finally, Huike (Eka) made three prostrations and then stood at his position.

The Ancestor said, "You have attained my marrow."

Then, [Bodhidharma] made him the Second Ancestor and transmitted the Dharma and the robe.[18]

This story appears in the section on Bodhidharma in *The Record of the Transmission of the Lamp*. The structure of this story is very similar to that of the story of Vimalakirti's thunderous silence. Bodhidharma asked his disciples to speak of what they had attained. Like the many bodhisattvas in the story of Vimalakirti, the first three disciples spoke of their understandings, which were indeed not mistaken views. What the third disciple said is the same as Manjushri's statement that the Dharma of nonduality cannot be spoken of in any way. Finally, Huike did exactly the same as Vimalakirti did; without saying anything, he made three prostrations in front of his master and returned to stand at his seat.

Dogen, the founder of the Japanese Soto Zen tradition, quoted this story in *Shobogenzo Katto* (Entanglement) and made unique comments on it. Usually, this story is interpreted to mean that Huike's understanding was superior to that of the other three disciples—that is, silent action is superior to expressing one's understanding using words. However, Dogen said that all four of them received Bodhidharma's heart/mind without anything lacking. Expression using silent action or using language is neither superior nor inferior. As far as they are the expression of the Dharma, they are equal. Later, I will discuss this understanding of Dogen, which is different from the common understanding of this story in the Zen tradition.

The World Honored One Ascends the Seat

One day the World Honored One ascended the seat. Manjushri struck the wooden sounding block and said, "Clearly see the Dharma of the Dharma

King; the Dharma of the Dharma King is thus." The World Honored One then descended from the seat.[19]

This story is Case 1 of the *Book of Serenity (Shoyoroku)*. It's the same kind of story as that of the Buddha picking up a flower and Mahakasyapa smiling. In this story, instead of Mahakasyapa smiling, Manjushri struck the wooden block and declared that the Buddha's Dharma can be expressed only in silence.

There are numberless similar stories in Zen literature. We can see that the essential point of these stories is the same as the point I introduced through the examples of Buddhist theories from early sutras about Shakyamuni Buddha, Mahayana sutras such as the *Vimalakirti Sutra*, Nagarjuna, Yogacara, and *tathagata-garba* theory. All of them discuss the relationship between the Dharma beyond thinking and the teachings that express the Dharma using words and letters. The relationship between the second and the third reasons of why "thinking" is a problem is the main points of these koans.

Mazu Daoyi (Baso Doitsu) and Shitou Xiqian (Sekito Kisen)

Chinese Zen is largely influenced by the *tathagata-garbha* (buddha-nature) theory mentioned in *The Awakening the Faith in Mahayana*. For example, one of the most important Zen masters in the T'ang Dynasty, Mazu Daoyi (Baso Doitsu, 709–88), said in his discourse:

> All of you should believe that your mind is Buddha, that this mind is identical with Buddha. The Great Master Bodhidharma came from India to China, and transmitted the One Mind teaching of Mahayana so that it can lead you all to awakening. Fearing that you will be too confused and will not believe that this One Mind is inherent in all of you, he used the *Lankavatara Sutra* to seal the sentient beings' mind-ground. Therefore, in the *Lankavatara Sutra*, mind is the essence of all the Buddha's teachings, no gate is the Dharma-gate.[20]

This One Mind, which is beyond what is experienced and the one who experiences, came from *The Awakening of Faith*. As is mentioned in that text, One Mind is the original reality beyond thinking; however, this Mind becomes *alaya* consciousness when it is influenced by the wind of ignorance and the waves (thinking) of karmic discriminating consciousness emerge. Basically, Zen practice based on this theory is to return to and restore the original One Mind by stopping one's involvement with thinking. Zen masters' direct actions, such as shouting or hitting someone with a staff, and their nonsensical answers to questions put to them are methods to liberate students from a discriminating, conceptual way of thinking. This method was used by many Zen masters in the Hongzhou school founded by Mazu Daoyi.

Shitou Xiqian (Sekito Kisen, 700–790) was a contemporary of Mazu. He was a well-known Zen master, but his school was much smaller than Mazu's. Later people characterized Mazu's style as a miscellaneous goods store and Shitou's as a true gold shop. Shitou did not used direct and violent methods but wrote wonderful poems such as *Merging Difference and Unity (Sandokai)*, in which he expressed the relationship between the ultimate truth (*ri*) beyond words and letters and the concrete and conventional truth (*ji*). For example, he wrote in *Sandokai*, "The spiritual source shines clearly in the light; the branching streams flow in the darkness."[21]

Linji (Rinzai) and Caodong (Soto)

In the Song Dynasty (960–1279), prestigious Chinese Buddhist monasteries were dominated by Zen Buddhism. Among the five schools of Zen established in the Tang Dynasty, only the Linji and Caodong schools survived until the Song Dynasty. The Linji school was from Mazu's lineage, while the Caodong school was from Shitou's lineage. Koan collections and commentaries were produced in this period in both Linji and Caodong. In the Linji school, *Blue Cliff Record (Hekiganroku)* and *Gateless Barrier (Mumonkan)* are the most important, and they are still used today. In the Caodong school, though several collections were made by various masters, *Book of Serenity (Shoyoroku)* is the most well known and still used.

However, these schools had different approaches to the koans. In the Linji tradition, *kanhua* (*kan-na*, "watching the koan story") Zen was developed. Linji masters, particularly Dahui Zonggao (Daie Soko, 1089–1163 CE), put emphasis on experiencing *kensho* ("seeing the original nature") through focusing on *huatou* (*wato*, a single word or phrase as the essence of each koan story). *Kensho* is a kind of psychological breakthrough experience that enables practitioners to see the original nature of Mind with no thinking arising. The most famous example of this practice is "*wu* (*mu*)" in the koan of Zhaozhou's "Dog's Buddha-nature." Dahui criticized Caodong Zen masters such as Zhenxie Qingliao (Shinketsu Seiryo, 1089–1151 CE) and Hongzhi Zheingjue (Wanshi Shokaku, 1091–1157 CE) and called their style of practice "Silent Illumination Evil Zen." This is the origin of the long-lasting argument between the Linji (Rinzai) and Caodong (Soto) schools continuing even today.[22]

The "Dog's Buddha-Nature" Koan in the Linji Tradition

To understand the characteristics of these two schools in Chinese Chan (Zen), it's interesting to compare their approaches to the same koan. We can see their attitudes toward thinking (karmic consciousness) and awakening to the reality beyond-thinking. One of the most famous koans is "Dog's Buddha-nature" (also called "Zhaozhou's *Mu*"), found in the *Gateless Barrier*. The story is very short: A monk once asked Master Zhaozhou, "Has a dog buddha-nature or not?" Zhaozhou said, "No (*Mu*)!" Wumen (Mumon)'s comment is:

> In practicing Zen, you must go through the barrier set up by ancestral masters. To attain the wondrous realization, you have to completely cut off the path of the mind (discriminating thinking). If you have not gone through the ancestors' barriers and cut off the path of the mind, you are simply phantoms haunting grasses and trees. Now tell me, what is the ancestors' barrier like? Simply this one character of *Mu* is the single barrier in the gate of our tradition. . . . Don't you want to break through the barrier? With your 360 bones and 84,000 thousand pores, throughout your entire body, arouse this doubt, and be attentive to this character *Mu*. Hold it day and night, and never have the view of voidness, or the dualistic view of being (*u*) and nonbeing (*mu*). It is like having swallowed a red-hot iron ball and even if you try to vomit it up, you cannot do it.[23]

To break through this koan, practitioners had to completely cut off thinking, both subjective and objective. D. T. Suzuki introduced how the Chinese Zen Master Wuxue Zuyuan (Mugaku Sogen, 1226–1286) practiced with *mu* in his essay "On Satori: The Revelation of a New Truth in Zen Buddhism."[24] It took him more than six years to pass through this koan. In the Rinzai tradition, people sit in the zendo or elsewhere and always focus on *mu*. When miscellaneous thoughts come up, they just return to *mu*. According to a modern Japanese Rinzai Zen master, until practitioners go through Zhaozhou's *mu* or a few other koans for beginners and attain a *kensho* experience, their masters prohibit them from reading any Buddhist texts. They do this because they consider reading and thinking (even about Buddhist teachings) an obstacle to being free from intellectual thinking. After several years of such practice, this Japanese master experienced a state in which no thoughts were aroused at all. He called that his *kensho* experience. That was not the goal of Rinzai practice but the starting point of the next stage of practice. In the Rinzai koan practice curriculum established by Hakuin (1685–1768), practitioners need to pass through hundreds of koans, and to work on those koans they need to study not only Buddhist teachings but also Daoist and Confucian texts. Once they really go beyond thinking, they start to study the Dharma with words and letters, and when they complete koan study, they practice outside of the temple in order to work with people in the world. This is called "practice after enlightenment" or "returning to the market place." In Rinzai practice, there are steps: first, practitioners go beyond thinking; then they study teachings using words and letters; and finally they return to the actual world to work with people.

"Dog's Buddha-Nature" Koan in Caodong Tradition

In Case 18 of the *Book of Serenity* produced within the Caodong school, the koan story is much longer.

A monk asked Zhaozhou, "Does a dog have a buddha-nature or not?"
Zhaozhou said, "Yes."
The monk said, "Since it has, why is it then in this skin bag?"
Zhaozhou said, "Because he knows yet deliberately transgresses."
Another monk asked Zhaozhou, "Does a dog have a buddha-nature or not?"
Zhaozhou said, "No."
The monk said, "All sentient beings have buddha-nature—why does a dog have none, then?"
Zhaozhou said, "Because he still has impulsive consciousness."[25]

A monk asked Zhaozhou exactly the same question as in the *Gateless Barrier* version: *"Does a dog have buddha-nature or not?" Zhaozhou said, "Yes."* This "yes" is *u*, so it means "Yes, it has." But in this version, the monk asked again: *"If the dog has buddha-nature, why is it then in this skin-bag?"* "Skin-bag" is the dog's body. If the dog has buddha-nature, why does it have to transmigrate and be born in the realm of animals and live as a dog? If a dog has buddha-nature, why does this living being need to be a dog, that is, to be part of the six realms of samsara? Buddha-nature is unconditioned, and the dog's body is conditioned within life and death and within time and space. Why does unconditioned buddha-nature need to be in the conditioned body of the dog? Zhaozhou said, *"Because he knows yet deliberately transgresses."* Zhaozhou is saying that this living being is a bodhisattva and therefore it surely has buddha-nature. As bodhisattvas, we need to take the four great bodhisattva vows. The first one is "Living beings are numberless; we vow to save them." "Save them" means to save them all. The first of the four bodhisattva vows means that until all living beings reach the cessation of suffering and enter nirvana, we vow not to enter ourselves. All bodhisattvas need to work within samsara until all beings enter the other shore. This is why bodhisattvas deliberately take on a conditioned body and mind and live in this world of samsara. The first bodhisattva vow means that we find nirvana within samsara. As bodhisattvas, we should continue to be in samsara without entering nirvana.

This means that we need to take certain forms as living beings; in our case, we have taken human form, but some bodhisattvas take the bodies of dogs, cats, or some other form. Some bodhisattvas intentionally create a certain kind of karma that brings about a future existence and become dogs. The dog can be a form of a bodhisattva. Because it intentionally or deliberately transgressed in making karma, it was born as a dog. In order to walk together and help others, we intentionally make karma. Therefore we need to take a certain form of living being; we cannot be formless. The dog as it is, even though it has karmic consciousness, is a bodhisattva. That is what Zhaozhou's answer means; the dog intentionally became a dog and got into the dog's skin-bag as a bodhisattva practice.

Then another monk asked Zhaozhou the same question: *"Does a dog have buddha-nature or not?"* This time Zhaozhou said, *"No (mu)."* First he said *u*, but to the next monk he said *mu*, and the conversation continued. This is different from the version in *the Gateless Barrier*, in which *"mu"* is all Zhaozhou said.

The monk asked again, *"All sentient beings have buddha-nature—why does a dog have none then?"* Then Zhaozhou said, *"Because he still has impulsive consciousness."* Impulsive consciousness is the same as *gosshiki* (karmic consciousness, or activating consciousness), which appears in the section of *The Awakening of Faith* that I discussed earlier. In the Rinzai approach, only *mu* is important, but in the Caodong approach, it's important to see both sides: *u* and *mu*.

There is an introduction to this story by Wansong Xingxiu (Bansho Gyo-shu, 1166–246 CE), the Chinese Caodong Zen master who compiled *Book of Serenity*. It says:

> A gourd floating on the water—push it down and it turns; a jewel in the sun-light—it has no definite shape. It cannot be attained by mindlessness, nor known by mindfulness. Immeasurably great people are turned about in the stream of words—is there anyone who can escape?[26]

This mindlessness is *mu-shin* (無心), and mindfulness is *u-shin* (有心); again there is a pair of *mu* and *u*. The point in the Caodong approach is to inquire why Zhaozhou gave opposite and contradictory answers to the same question. In this introduction, Wansong said that it's like a gourd. A gourd is emptied and dried and used as a water container. It's like a plastic bottle. When it is empty and floating on the water, if we push down, it turns around. That means that buddha-nature is like the empty bottle floating on the water. When we push it, it turns, and sometimes it appears as *u* and sometimes as *mu*. We cannot say whether it is definitely *u* or *mu*. In this case *u* and *mu* are a pair and opposites, and this pair is always turning. We see buddha-nature from *u* and *mu* without clinging to either of them. When we see it from one angle it is like *mu*, and from another angle it is like *u*. When seeing it from one perspective, buddha-nature is there: the dog has buddha-nature. But from another perspective, there is no such thing as buddha-nature. That is what Chinese Caodong (Soto) Zen points out in this koan. In this case, Caodong masters enable their students to awaken to the reality beyond duality, beyond thinking, by showing two sides that are opposite and negate each other.

There is another point in the *Book of Serenity* version. In his verse on this koan, Hongzhi interpreted Zhaozhou's answers of *u* to the first monk and *mu* to the second monk as a method of education. Hongzhi thought the first monk was a beginner and therefore Zhaozhou said a dog has buddha-nature as a kind of encouragement. To the second monk, who was a more experienced practitioner, he took buddha-nature away as a method to help the monk free himself from clinging to the concept of "buddha-nature." This is the same method as Mazu used. His famous saying was "The mind is itself Buddha," but later he said, "Neither the mind, nor the Buddha." First, he gave a yellow leaf to a crying baby saying it was gold; then later, when the baby stopped crying, Mazu took it away.

DOGEN

Dogen's View about Buddha-Nature

Dogen's interpretation of buddha-nature is very different from the ones in *Gateless Barrier* and *Book of Serenity*. In the very beginning of *Shobogenzo Bussho (Buddha-nature)*, Dogen discusses his basic understanding of what buddha-nature is and is not.

There Dogen quotes the well-known statement from the *Mahayana Parinirvana Sutra* that says, "All living beings without exception have buddha-nature." The statement in the *Parinirvana Sutra* is: "*Issai shujo shitsu u bussho* (一切衆生悉有佛性)." *Issai* is "all," *shujo* is "living beings," *shitsu* means all of them without any exception, *u* means "to have," and *bussho* is buddha-nature. All living beings without exception have buddha-nature. This is a very clear sentence. There is no question.

But Dogen reads *shitsu* and *u* in a completely different way. This is an example of how he plays with words. He even ignores Chinese grammar. He reads *shitsu-u* as one word, as a kanji compound and as a noun. *U* can be read as "to be" or "being" instead of "to have." *Shitsu* can be read as the adjective "entire" or "whole." He reads this as a compound, *shitsu-u*, that is, "entire-being." Thus, he reads this sentence as "All living beings, entire-being is buddha-nature," instead of "All living beings have buddha-nature." Dogen's point is that buddha-nature is not something owned by living beings or hidden within them. It is not like a diamond hidden within rocks and dirt. This is the difference between a common understanding of buddha-nature and Dogen's understanding. One of the most important sayings in Dogen's teaching is "Nothing is hidden." That means buddha-nature is not something hidden. The common understanding of buddha-nature from the *Tathagata-gharba Sutra* is that even though we have it, it is hidden because it is covered with our delusive thinking; therefore we usually cannot see it and we have to discover it. To discover this hidden diamond, buddha-nature, is called *kensho* in Rinzai practice. However, from Dogen's point of view, buddha-nature is not something like the diamond hidden within delusion or dirt. Instead the entire-being of all living beings is buddha-nature. He discusses this in the beginning of *Shobogenzo Bussho* (*Buddha-nature*):

> Though we may call them living beings, sentient beings, various groups of living beings, or various kinds, the word "entire being" refers to living beings, or various beings. That is, "entire being" is buddha-nature. I call one entirety of "entire being" a living being. At the very moment of thusness, inside and outside of a living being is nothing other than "entire being" of buddha-nature.[27]

Dogen is saying that in Mahayana teaching, we all exist as knots of Indra's net, and everything is connected within this net. When we touch one knot, we touch the entire net. One includes everything, one is connected with all beings, all beings are reflected in this one, and this is true for each and every being. This is how entire-beings exist, and this reality itself is buddha-nature. Buddha-nature is not something hidden in individual living beings; the way things are, as a network of interdependent origination, is itself buddha-nature. "At the very moment of thusness" means when things are within this interconnectedness. Each and every being within this network is buddha-nature. This is a very basic understanding of buddha-nature according to Dogen, which is different from both the Chinese Linji and Caodong approaches.

Considered from Dogen's point of view on buddha-nature, the common interpretation of these conversations between Zhaozhou and the two monks does not make sense at all because they are discussing whether a dog "has" buddha-nature or not. According to Dogen, buddha-nature is not something dogs or human beings can own like a hidden jewel within the self. Because Dogen is within the Soto tradition and he respects Hongzhi, he quotes the same conversation used in the *Book of Serenity*. Yet he carefully makes a small change, and he reads the same conversation in a unique way. He ignores even the grammar, and he reads each Chinese character very unconventionally.

Dogen's Comments on "Dog's Buddha-Nature"

Dogen's comments on this koan are long and unique. It is very clear he is not bound by either Chinese Chan tradition in interpreting this koan. His unusual comments come from his unique understanding of buddha-nature, and this shows another Zen approach to the problem of "thinking." The Linji tradition focuses on the *huatou*, the essential point of the koan, and cuts off the path of thinking by really experiencing the cessation of thinking. In the Caodong tradition, buddha-nature is seen from positive (*u*) and negative (*mu*) perspectives in order to enable practitioners to free themselves from attachment to either side and awaken to the reality beyond thinking. Dogen interprets this koan story as the exact depiction of bodhisattva practice.

First of all, for Dogen, the question of whether or not the dog has buddha-nature does not make sense at all. He does not read this koan story as a teaching tool as Hongzhi does, and therefore he deliberately changes the order of the conversation. In Dogen's version, first Zhaozhou said *mu*, and then to the second monk he said *u*. Now I will introduce Dogen's comments on the koan with some explanations.

> *A monk asked Great Master Zhenji of Zhaozhou, "Does a dog have buddha-nature or not?"* We should clarify the intention of [the monk who is asking] this question. Gouzi means "a dog." [The monk] is neither asking if [a dog] has buddha-nature, nor asking if [a dog] has not buddha-nature. He is asking if an iron man also studies the Way. Although [the monk] may deeply regret having been seized unexpectedly by [Zhaozhou's] poison hand, he did it in the excellent style of finally seeing half a sage after thirty years.[28]

"*Gouzi* (狗子, *kushi*)" is the Chinese word used in the monk's question. Dogen translates this into the Japanese word *inu* (いぬ、犬) without using Chinese characters, possibly so that his Japanese audience could be certain that a dog was meant. The expression "an iron man" (鐵漢, *tekkan*) means a very determined bodhisattva. For a determined bodhisattva there is no question of whether or not he continues to practice. Precisely because he is ceaselessly practicing, he is called the iron man. Dogen is saying that this is not a question but a statement. Dogen doesn't think the monk asks this question because he doesn't know the answer; the monk is saying that because the dog is an iron man, it is always practicing. The dog is a bodhisattva. To be a dog is its way of practice, and it is expressing buddha-nature as an iron man.

By asking this question, the monk was caught with "[Zhaozhou's] poisoned hand." However, Dogen points out that the monk's seemingly foolish question is not in vain. "His resentment may be intense" means the monk didn't really want to ask such an obvious question, but it was a means of "seeing half a real saint at last, after thirty years," of bringing out Zhaozhou's answer. The monk intentionally made a mistake to help Zhaozhou to express how a bodhisattva practices with all beings, including the realm of animals. Zhaozhou's answering this question is the same way that Shakyamuni Buddha stood up from the diamond seat under the bodhi tree after his awakening and walked to Deer Park to teach the five monks. The Buddha also intentionally made a mistake when he tried to teach using words about something beyond thinking, but without this mistake, Buddhism would not exist. The

Buddha returned to the marketplace to teach. This is also the same as Vimala-kirti's sickness, which allowed him to preach the dharma.[29]

Zhaozhou said, "It does not have (mu)." Hearing this saying, there must be a path to study [we should follow]. The "mu" that buddha-nature itself speaks must be said in such a way; the "mu" that the dog itself speaks must be said in such a way; the "mu" that a bystander cries out must be said in such a way. The "mu" will have a day when at the very least it melts stone.

Dogen says this *mu* is really important. *Mu* is the way to express the reality of each and every being within interdependence. When we see ourselves as individuals, we exist as karmic people. I was born seventy-three years ago in Japan and I have been living in a particular way as a zazen practitioner, so I am kind of a unique person. Now I am writing about my understanding of Dogen's teaching. I am here and now as Shohaku, this collection of five aggregates is here as Shohaku, but actually there is no such fixed entity called Shohaku existing without relation to others. In this sense each and every thing is *mu*, but also there is no such entity as a whole of interconnectedness. *Mu* is one of the ways to see this reality. There is no individuality, and also there is no whole. Interconnectedness is the only thing there. Yet later on, Dogen talks about this reality as *u*. Basically, his idea is a continuation of the Chinese Caodong (Soto) Zen teachings, but he deconstructs the concept of buddha-nature and then reconstructs it. He writes that this reality of inter-dependent origination is itself buddha-nature, and *u* and *mu* are two ways of viewing this one reality. One being can be a dog, and another being can be a human being or a cat or a desk or a glass of water. Everything is there as it is, and yet these things are really not there. This *mu* is the complete expression of buddha-nature and also the complete expression of how a dog is and how a human being is. This is what Zhaozhou means by saying *"mu."*

In this passage, "bystander" means those who are thinking about what Zhaozhou said, or about the meaning of this conversation. We are bystand-ers. Bystanders are also *mu*. This *mu* has a stone-melting power. It is said that when the sun is really powerful, even the stones will melt like snow. This means that *mu* can completely melt away our karmic nature. When we really see the emptiness of all beings, we are liberated from our grasping or attach-ment to ourselves and we can be free from our self-centeredness. The five aggregates of attachment (*panca upadana skandha*) become liberated from attachment to themselves and can be simply five aggregates (*panca skandha*) that are empty.

The monk said, "All living beings, all of them have buddha-nature, why does the dog not have?" The essential principle is that if all living beings are "mu," buddha-nature also must be "mu," and the dog also must be "mu." [The monk is asking] what is such an essential principle like? Why should the dog's buddha-nature have to wait for "mu"?

This is Dogen's comment about the second question by the monk. What Dogen means is that all beings, not only dogs, are *mu*. Even buddha-nature is *mu*, and even living beings are *mu*. "No sentient beings" means sentient beings are *mu*. Everything has disappeared completely; even the dog has disappeared. "What" is the translation of the word *somosan* (作麼生). This word is used in Zen literature to refer to something that cannot be named or defined in any way, that is, this reality of interdependent origination itself that is often translated as "thusness." "What" is this thing? This means the entirety of interdependent origination. In Dogen's version of this koan, first Zhaozhou points out the side of *mu*. If everything is *mu*, it doesn't need to be called *mu*, and even the word *mu* disappears.

Zhaozhou said, "Because it has karmic consciousness." What this saying means is that "being for the sake of others" is [being] with karmic consciousness. Even if "being (*u*) with karmic consciousness" or "being (*u*) for the sake of others," the dog is "nonbeing (*mu*)," and buddha-nature is "nonbeing (*mu*)." Karmic consciousness has not yet understood the dog; how could the dog meet with buddha-nature? Whether we let go of the two ["being (*u*)" and "nonbeing (*mu*)"] or take in the two, it is still the beginning and end of karmic consciousness.

This is Zhaozhou's answer to the second question from the first monk. Again, Dogen reads the original Chinese sentence in a unique way. The Chinese sentence is very short: *i ta u gosshiki zai* (為他有業識在). In a common way of reading this Chinese sentence, *i* is "because," *ta* shows third person, *u* is "to have," *gosshiki* is "karmic consciousness," and *zai* means "to be"— "Because it (the dog) has karmic consciousness." This is the common way of reading this sentence. However, in the next sentence Dogen says, "What this saying means is that 'being for the sake of others' is [being] with karmic consciousness." When we only read this English translation, it's not clear where this expression, "existence for the sake of others," comes from, but when we read this in Chinese, we can see that Dogen reads the first three words of the sentence in a very creative way. Another meaning for this character *i* is "for the sake of," *ta* can be "others," and instead of "to have," *u* can mean "being." Thus, it is possible to read these three Chinese characters (為他有) as "existence for the sake of others." "A being for the sake of others" is a bodhisattva. In order to work with all beings, to carry out the bodhisattva vows, to help others to cross over the river between this shore and the other shore, all bodhisattvas need karmic consciousness. That is how Dogen reads this sentence. He reads this as "Because the dog or the bodhisattva is an existence for the sake of others, in order to work with others in this world, the dog needs karmic consciousness." When we only read the English translation, we cannot really understand why Dogen could read this sentence in this way.

To understand Dogen's writing only in translation is very difficult—almost impossible.

An existence for the sake of others, a bodhisattva, needs to have karmic consciousness. Dogen uses "karmic consciousness" in a positive way. Commonly in Buddhism, karmic consciousness is a cause of transmigration within samsara that creates karma and results in our continued suffering, and we try to eliminate it or be liberated from it. What Dogen is saying here is the opposite. We need karmic consciousness in order to be bodhisattvas. Because of the bodhisattva vow, we have to stay in samsara and we vow not to enter nirvana. In order to work on this shore, to help others, we need karmic consciousness. Our practice is not to eliminate karmic consciousness; instead we need to learn how to use karmic consciousness for the sake of others.

Dogen says, *"Karmic consciousness has not yet understood the dog,"* because karmic consciousness is the dog itself. Without the discriminating thinking that is the function of karmic consciousness, the dog disappears. It is not a matter of how karmic consciousness understands the dog. "Karmic consciousness is itself the dog" means that there is no subject/object separation or relationship. There is no way to understand the dog as an object. A dog cannot see the dog itself. Karmic consciousness cannot see karmic consciousness itself, as our eyes cannot see themselves.

Nor can the dog encounter buddha-nature; Dogen says, *"How could the dog meet with buddha-nature?"* Karmic consciousness, the dog, and buddha-nature: all are exactly one thing. It is not a matter of karmic consciousness understanding the dog, or the dog encountering buddha-nature. Whether we see that we are deluded, self-centered beings, or whether we think we exist for the sake of others as bodhisattvas, both are actually there, and we are 100 percent both. It's not a fifty-fifty split. Karmic consciousness and buddha-nature are really one thing. We are 100 percent karmic consciousness, conditioned karmic people, individual deluded people, and we are also 100 percent buddha-nature. In order to work within this shore of samsara, buddha-nature needs karmic consciousness—buddha-nature needs to manifest itself as a karmic consciousness. This is Dogen's interpretation of the first conversation between the monk and Zhaozhou. *A monk asked Zhaozhou, "Does a dog have buddha-nature or not?"* This question is about the principle for this monk to get hold of Zhaozhou. Therefore expressing and asking buddha-nature is ordinary tea and rice of the buddha-ancestors.

Then another monk asked Zhaozhou exactly the same question. Again, according to Dogen, this is not a question. It's a trap for the monk to test and get hold of Zhaozhou, and Dogen says the monk is successful. In the previous part of *Shobogenzo Buddha-nature*, Dogen complained about the ancient Chinese Zen masters, saying that they only discussed whether a dog has buddha-nature or not, not what buddha-nature actually is. Here he is trying to discuss what buddha-nature is. According to him, this discussion is carried out in day-to-day ordinary things, like eating rice three times a day or drinking tea every day. We need to inquire what buddha-nature is within our daily activities instead of in some mystical space or otherworldly realm.

Zhaozhou said, "It has (u)."[30] The way this "being (*u*)" exists is not the same with "existence" of the commentary masters in the teaching schools; is not the same with "existence" discussed in Sarvastivadin (Existence School). We should further advance and study buddha-being (*butsu-u*). Buddha-being is Zhaozhou-being; Zhaozhou-being is dog-being; dog-being is buddha-nature-being.

This time, Zhaozhou answered, "It has," or *u*. Sarvastivadin is one of the twenty schools of Buddhism that existed before Mahayana Buddhism. This school put emphasis on *u*. In their Abhidarma texts[31] such as the *Abhidharmakosa-shastra*, Sarvastivadins analyzed dharmas (beings) into seventy-five kinds, and they said that there is no *atman* or self; the seventy-five dharmas are really *u*, "being," and they exist substantially and permanently in the past, present, and future. The Japanese translation of the name Sarvastivada is *Setsu issai u bu* (説一切有部), "the school that insists that all dharmas are *u*."

This is the main doctrine of Abhidharma teaching that Mahayana Buddhism and especially Nagarjuna criticized. Nagarjuna's teaching of emptiness is a negation of this *u*. What Dogen is saying here is that the *u* of which Zhaozhou is speaking is not the kind of metaphysical *u* described by the Sarvastivadins, a fixed, permanent entity. Instead *u* is one side of emptiness. I am here as Shohaku and I am *u*, but this *u* as a collection of five aggregates that is a phenomenon is not a metaphysical *u*, a fixed independent entity that can exist without relationship to others. This collection of five aggregates is empty. *U* and *mu* are two sides of emptiness, and emptiness is also neither *u* nor *mu*. That is what Dogen wants to say. This way of being is what buddha-nature is. The way all things are, as both *u* and *mu*, and neither *u* or *mu* is buddha-nature. Therefore he also used the expression "*u*-buddha-nature" and "*mu*-buddha-nature" in the later part of *Shobogenzo Buddha-nature*. *U* is one side of buddha-nature and *mu* is another side.

An important point is that these sides are not half and half; from one side, everything is really there as a collection of all different kind of elements. Yet because it is just a collection of various elements, it is not really there, and in that sense, it is *mu*. Without relationship with all other beings, each and every thing cannot exist for even one moment.

This is what Dogen expresses for example in *Genjokoan*, when he says that the entire vastness of the moon's light is reflected in every drop of water. This reflection refers to the connection. In each and every being, the entirety of the network of interdependent origination is reflected or illuminated. Each thing is illuminated by everything. This is the way the buddha-nature is, and we are part of this entirety.

Another expression Dogen uses is *zenki* (全機). *Zen* here means "total" or "entire" and *ki* is "function." This is not simply a network but a dynamic working. This *ki* is function or work, but *ki* also can mean a machine or mechanism. For example, the oldest machine in China is the weaving machine. When we push one part of the machine, the treadle, the entire machine moves and works and makes the fabric. When a loom is used in Zen literature as a metaphor, often the vertical thread (warp) is referred to as time and the horizontal thread (weft) is referred to as space. This entire network is always working, functioning, and moving, and this dynamic movement throughout time and space is how buddha-nature works. Each of us is a part of that total function. That is how Dogen sees our life and this world in which we live. Dogen is saying that our lives operating as part of total function is not the metaphysical *u* discussed in Sarvastivadin teaching.

All beings are part of this entirety of interconnectedness within time and space; that is Buddha's Dharma body. As is said in the *Sutra of Buddha's Final Discourse*, after Shakyamuni's death, when we practice following the Buddha's teaching, the tathagata's dharma-body is always manifested within our practice and is indestructible. "Buddha-being" means the way things are as emptiness. Zhaozhou, the dog, and each of us are all buddha-nature-being. Our practice is to participate in this total function and manifest the dharma body intentionally and actively.

The monk said, "Since [the dog] already has it, why did it enter forcibly into this skin-bag?" In asking if what this monk expresses is present-being, ancient-being, already-being, although already-being resembles various beings, already-being is solitary and bright. Should already-being enter forcibly or not enter forcibly? The action of entering forcibly into the skin-bag is not a vain, mistaken effort.

This "entering forcibly into" means to be born as a dog and get into a dog's skin-bag. Because of the bodhisattva vows, we take this form of a dog or a human being. In a sense, all of us are bodhisattvas whether we become Buddhists or not. We are living for the sake of others, we are supported by all beings, and because we are part of the network of all beings, we also support others. We cannot be completely independent and have no relationships with others. This way of being is the basis of the bodhisattva vows. In another sense, to become bodhisattvas means that we awaken to and accept that reality and intentionally or actively try to support others instead of being harmful to others.

We need to be dogs or some other forms of life. We are already born as dogs or human beings with certain conditions. We have to accept this and to live together with others. This "deliberately" or "intentionally" doesn't refer to an individual person's intention but to Buddha's intention. Buddha in this case means this entire network. This network's intention allows all beings to be bodhisattvas. That is the only way we can be. To be born into a dog's skin-bag is not a mistake. A bodhisattva needs some kind of skin-bag in order to work with others. Life is something formless; to be living beings, we need certain conditioned forms within time and space. This is what Dogen means when he says in *Genjokoan*, "We should know that [for a fish] water means life, [for a bird] sky means life. A bird is life; a fish is life. Life is a bird; life is a fish."

According to Dogen, the bodhisattva is born into the skin-bag on purpose. He is saying that the word "entering forcibly into" is not necessary, because put this way it means that something that is not a dog was born as the dog. There is separation of the bodhisattva and dog's skin-bag. The bodhisattva is the skin-bag itself. To live in a skin-bag and practice as a bodhisattva is itself the daily activity that constitutes the emancipated body of suchness. Because we live with certain particular forms of living beings, we are conditioned and live with karmic consciousness with which we need to think. Yet when we arouse bodhi-citta and study and practice the Buddha's teachings based on the four bodhisattva vows, we are bodhisattvas.[32]

Our practice as not-matured bodhisattvas is full of mistakes, and yet that is a part of "the dog entering forcibly into such a skin-bag." This is exactly how buddha-nature works. Dogen transforms the meaning of transmigrating within samsara life after life. This life with the human skin-bag is not something from which we need to escape; we need to live within this skin-bag to continue bodhisattva practice.

We can see how Dogen's interpretation of dog's buddha-nature koan is different from that of Chinese Rinji and Caodong traditions. For Dogen, in this koan the monks and Zhaozhou together depict how a bodhisattva continues to practice in this actual world as a conditioned person. As conditioned people, we need karmic consciousness and thinking. Thinking is not something we have to throw away, but we need to study how to live with thinking without being deceived by it.

CONCLUSION: BEYOND THINKING

According to Dogen's manual of zazen practice entitled *Universal Recommendation of Zazen (Fukanzazengi)*, there are three important points in this sitting practice: harmonizing body, harmonizing breath, and harmonizing mind.

As for harmonizing mind, he only wrote: "Think of not-thinking. How do you think of not-thinking? Beyond-thinking." This is a quote from a koan that is a dialogue between Yaoshan Weiyan (Yakusan Igen,751–834, a disciple of Shitou Xiqian) and a monk:

When Great Master Yaoshan Hongdao was sitting, a monk asked, "What is thinking in steadfast immovable sitting?"
The Master replied, "Thinking of not-thinking."
The monk said, "How is the thinking of not-thinking?"
The Master said, "Beyond-thinking."[33]

In the beginning of *Shobogenzo Zazenshin* (Acupuncture Needle of Zazen), he makes comments on this conversation to express the essential meaning of zazen. His way of reading this conversation is again unique. He reads "Think of not-thinking" as "Thinking is nothing other than not-thinking" and says, "Thinking is the skin, flesh, bones and marrow [of zazen]. Not-thinking is the skin, flesh, bones, and marrow [of zazen]." This means both thinking and not-thinking are the entirety of zazen. In common logic, thinking and not-thinking are opposite and negate each other; therefore it is not possible that both of them are there at the same time. However, Dogen says thinking and not-thinking completely interpenetrate each other within zazen. In this point, Dogen is more radical than Nagarjuna, who said, "Without relying on everyday common practice (i.e., relative truths), the absolute truth cannot be expressed. Without approaching the absolute truth, nirvana cannot be attained." Yet Dogen goes even further by saying that the absolute truth and the conventional truth, nirvana and samsara, are one and all are the entirety of just sitting zazen.

He reads, "How do you think of not-thinking" as "Not-thinking is thinking of how." In this case, the word "how" is interpreted not as an interrogative but a noun that refers to the way things are as thusness. Both thinking (the relative truth) and not-thinking (the absolute truth) are nothing other than the true reality of all beings, and both thinking and not-thinking are beyond-thinking (*hi-shiryo*). He uses the same logic as he did when writing that emptiness is neither "*u*" nor "*mu*" but both "*u*" and "*mu*."

In zazen, we sit in the upright posture facing the wall. We keep our eyes open, breathe through the nose deeply and smoothly from the abdomen without making noise, and let go of thoughts. Even when we sit in this posture, all different kinds of thoughts, emotion, daydreams, etc. are coming and going, arising and perishing. When we become aware that we are thinking about them, we stop thinking and return to the posture, breathing, and letting go. We simply repeat this millions of times in zazen.

In zazen, we don't have any external object. We sit facing the wall, but the wall is not an object; we don't gaze at the wall. Neither do we have any internal object on which we concentrate the mind. However, those thoughts coming and going often become objects and we start to interact with them. In such a circumstance, the mind becomes divided into two pieces, subject (the person sitting) and objects (the thoughts). As soon as we become aware of such a separation within our minds, we return to just sitting and become one piece. Because during zazen we have no internal and external objects, it is very clear that when we are thinking, those thoughts are illusion, not reality. Then we let go of them. Even though we let go and return to just sitting, in the next moment thoughts come back, and we let go of them again.

Even when we sit in this posture, all the other parts of our body continue to function; our stomachs are digesting, our hearts are beating and circulating blood, and all the billions of cells in our bodies are still working. There is no reason for only our brains to stop working when we sit in zazen. The function of our brains is to produce thoughts. It is very natural that thoughts welling up from our brains (in Buddhist terms, from the karmic consciousness) are coming and going. When we grasp any of these thoughts as objects, then we are thinking. It is different from thoughts just coming and going like clouds in the sky.

In zazen, we don't grasp any thoughts but let go of them. Thoughts are there but "I" don't think. These are simply secretions from our brains or karmic consciousness. When one drives a car and puts it into a neutral gear, the engine is still moving but the car does not move. Similarly, in zazen we don't take any action based on the thoughts that are coming and going. When we grasp some thoughts and take action, we make karma; when we let go of them and do not take any action, no karma is made. We are free from karmic consciousness, although karmic consciousness is still working. We don't escape from karmic consciousness or fight against it to eliminate it, but we are not deceived by thoughts. We simply let go of them and just sit. Dogen calls this practice *shikantaza*, just sitting.

In the early Buddhist teaching, the five skandhas of attachment (*panca upadana skandha*) are themselves suffering. There is no sufferer beside the five aggregates.[34] During zazen, we are simply being five skandhas; we don't grasp the five skandhas as "I." Five skandhas are simply five skandhas. This is when we (five skandhas) cease to be five "skandhas of attachment." The first sentence of the *Heart Sutra* says, "Avalokiteshvara Bodhisattva, when deeply practicing *prajna paramita*, clearly saw that all five skandhas are empty, and thus relieved all suffering." This sitting is itself *prajna paramita*, and also clear seeing. "Five skandhas of attachment" is Mara, the demon conquered by the Buddha when he attained awakening, but "five skandha of emptiness" in our zazen is Avalokiteshvara, the bodhisattva of wisdom and compassion.

All of the Buddhist traditions have some kind of meditation practice. Zazen in Dogen's tradition is also considered to be a kind of meditation, but this is a very unusual meditation practice. First of all, zazen has no object of meditation on which to focus the mind. We don't use meditation techniques such as counting breaths, watching breath, visualization, chanting mantras, etc. Commonly, meditation practice is considered to be a method to attain "altered states of consciousness that are ecstatic, aimed initially at withdrawing the practitioners' senses and thoughts from interaction with the external world and finally at bringing all mental activity to a halt."[35] In zazen, we don't aim at attaining some altered states of mind. We simply return to here and now whenever we find that our minds have gone somewhere else.

All of the four reasons why thinking is always a problem in Buddhism that I mentioned in the beginning of this article are taken care of within this simple practice. We let go of both subjective thinking, which makes our lives samsara (physical eye, the first of five eyes), and objective thinking that creates our fixed system of values and our picture of world (divine eye). We are not deceived by them. The practice of letting go in our sitting helps us to let go of our biased and fixed ideas about things that hook us to certain objects. Even when we are not sitting and just moving through our daily lives, this practice enables us to let go of our stereotyped concepts and allows us to be flexible.

Just sitting is itself the *prajna* eye that does not see anything from a fixed point of view. By helping us to let go of our subjective thinking and rational thinking, even including Buddhist teachings and our understanding of the Dharma, zazen enables us to sit on the ground of reality in which everything is connected with everything. Zazen is practice, not a theory about reality or truth. We need to continue to practice endlessly. Finally, the practice of "thinking of not-thinking; beyond thinking" enables us to use thinking freely and creatively as Dogen did in many of his writings. This just sitting is itself the Dharma eye. Within this simple practice, the Tathagata's dharma body manifests itself.

NOTES

1. In writing this article, I received help from Shoryu Bradley, Hoko Karnegis, and David Thompson. I would like to express my heartfelt appreciation to them. Please see the appendix for translation notes.

2. The six realms of samsara are heavenly beings, *asuras* (fighting spirits), humans, animals, hungry ghosts, and hell dwellers.

3. *The Diamond Sutra*, translation by Red Pine (New York: Counterpoint, 2001), 307. The translation of the following comments by Nagarjuna are from the same book (310–13).

4. A bodhisattva is a being who has aroused the aspiration to awaken but has vowed not to leave the world of samsara until all other beings have themselves awakened.

5. Yogacara is a school of Indian Mahayana Buddhist philosophy that explains how our human experience is constructed by the mind.

6. Hajime Nakamura, *Gotama Buddha: A Biography Based on the Most Reliable Texts* (Tokyo: Kosei Publishing Co., 2000), 228.

7. Kenneth K. Inada, *Nagarujuna: A Translation of His* Mulamadhyamakakarika *with an Introductory Essay* (Tokyo: The Hokuseido Press, 1970), 146.

8. I paraphrased and shortened the story from *The Vimalakirti Sutra*, trans. Burton Watson (Columbia University Press, 1997), 104–11.

9. *The Vimalakirti Sutra*, 310–13.

10. The other two are the *nirmanakaya*, the physical body that manifests in time and space, and the *sambhogakaya*, the reward body.

11. *Gotama Buddha*, 252.

12. The Madhyamaka school holds that all things are empty of any essence that gives them an existence independent of all other things because they cannot arise and come into being on their own. The Yogacara school asserts that the ordinary operations of the consciousness are the root of our delusion because they create separation into subject and object.

13. Tathagata (Skt.) means "one who has thus gone." It is another term for a buddha.

14. *The Awakening of Faith: Attributed to Asvaghosha*, trans. Yoshito S. Hakeda (Columbia University Press, 1967), 31.

15. A koan is a paradoxical story or question designed to release a practitioner from habituated ways of thinking.

16. This is my translation. Another translation is in Zenkei Shibayama, *Zen Comments on the Mumonkan* (New York: Harper & Row, 1974), 58.

17. This is my translation from Case 169 of *Shinji Shobogenzo*. Another translation is in Zenkei Shibayama, *Zen Comments on the Mumonkan*, 158.

18. This is my translation from *Shobogenzo Katto* (Entanglement). Another translation is in Andy Ferguson, *Zen's Chinese Heritage: The Masters and Their Teachings* (Boston: Wisdom Publications, 2000), 16–17.

19. My translation. Another translation is in Thomas Cleary, *Book of Serenity: One Hundred Zen Dialogues* (New York: Lindisfarne Press, New 1990), 3.

20. Cheng Chien Bhikshu, *Sunface Buddha: The Teachings of Ma-tsu and the Hung-chou School of Ch'an* (Berkeley: Asian Humanities Press, 1992), 62.

21. For a discussion, see chapter 7 in Shohaku Okumura, *Living by Vow* (Boston: Wisdom Publications, 2012), 207.

22. About Dahui's criticism of Caodong's silent illumination Zen, see Morten Schlutter, *How Zen Became Zen: The Dispute over Enlightenment and the Formation of Chan Buddhism in Song-Dynasty China* (University of Hawaii Press, 2008).

23. This is my translation. Another translation is in *Zen Comments on the Mumonkan*, 19.

24. D. T. Suzuki, *Essays in Zen Buddhism First Series* (New York: Grove Press, 1949), 255–56.

25. Translation by Cleary, *Book of Serenity*, 76.

26. Cleary, *Book of Serenity*.

27. This is Okumura's unpublished translation. Another translation is in *The Heart of Dogen's Shobogenzo*, trans. Norman Waddell and Masao Abe (State University of New York Press, 2002), 61.

28. Dogen's comments in this section are Okumura's unpublished translation. Another translation is in *The Heart of Dogen's Shobogenzo*, 91–94.

29. The character of Vimalakirti is a wealthy layman and an advanced Buddhist practitioner. He feigns illness in order that various humans and bodhisattvas will visit him, giving him the chance to expound the teachings.

30. This "it has" and the "has" in the monk's quotation is *u*, and here this means "being." I changed the translation from "has" to "being" and also added *u* to read this passage.

31. The Abhidharma texts are made up of summaries and systematic lists of material appearing in the sutras.

32. Bodhi-citta is one of the key concepts in Mahayana Buddhism. This word is translated into English variously, for example, "awakening mind," "thought of awakening," "aspiration to awakening," "way-seeking mind," etc. A person who has aroused this mind is called a bodhisattva. This is a basic motivation of bodhisattva practice to seek awakening and help others to do so. Dogen wrote in *Shobogenzo Hotsu-bodaishin* (Arousing Bodhi-citta), "To arouse the bodhi-mind means to take a vow that, 'Before I myself cross over, [I will] help all living beings cross over [the river between this shore of samsara and the other shore of nirvana]' and strive to [fulfill this vow]. Even if their outside appearance is humble, those who have aroused this mind are already the guiding teachers of all living beings."

33. Okumura's translation.

34. See Walpola Rahula, *What the Buddha Taught* (New York: Grove Press, 1959), 20.

35. Paul J. Griffiths, *Indian Buddhist Meditation (Buddhist Spirituality)*, ed. Takeuchi Yoshinori (New York: Crossroad, 1993), 36–37.

Chapter 11

Introduction to J. Krishnamurti[1]

David Bohm

My first acquaintance with Krishnamurti's work was in 1959 when I read his book *The First and Last Freedom*. What particularly aroused my interest was his deep insight into the question of the observer and the observed. This question had long been close to the center of my own work, as a theoretical physicist, who was primarily interested in the meaning of the quantum theory. In this theory, for the first time in the development of physics, the notion that these two cannot be separated has been put forth as necessary for the understanding of the fundamental laws of matter in general. Because of this, as well as because the book contained many other deep insights, I felt that it was urgent for me to talk with Krishnamurti directly and personally as soon as possible. And when I first met him on one of his visits to London, I was struck by the great ease of communication with him, which was made possible by the intense energy with which he listened and by the freedom from self-protective reservations and barriers with which he responded to what I had to say.

As a person who works in science I felt completely at home with this sort of response, because it was in essence of the same quality as that which I had met in these contacts with other scientists with whom there had been a very close meeting of minds. And here I think especially of Einstein who showed a similar intensity and absence of barrier in a number of discussions that took place between him and me. After this, I began to meet Krishnamurti regularly and to discuss with him whenever he came to London.

We began an association which became closer as I became interested in the schools, which were set up through his initiative. In our discussions, we went quite deeply into many questions which concerned me in my scientific work. We probed into the nature of space and time, and of the universal, both with regard to external nature and with regard to mind. But then we went on to consider the general disorder and confusion that pervades the conscious-ness of mankind. It is here that I encountered what I feel to be Krishnamurti's major discovery. What he was seriously proposing is that all this disorder, which is the root cause of such widespread sorrow and misery, and which prevents human beings from properly working together, has its root in the fact that we are ignorant of the general nature of our own processes of thought. Or to put it differently, it may be said that we do not see what is actually hap-pening when we are engaged in the activity of thinking. Through close atten-tion to and observation of this activity of thought, Krishnamurti feels that he directly perceives that thought is a material process, which is going on inside of the human being in the brain and nervous system as a whole.

Ordinarily, we tend to be aware mainly of the content of this thought rather than of how it actually takes place. One can illustrate this point by consid-ering what happens when one is reading a book. Usually, one is attentive almost entirely to the meaning of what is being read. However, one can also be aware of the book itself, of its constitution as made up out of pages that can be turned, of the printed words and of the ink, of the fabric of the paper, etc. Similarly, we may be aware of the actual structure and function of the process of thought and not merely of its content.

How can such as awareness come about? Krishnamurti proposes that this requires what he calls meditation. Now the word meditation has been given a wide range of different and even contradictory meanings, many of them involving rather superficial kinds of mysticism. Krishnamurti has in mind a definite and clear notion when he uses this word. One can obtain a valuable indication of this meaning by considering the derivation of the word. The roots of words, in conjunction with their present generally accepted meanings often yield surprising insight into their deeper meanings. The English word meditation is based on the Latin root *med* which is to measure. The present meaning of this word is to reflect, to ponder (i.e. to weigh or measure) and to give close attention. Similarly the Sanskrit word for meditation, dhyana, is closely related to dhyati meaning to reflect. So at this rate to meditate would be to ponder, to reflect, while giving close attention to what is actually going on as one does so.

This is perhaps what Krishnamurti means by the beginning of meditation. That is to say, one gives close attention to all that is happening in conjunction with the actual activity of thought, which is the underlying source of the gen-eral disorder. One does this without choice, without criticism, without accep-tance or rejection of what is going on. And all of this takes place along with reflections on the meaning of what one is learning about the activity of thought. It is perhaps rather like reading a book in which the pages have been scrambled up, and being intensely aware of this disorder, rather than just "trying to make sense" of the confused content that arises when one just accepts the pages as they happen to come. Krishnamurti has observed that the very act of meditation will, in itself, bring order to the activity of thought without the intervention of will, choice, decision, or any other action of the thinker. As such order comes, the noise and chaos which are the usual background of our consciousness die out and the mind becomes generally silent. Thought arises only when needed for some genuinely valid purpose, and then stops, until needed again.

In this silence, Krishnamurti says that something new and creative happens, something that cannot be conveyed in words, but that is of extraordinary significance for the whole of life. So he does not attempt to communicate this verbally, but rather he asks of those who are interested that they explore the question of meditation directly for themselves, through actual attention to the nature of thought.

Without attempting to probe into this deeper meaning of meditation, one can however say that meditation, in Krishnamurti's sense of the word, can bring order to our overall mental activity, and this may be a key factor in bringing about an end to the sorrow, the misery, the chaos and confusion that have over the ages been the lot of mankind and that are still generally continuing without visible prospect of fundamental change.

Krishnamurti's work is permeated by what may be called the essence of the scientific approach, when this is considered in its very highest and purest form. Thus he begins from a fact, this fact about the nature of our thought processes. This fact is established through close attention, involving careful listening to the process of consciousness, and observing it assiduously. In this, one is constantly learning, and out of this learning comes insight, into the overall or general nature of the process of thought. This insight is then tested. First one sees whether it holds together in a rational order. And then one sees whether it leads to order and coherence, on what flows out of it in life as a whole.

Krishnamurti constantly emphasized that he is in no sense an authority. He has made certain discoveries and he is simply doing his best to make these discoveries accessible to all those who are able to listen. His work does not contain a body of doctrine, nor does he offer techniques or methods for obtaining a silent mind. He is not aiming to set up any new system of religious belief. Rather it is up to each human being to see if he can discover for himself that to which Krishnamurti is calling attention, and to go on from there to make new discoveries on his own.

It is clear then that an introduction, such as this, can at best show how Krishnamurti's work has been seen by a particular person, a scientist, such as myself. To see in full what Krishnamurti means, it is necessary, of course, to go on and to read what he actually says, with that quality of attention to the totality of one's responses, inward and outward, which we have been discussing here.

NOTE

1. Content reproduced with permission. Permission to quote from the works of J. Krishnamurti or other works for which the copyright is held by the Krishnamurti Foundation of America or the Krishnamurti Foundation Trust Ltd. has been given on the understanding that such permission does not indicate endorsement of the views expressed in this media. For more information about J. Krishnamurti (1895–1986), please see www.jkrishnamurti.org.

Chapter 12

Banaras Fifth Public Talk (Sunday, February 6, 1955)[1]

J. Krishnamurti

Perhaps it might be worthwhile to find out what is the function of our thinking, because without understanding the whole process of our thought, conscious as well as unconscious, the mind cannot be free to discover what is true. We may search for truth, but our search will be in vain if we do not understand the content or the background of the reaction which we call our thinking. Our thinking is obviously supposed to guide our action, but our action is now so automatic that there is hardly any thinking at all. Besides, through various forms of education, the education that we receive at school and college, as well as the whole education imposed by society, our minds are conditioned to adjust or submit to the demands of a particular culture. We accept certain things as inevitable, depending on our sociological, religious, or economic background, and having accepted, we act; hence our action becomes almost automatic. Thinking is hardly necessary any more, and it seems to me very important to re-examine the whole process of our thinking and see if we cannot totally break away from the background in which we have been brought up, thereby bringing about a revolution in our lives which will in turn create a different kind of culture altogether. Real revolution is not Communist, Socialist, Capitalist, or anything of that kind, because it can only be based on the search for reality, for God, or what you will. That search is in itself the revolution, but such revolution cannot take place as long as our thinking is merely the repetitive reaction of a certain form of conditioning.

So, it is obviously very important for all of us to find out how our minds operate, which is to have self-knowledge. If we don't know the ways of our own thinking, if we are unaware of our reactions and of how our thought is conditioned by the culture in which we have been brought up; if the mind does not penetrate deeply into the whole problem of its own background, which is really the "me," the self, then surely all knowledge, except perhaps

mechanical knowledge, becomes detrimental and mischievous. Is it not possible, then, to investigate the process of our thinking, not according to any
formula, guide, or guru, but for ourselves, and thereby find out how the mind
works? Now, what is thinking? Can thinking ever be original, or is it always
a repetitive process, the reaction of a background? Can thought lead us to
reality, to God, to that extraordinary something which is beyond the process
of the mind and which we call the ultimate, the absolute, or is thought a hindrance to the discovery of that reality?

Please, may I suggest that you are not merely listening to a talk. You cannot help listening because you are here and I am talking, but if in the very
process of listening you observe how your own mind works, then these talks
will have significance. What I am saying is nothing extraordinary, it is merely
a description of the ways of the mind so that as we are listening each one of us
can be aware of the process of his own thinking. If one merely listens to a set
of words and phrases and tries to catch their meaning, a talk of this kind will
have no great depth; but if in the process of listening one can pursue one's
own thinking and discover from what source it springs, then listening will be
a self-revealing process, not just an acceptance or denial of what is being said.

Can thinking ever be the means to find out what is true, what is God?
Surely, if we do not find out for ourselves what that reality is, mere reform or
amelioration within the social structure can only lead to further misery. After
all, man exists to find that supreme thing which is the foundation of all foundations; and without search, inquiry, without the constant watchfulness of our
reactions, our thoughts and feelings, to see if they lead to that ultimate reality,
to that something beyond the mundane, all our beliefs and religious activities
become utter nonsense, mere superstitions leading to further mischief.

Does thought lead to reality, that reality which is never constant, which
cannot be qualified in terms of time but must be discovered from moment to
moment? To seek that reality, the mind must also be of that quality, otherwise
it cannot have the comprehension or the feeling of what is true. So, can thinking help to discover that reality? And can thinking be original, or is all thinking imitative? If thinking is imitative, then obviously thinking cannot lead to
that reality, it is not the way out, it is not a process by which to uncover what
is true. And yet our whole process of search is the cultivation of thinking, of
various practices, disciplines, which are all based on thought. If thought can
open the door to reality, then it has significance; but thought may be a barrier
to reality, so one must find the truth of the matter for oneself, and not merely
accept or reject.

Surely, what we call thinking is the response of memory. That is fairly
obvious. You have been brought up in a certain tradition; as a Hindu, a
Christian, a Buddhist, a Communist, or whatever it be, you have various associations, memories, beliefs, and that background responds to any

challenge, which is called thinking. So the background is not different from thinking; thinking is the background. When you are asked a question about your religion, what you believe in, immediately your mind responds according to your conditioning, in terms of the various traditions, experiences, and beliefs that you have. You respond according to your particular background, as a Christian or a Communist also does. So thinking is an impediment in the sense that it is merely the response of the background, of a particular conditioning. Surely, that again is obvious. Such a response, which we call thinking, definitely cannot open the door to reality. To find out what reality is, one must totally cease to be a Hindu, a Christian, a Communist, this or that, so that the mind is no longer conditioned and is therefore free to discover what is true.

Is it possible for the mind to be free from its whole conditioning as a Hindu, a Moslem, a Christian, or whatever it be? And who is the entity that is going to free the mind from its background? Do you understand the question? When you say, "I must be free from my conditioning as a Hindu," who is the entity that is going to bring about this freedom? Who is the analyzer of the background? Can the analyzer break up the background? Am I making myself clear?

As a Hindu I have certain formulas, concepts, beliefs, traditions, and I see the necessity of being free from them all, for if I am not, it is obviously impossible to find out what reality is. If I am conditioned as a Communist, or if my mind is moulded according to any other belief, how can I ever find out what is real? Such a mind can only experience that to which it has been conditioned. Unless the mind is free from all conditioning, its search is merely a sociological reaction and it will find only what it has been conditioned to. Then how am I to free myself from all conditioning? Is there an entity who is going to help me to free myself from conditioning? That is, is there in me a thinker, an analyzer, an observer, who is not contaminated by my conditioning?

You see, so far we have assumed that there is a thinker apart from thought, have we not? We are used to the idea that there are two separate processes, one being a permanent state as the thinker, the analyzer, the observer, and the other being the movement of thought. We have always believed that there is the Paramatman, a permanent spiritual entity who by analyzing the process of thinking is going to reject whatever is false and keep only what is true. Now, is there such a permanent entity apart from impermanent thought? Or is there only thinking, which is entirely impermanent and therefore creates the thinker in order to make itself permanent? Surely, thinking creates the thinker, it is not the thinker who creates the thought. This is really very important to understand for oneself, it is not a thing to accept or reject. Has not thinking created the thinker, and not the other way round?

After all, if there were no thinking, would there be a thinker? It is thinking that gives rise to the thinker, and the thinker then becomes the permanent analyzer, the observer who is untouched by time; but that entity has been created by thought, surely. It is like a diamond. The qualities of the diamond make the diamond. Remove the qualities of the diamond, and there is no diamond at all. Similarly, various desires, urges, compulsions create in their movement the entity which becomes the actor, the embodiment of will, which is the "I" of assertive action, of assertive thought. But that will is made up of many desires. If there were no desires, there would be no will, no "I."

So, if there is only thinking and not the thinker, then the thinker who says, "I will free myself from my conditioning" is himself the outcome of conditioned thought; therefore the thinker, the observer, the analyzer, the experiencer, cannot free the mind from its conditioning. The mind may separate itself as the thinker and the thought, as will and desire, as the good and the bad, as the higher self and the lower self, but that whole process is still within the field of thought, it is only a self-deception leading to a great deal of mischievous action. The question then is, can the mind free itself from its own conditioning when there is no censor, no analyzer, no superior self who is going to cleanse the mind?

Are you following this? Please, if this much is not clear, to go further will have no meaning. It is essential to understand this, otherwise you will cling to the idea of a higher self, a spiritual something which is God given, timeless, but encased in ignorance, and which is always pushing away the ignorance that is coming upon it which is all absurd. And if there is no permanent self at all, but only thinking which creates the permanent self in different forms, then can thinking free the mind to find out what is true?

As long as we have not found out what is true, what is God, what is that extraordinary something which fills life with greatness, goodness and beauty, all our activities at whatever level can have only a superficial meaning. Unless we are directly experiencing that which is true from moment to moment, our culture becomes mechanical and therefore destructive. Surely, man exists to find God, not merely to earn a livelihood and adjust himself to a particular pattern of society. Society does not help man to find truth. On the contrary, society prevents man from discovering what is true, because society is based on the desire to be secure, to have permanency, and a mind that is secure, safe, that is seeking permanency, can never find reality. But the man who understands what is true, who is experiencing reality from moment to moment, helps to bring about a totally new society. Reformation, adjustment, or any form of revolution within the framework of society can only lead to further misery and destruction as is shown in the world at the present time, where every effort to solve one problem leads to a hundred more. Whereas, if the mind can understand what is true, experience it directly, then that very understanding creates its own action which brings about a new culture.

Our question then is, can the mind free itself from its own conditioning? If there is no "I," no self, no Atman to free it, then what is it to do? Do you follow the problem? We have invented the "I" which is going to free the mind from conditioning. But as we investigate the process of the "I," we discover that the "I" has no reality, it is merely a product of thought, which is a reaction of the background. So there is only thinking, thinking according to the background. Thinking is the response of the background, which is the mind's conditioning as a Christian, a Buddhist, a Hindu, and so on. If thought is the response of the background, and all background is conditioning, then thought cannot lead to freedom; and it is only in freedom that you can find out what is true.

So, to find what is God, what is true, thought must come to an end. Please, this is not only logical, it is factual. Thought must come to an end. But the moment you ask, "How am I to end thought?" there is an entity who operates, who practices the "how" in order to put an end to thinking. So there is no "how" at all, and this is very important to understand, because for all of us the "how" is the most important thing. We say, "How am I to do this, what is the discipline I must practice?" and all that business, which we now see has no meaning. So at one sweep we get rid of this whole problem of the "how."

This may sound too facile, but it is not facile, it is not easy; on the contrary, it demands a great deal of attention, not concentration but attention. Concentration is exclusive because it implies a motive, an incentive, whereas attention has no motive and is therefore not exclusive. In the mind's observation of itself there comes self-knowledge, which is not the knowledge of the higher self. The higher self is an invention of the mind that wants to escape from the actuality of thought in relationship to people, to things, and to ideas. When it wants to escape from what is, the mind goes off into all kinds of absurdities. But when the mind begins to inquire into the process of its own being, when it sees the implications of thought and how thought comes into being, then that very perception puts an end to thought. There is no thinker who puts an end to thought, therefore no effort is involved. Effort arises only when there is an incentive to gain something. If the mind has an incentive to break away from its conditioning, then that incentive is the reaction of that conditioning in a different direction.

So, it is very important to understand the whole process of our thinking, and the understanding of that process does not come through isolation. There is no such thing as living in isolation. The understanding of the process of our thinking comes when we observe ourselves in daily relationship, our attitudes, our beliefs, the way we talk, the way we regard people, the way we treat our husbands, our wives, our children. Relationship is the mirror in which the ways of our thinking are revealed. In the facts of relationship lies truth, not away from relationship. There is obviously no such thing as living in isolation. We may carefully cut off various forms of physical relationship, but the mind is still related. The very existence of the mind implies relationship, and self-knowledge lies through seeing the facts of relationship as they are without inventing, condemning, or justifying. In relationship the mind has certain evaluations, judgments, comparisons, it reacts to challenge according to various forms of memory, and this reaction is called thinking. If the mind can just be aware of this whole process, you will find that thought comes to a standstill. Then the mind is very quiet, very still, without incentive, without movement in any direction, and in that stillness reality comes into being.

NOTE

1. Content reproduced with permission. Permission to quote from the works of J. Krishnamurti or other works for which the copyright is held by the Krishnamurti Foundation of America or the Krishnamurti Foundation Trust Ltd. has been given on the understanding that such permission does not indicate endorsement of the views expressed in this media. For more information about J. Krishnamurti (1895–1986), please see www.jkrishnamurti.org.

Chapter 13

Beyond Thinking

Jac O'Keeffe

We teach our children how to take care of their bodies and their property. We teach our children how to communicate, and we give them tools so that they can manage in the world. In good faith, we pass on beliefs, behaviors, and ideas about themselves and the world. We fill their minds with thoughts and neglect to teach them how to think. Why? Because we have not learned how to use our minds efficiently and effectively. Through the experience of living, we realize that many of our thoughts create suffering in ourselves, in others, and in our relationships. Understanding the mind and learning how to navigate through the process of thinking is a basic and crucial skill for living a happy life.

When suffering happens, there is one thought in the mix of our beliefs that consolidates the experience of suffering. That thought is the personal "I" or "me"! Any experience must happen to "me" in order for it to register as a personal event. Suffering always requires personal ownership of an experience for an otherwise benign experience to be perceived as suffering. Suffering can only happen to one who believes in the personal "I" or "me."

This is an invitation to you, the reader, to explore how your thinking mind works. If you can better understand your mind and its components, then the steps you need to take to end personal suffering will become clear to you.

There is a circuit of neurological pathways in your brain called the default mode network (or DMN). Brain imaging has taught us that when the DMN is firing, your thoughts are self-referenced.[1] In other words, whatever thoughts are processed through your DMN are also integrated with your personal response, opinion, emotional reaction, and so on. Every DMN-based thought has something to do with "me." The personal "I" is readily available, and these thoughts add qualitatively to the story about "me," regardless of their content. When life is good, positive experiences are happening to "me" and there is nothing to complain about. However, good times don't last, and the high that the personal "I" enjoys can be matched by cycles of internal, deeply painful experiences because bad things can happen also. Emotional and physical pain happen to the personal "I." When the DMN is processing our thoughts, we operate from a dualistic perspective. Subject-object (or "I am–that is") perception prevails and what I can name appears to be separate from me. This is duality ("I am . . ." and "that is . . ."). Labeling begins. The DMN is also responsible for our ability to place ourselves within the context of linear time. It offers us a reference point for operating more efficiently within the humanly shared idea of time. Therefore the DMN consolidates a particular sense of who we are in the world. But is this our identity or simply neurology that has evolved from viewing the world through the subject-object (dualistic) perception?

Life presents a series of experiences. Some folks are mildly scathed with negative impact or trauma. Others grapple with perceived immense suffering for substantial parts of their lives. Whichever way it runs for you, the personal "I" is a perspective that is not required by you to live a full and meaningful life. When there is no awareness of your thoughts or understanding of how your mind works, your self-referencing neurology (the DMN) will over-ride any available objectivity. Then you will believe your thoughts to be a true perception of what is happening. Furthermore, the personal "I" thought causes you to believe that you are who you *think* you are.

The personal "I" (that's the one your mind tells you is you) is not content by nature. Generally, it seeks excitement in its early years and harmony with age. It always requires acceptance and approval. It invests in its self-image, and it seeks love. The personal "I" is often referred to as the ego. It is needy and self-centered. It is the birthing place of self-righteous ideas that when verbalized often contain the word "should." It generates all desires, and its appetite is insatiable. If your DMN is very active, you will recognize these patterns in your thinking. You are not who you think you are, however. Your brain works this way when you have not learned how to use your mind well.

The personal "I" takes everything personally. It is after all a self-referencing mechanism. When one is self-confident and emotionally mature, there is a substantial reduction in the number of life events that are taken personally. However, this pattern can and will revert to an "all about me" perspective if life throws a curve ball.

There is another network of neurological pathways in the brain better equipped to deal with life. This is called the task-oriented network. The DMN and the task-oriented network can be thought of as the thinking mind and the working mind, respectively. The thinking mind uses the DMN, and the work-ing mind uses the task-oriented network. For example, thoughts that involve planning, problem solving, analysis, etc. are undertaken by the working mind; these are tasks.

When you effectively use your mind, thoughts no longer control or influence your state of well-being. When you use your thinking capacity in a healthy and informed way, you will recognize that your mind is a tool to be picked up and set down as needed. Then thinking ceases to be a problem. There is an openness to life because your attention is available. The incessant chatter of the thinking mind reduces in volume and, for some, disappears totally. There is a natural innate peace and calm in your disposition regardless of what life throws your way. What we are exploring here is not avoidance, nor does it reduce your capacity to engage with life. Rather, it is a path to being fully human, being available and open to whatever presents. It is an invitation to be fully present. This is possible when your mind is not wandering and coloring what is perceived through the filter of its own (usually unconscious) personal agenda.

Have you noticed that fantasy and chasing a desire in your mind can make you suffer? Have you seen that the feel good factor of living in your head is short lived and that the judgment of life being a disappointment is a direct result of listening to and believing the thinking mind? Fantasy is the mind's attempt to create an alternate reality. To do so, it must first reject what is here now. There is nothing wrong with life; it is our resistance to and rejection of it that creates our discontentment. The thinking mind, the personal "I," is the one who rejects what is (that is, the present moment). The working mind changes what needs changing, from a practical perspective, and does not operate from desire-based motivations. The working mind is objective and draws on your own wisdom and responds in the moment.

The thinking mind, on the other hand, is a contracted perspective in several ways: energetically, mentally, and physically. Our perception and often our bodies are highly contracted in order to maintain the localized perception of the personal "I," in full view. In dropping the personal "I" perspective, your body will begin to relax. As your perspective broadens, ease comes to your life. You may find that your opinions soften, and your tolerance of others increases. Without the personal "I," you will begin to develop patience. It is the personal "I" who is intolerant and impatient. It is the personal "I" who is critical and judgmental because it seeks to assert itself continually and does so at the expense of others, albeit in the silence of your own mind.

When you drop the personal "I" agenda, the character or personality undergoes some changes. Your personality will no longer be assumed to be an authentic representation of who you are. It repositions itself to be a wonderful interface between you and the world. Changes will come and these will be welcome consequences that allow you to be more fluid in your response to life.

The personal "I" thrives on drama. Can you recognize that the personal "I" is heavily invested in a story? All thoughts that cruise by your thinking mind comprise a story, a story that directly or indirectly involves you. If you believe that you are who you think you are, then who and how you are right now is dependent upon the momentary thoughts being entertained by your thinking mind. Dropping the thinking mind requires you to drop your investment in your story. When required by life, you will be able to pick up and set down your story without attachment. Defending yourself and being attached to your opinions will cease. The working mind can facilitate all effective functioning, and it does so with ease and fluidity.

Can you let go of your story? Your mind might tell you that your needs will not be met, and you will have to take this risk as well as other mind-created and mind-perceived scenarios. Find out for yourself if there is risk in letting go of the personal "I" thought mechanism. Self-pity might arise—pay no attention. Be careful where you place your attention because whatever thoughts gain your attention will inevitably present as real to you, and this creates your experience of life. Your mind is potent, and its potency is dependent upon the amount of attention that it receives (from you). If you are interested in the stories that your mind creates, they will claim your attention. First your attention follows your thoughts. Then your thoughts are believed to be true if all your attention is absorbed in the content of these thoughts. This is how the thinking mind works when it uses the self-referencing mechanism in an unmanaged and inefficient way. It is the root of all suffering.

Can you live without personal drama? Can you embrace how that might unfold in daily living? Life and how you live it will feel lighter. Consequentially, you may not have as many stories to share with others, and your interest in the personal stories of others will reduce also. Drama will cease to be a juicy engagement for your mind. Stories other people tell about themselves will have similar impact to watching a movie. Nothing sticks. Can you allow yourself to slip into the background at home and in your social group? The personal "I" is the one who seeks attention from others. The working mind knows nothing of this motivation. Living without personal drama yields an experience of life that is approached with ease from a naturally calm inner state. This is the beginning of embracing what it means to be truly human. Life beyond thinking is a life beyond suffering.

If your story is dropped, your perspective will naturally widen. Your bandwidth expands. Objectivity comes into play. When you are truly objective, a personal agenda is not influencing your perception. You can practice being objective as a technique that will shift your attention from the content of your thinking mind. When you are objective, you are observing life itself. Thoughts come and go and they are recognized to be thoughts because their content is not of interest to you. You can observe your mind presenting stories, opinions, and judgments; it will vie for your attention. If you retain some objectivity and see the tricks of your thinking mind at play, you will not be sucked into believing the ceaseless radio play of your thinking mind. Your thinking mind recycles opinions, judgments, and commentaries continuously. Learn to recognize the tricks and loops of your thinking mind. The distance that comes from not believing your thoughts offers relief. You are no longer under the hypnosis of your thoughts. Living shows itself to be a light-filled and naturally flowing exercise. Your thoughts are subjective perceptions, and there is no occasion in life where one is required to believe one's thoughts to be the truth. Subjective perception is one of many viewing points through which you can perceive the world. One must recognize the thinking mind as that which glues the personal "I" thought to your experience, and in turn creates suffering. Can you sense the freedom that comes with this recognition? Observe your thoughts without judgment and remember only the personal "I" judges thoughts to be right or wrong according to "my" standards. The moment you realize that you are lost in your thinking mind, take the opportunity to shift your perception into the observer mode.

When you read that your life story is simply a story, did you want to defend it? Did defining your personal life as a story feel belittling to you, or even disrespectful? If this is the case, then your investment in the personal "I" is substantial. The inability to accept the idea that your story is a story indicates that some personal development is needed. Some emotional maturation is needed when you cannot detach from the personal. Allow for the possibility that the personal "I" is not ready to let go of its own story. The personal "I" will always want to hide and entice you to believe in new stories and more judgments. This is its effort to continue its status quo.

Stepping back from the personal "I" is the first movement toward becoming the manager of your mind. You may already be able to see that the thinking mind is the source of all problems. When the personal "I" is active, there is ownership and something to defend or advocate internally or externally. The personal "I" always takes a position. It is thus rooted in separation. There is me and there is you. Subject-object perception prevails. Whatever connects us at a deeper level is not visible or accessible, as the personal agenda clouds all perception. Remember, if suffering is to happen, there must be one who suffers. Without the personal "I" story, who is it that suffers? When the self-referencing mechanism no longer functions, pain can still occur, but it passes quickly, and it does not destabilize your core. For example, pain happens to the body, and no matter how severe, it will not absorb all your attention. Without the thinking mind coloring your perception, you can know that you are not your body. The body can feel intense pain, but you remain okay and untouched. Suffering cannot happen without a "me" who is available to suffer.

The mind is a tool for your use, as a body-mind organism. As human beings we function with a great dependency on stories. We communicate with language that requires stories for communication. Stories are an essential aspect of what makes us human. Stories are not a problem; believing them creates big problems! The invitation here is not to flip a switch and choose not to believe stories. Rather, the pointer is to see that your stories about you are not an accurate depiction of who you are. Stories assist in functionality. They do not offer identity or definition. Stories that are believed into your reality create the one who suffers. If you approach this viewpoint intellectually, you might think that to recognize and dismiss the activity of your thinking mind would help alleviate suffering. You would have partial success and would have to remind yourself not to believe your thoughts for some sustained lasting inner relief. Why? Because if you were to not believe your own stories, then there would be a personal identity who is taking a position. In this case, the personal "I" is already believed into reality in order to take the position of not believing all other stories! This approach is ineffective. What we are about in this chapter is subtle. See through the mistaken identity of taking yourself to be the culmination of your stories by realizing that the personal "I" is a product of your mind. If you can see the world as a matrix, note there is a crack appearing in its fabric. Peeping through that crack happens when you see that the believability of the personal "I" creates all suffering.

You are not who you think you are. Are you the observer of the personal "I" thoughts? Are you an impersonal "I"? Perhaps we can consider that these are viewpoints also. What then are you, or who are you if your story no longer defines you? If your story is no longer believed to be the essence of who you are, then to what do you refer? The one who is thinking, the one who entertains stories is also a story. That is the turning point that leads away from suffering permanently. There is a qualitative difference between seeing through the stories of your mind and seeing through the one who gives attention to these stories. The latter is a giant step on the spiritual path, and it is a perspective that brings stability, peace, and rest! This shift in perspective can cause the DMN to stop running. The mind is no longer believed. There is freedom.

Recognizing that you are not who you think you are is a realization available to all on the spiritual path. There is distance and detachment from the thinking mind. Perception arises from a source that is prior to the conditioned, thinking mind. Beyond or prior to the thinking mind there is spaciousness. The shift in your point of perception automatically reorganizes how the world appears to you. The unifying forces throughout all aspects of manifestation are recognized, and separation is understood to be the overlay that assists us to function well as body-mind organisms. There is recognition that your body is a localized viewing point offering you an opportunity to participate in the world. However, the one who is seeing all of this must be seen through also.

The role and function of individual consciousness must be recognized and seen to function without personal ownership. When this leap happens, the self-referencing network (DMN) can turn off permanently. This is a physiological happening, and when this change happens in the physical brain, it is called enlightenment, awakening, or self-realization within spiritual contexts. For some this shift in perspective is not permanent and is enjoyed for a variable length of time before the DMN begins to fire again. In both cases, when the thinking mind has lost its believability, your reference point is no longer the personal "I." There is an innate knowing that what is the same in all of manifestation (essence of all that is) is also what you are. Furthermore, it is recognized that you never were the individual, autonomous, separate person that was created by erroneous thinking. There is freedom. Joy and bliss arise spontaneously.

Studies have shown that we have tens of thousands of thoughts every day, although we are consciously aware of a very small fraction of them.[2] Give yourself a break! Let yourself loosen and drop your interest in your thoughts. It is important to recognize that our minds are overstimulated and very active. Much is expected of us (or so we believe) when we are part of the commercially driven, contemporary culture. Opting out is not possible for most of us. It's worth noting that however attractive an alternate life, it rarely lives up to the fantasy. Why? Because if you get the chance to opt out, the mind together with its familiar loops stays with you! Changing the external environment can change your phenomenal experience, but your mind will revert to its old patterns after the newness of your environment becomes familiar. The potential to suffer continues regardless of external lifestyle shifts. However, shifting your internal attitude with regard to your thoughts will effectively turn around your experience of life. Recognizing that your thoughts are simply thoughts removes the power that you might have erroneously given to them.

There are many stimulants in our lives that increase thinking mind activity. Stress, lack of access to nature, chemicals in our food, caffeine, etc. all play a part in promoting an overactive thinking mind, to varying degrees, in each person. Taking time out and destressing are underrated. Taking time to reset your body and mind to a more organic and holistic pace that supports you can help every area of your inner and physiological life. Slowing down internally is easier when you slow down externally. Taking two or three minutes to breathe deeply and slowly will also help slow down the thinking mind. Other influences that shape your thinking patterns include your chemical physiology, which is largely influenced by your diet. Thus, there are many approaches one can take to offer some relief for an incessant thinking mind. You will be drawn to what makes sense for you. It is largely by trial and error that you learn to navigate the management of your own thinking mind.

The quality content of your thoughts is a culmination of many factors. Thinking patterns and beliefs are often inherited. Most were learned while we were children. We develop patterns of thinking in order to feel safe and secure in the world. If your early environments did not offer a sense of safety, your thinking mind will be excessively active, believing it can keep you safe. Your mind cannot keep you safe; this is outside its realm of control. Knowing that you are safe shows itself when attention is totally withdrawn from such beliefs. If your mind regularly entertains fear, this thought pattern can be underpinned by a belief that you are not safe. Our beliefs usually stem from our perception of the world that was set in motion when we were children. Few of us revisit and examine these beliefs effectively. If these foundational beliefs remain unexplored, you will not be able to recognize that these are thoughts that only serve to keep you in the prison of your own subjective, misguided perception. Your mind will attempt to maintain authority; it will want to be your leader and you will be its minion. Turning around this relationship does not happen overnight. Letting go of many foundational misunderstandings can be a journey. The objective is not to replace one set of beliefs for another; rather, it is to understand the role and function of the thinking mind. Recognize that your thinking mind is a liar. Spiritual work offers an objectivity to see that whatever the mind presents as story is invariably a subjective and tainted version of what is actually happening.

There are many practices to change the quality of your thinking. You can, for example, give up criticizing others and yourself or you can replace negative thoughts with positive thoughts. You can learn to recognize that fear, guilt, and shame are emotions created by thoughts and replace them with opposing belief systems. These techniques have their place and offer some relief. Permanent shifts in our thinking can only come by gaining an objective distance from the mind, recognizing its use and respecting its limitations.

Tenets of several religious practices encourage one to develop trust or to surrender to external deities. For some this is an effective way to learn how to trust and drop old beliefs. Religious practices often advocate nonjudgment of others, performing good deeds, etc. Religious guidance can help promote a lifestyle and an attitude that can positively influence the content of your thoughts. Spirituality is an upgrade from these practices. Spirituality turns the mind inward, preparing you to realize the truth that underpins all. Spirituality opens you as it broadens your perspective. The dualistic viewpoint weakens. The differences once perceived between you and others, right and wrong are lessened. Acceptance and tolerance increase. Life is understood to have more gray areas than black or white. Spirituality is not about taking on new beliefs or replacing one set of values and understandings for another. That is the domain of religion, which also has its place. Spirituality is an exploration of what lies deep within. It involves letting go of your often hard-earned ideas about yourself and the world. It requires you to be open and available so that you may shift your perspective from an "all about me" subjective viewpoint to a global, inclusive view of the totality.

Can you see your own thoughts and recognize them to be thoughts or stories? Right now, can you hear the voice in your head that is reading these words? Can you find the secondary voice that is ready with a comment regarding this material? If so, ignore the story that your mind is presenting about this text and notice from where this observation is coming. Can you sense your capacity to observe your thinking mind? Can you hear your mind give comments about what you are reading and not be attached to or readily believing these comments? Have no ownership of these comments. They will pass. On another day, these comments could be quite different. Let there be space for your mind to be fluid and not fixed to any one position. There are many shades of gray in life, very little is black or white. Be in the observer mode. Let your mind become an observer. When you observe, it is impossible to take things personally. The personal "I" idea created by the self-referencing network must be engaged to take things personally. Have no ownership and remain as the observer. Your working mind, the task-oriented capacity in your brain, allows you to function fully in life. The narrative from your thinking mind is a distraction and a waste of your energy when you offer it your attention.

Observe your thinking mind. Observe the endless narrative that offers thousands of concepts daily that vie for your attention. Don't buy into these thoughts. They are insignificant and a prerequisite to suffering. When you observe, you are not caught in any drama. Life is viewed from the audience rather than the perspective of a player on stage. There is calmness within. Something natural and latent within you is given space to open and reveal itself. Wisdom and creativity arise from this locale of no ownership of thoughts. You can play whatever role is required. The role of parent or manager or friend can be played without ownership of that role. There is nothing fake in allowing a role to be played. In taking the position of observer of your thoughts, there is a natural and healthy distance from a subjective perception and there is calmness and fluidity in your approach to life. You will be available to what is happening because your attention is available and present to what is, in any given moment. You will no longer be lost in daydreams, repetitive thoughts, or obsessions. There is no need to escape what is happening now because there is no resistance to life. Resistance requires ownership of an attitude and a position that is averse to what is already unfolding. If life itself is okay with what is happening, why bother to support the thinking mind that rejects and resists what is? Get to know the tricks of your own mind. Become wise to the thoughts that are sticky for you. Observe without comment and learn about your own thinking patterns.

What is it that observes? This is also your mind, but it's not the thinking mind. It's not the self-referencing network that filters all thoughts through the personal "I" story. Observing is a useful practice to help you to detach from the false sense of self-importance that is a consequence of believing your thinking mind. As you become more skillful at observing, your perspective widens, and an innate wisdom can develop. When observing, notice that your personality has likes and dislikes. This is fine. Do not attach to your preferences. There will be a natural move toward what works for you and away from what does not suit you. Aversions and desires arise only when the perspective has left observing and the personal "I" is asserting its position. The needs and wants of the personal "I" are insatiable. This is because there is infinite unease and no stability in the personal "I" thought mechanism. The personal "I" is not a healthy or natural perspective. It arises from identification with the thinking mind. This is misuse of the mind. Thoughts cannot offer you an identity; your thinking mind was never designed to fulfill this requirement. It is externally focused and has no capacity to switch itself off. When your attention is withdrawn from the external world, there is peace. Recognizing this fact is a useful step toward maturing out of the grip of the thinking mind. The mind plays many tricks, however, one being that the satisfaction of desires leads to happiness. For example, it may seem peaceful when desires are satisfied, but have you noticed that before long another desire arises? Entertaining desires is an unending cycle, and every desire leads to some calm that is nothing more than the absence of desire. Soon another desire will arise. Recognize this pattern within your own mind. Understanding the nature of desires softens their influence on your behavior.

The personal "I" offers mistaken identity. When it is active, you readily believe you are contained within your physical body and that you are who your mind presents you to be. It functions as a plausible identity, albeit available for both pleasure and pain. However, in observer mode you can observe this play of mind to be simply story and who you are is no longer so easily defined. In the impersonal observer the term "I am" stands alone, without a third word stating what you are. There is a sense of being, existing, resting without story or the need for story. I am is simply enough. I am this body or I am a person are fundamental beliefs, and once seen through, they cease being readily available to the personal "I." The observer does not hold to any defined sense of who you are. Its view is wider. You can feel there is a body and that it is for "your" use and you do not identify with it. The observer is quiet and there is calmness within. A sense of spaciousness develops with practice. It is easy to be in the present moment, and to be available to life itself. Acceptance is readily available. Something within says "yes" to life.

Thinking is no longer a problem when you observe your thoughts. But keeping yourself in observer mode indefinitely is impossible. Life presents situations and stories that give rise to an emotional charge. When previously unrecognized old patterns of thinking are stimulated, up pops the personal "I" again. In that moment, pull back to the observer to see what is creating the irresistible attraction for your thinking mind. Observing brings great relief. It is important to remember that the frequency with which you withdraw attention from the content of your thinking mind is more important than remaining for long periods in observer mode.

When you recognize that your thinking mind can be at times ridiculous in its attempts to reinforce a sense of self-importance, lightness in your attitude prevails. The first real glimpses of freedom from your story emerge. The observer presents I am, and from here, consider what it might be like if your view could be wider still. What if the am-ness of the I am were to fall away? It too is another story, albeit more subtle. Drop all attachment to subtle concepts of being and presence. For some, fear arises at this point. Do not go into the drama of fear. Fear passes if you do not resist it or cling to it. Only the personal "I" suffers with fear. There is no need to be fearful of fear. It is a human experience like all other expressions and emotions. If you do not shift into the personal "I" story, fear is a movement that passes through your body and mind without hindrance and with little or no impact. Somehow, everything is okay, always. Nothing happens to you unless your thinking mind personalizes and dramatizes an otherwise benign story.

Withdraw your attention from the "I am." Sense the perspective that is wider than the impersonal observer. Both the personal and impersonal capacity for story disappears. Your working mind enables functioning in daily life, and you will walk with ease in the world. There is no immunity from the turbulence of life, but how you meet such events is very different now. Therefore your direct experience of life is different also. Nothing touches your core, yet nothing is suppressed or denied. There is internal freedom and an ability to roll with whatever life places on your path. The thinking mind is not active and the volume of your thoughts is so low that they become barely noticeable. Either way, it doesn't seem to matter. There is stillness. Where is your attention that used to be fully invested in the thinking mind? Where is your attention that remained in the "I am," observing the tricks and chatter of the thinking mind? When we drop both the sense of being present and the observing mind, attention recedes within, resting at its source. There is peace and calm. There is stillness. Attention is readily available for the working mind. When a task is required, attention is available to perform what needs to be done to the best of your ability. When the task is complete, there is no attachment to the task or any associated projected outcome. Planning, doing, and performing are more efficient and without an agenda. There is no sense of *responsibility* because of ownership; it is replaced by an *ability to respond* to any given scenario—and one is accountable for how one responds.

Imagine a world where all people know how to effectively use their minds. Humanity would be transformed if we explored what lies beyond believing our thoughts. Paradoxically you cannot think about not thinking. All you can do and all you need to do is get a distance from your thoughts and stop dedicating your attention to the stories of your thinking mind.

What you really are is ever present, unaffected by events and experiences happening to the personality or body-mind organism. What you are is not thinkable or definable by your thoughts. Your ability to think is a human characteristic and does not define you, though the self-referencing mechanism works incessantly to do so, until it stops. What you are lies beyond thinking. What you are is present and available when the personal "I" is absent. This leads us to the conclusion that you must be other than both your story and the one who can observe that story. Everything passes through with ease when the "I" is not present to claim ownership of its perspective. All resistance to life comes from the personal agenda. Allow your thinking mind to be a tool for your use. Stop supporting the personal "I" and you will see how to get out of your own way. An exquisite experience of being fully human awaits.

NOTES

1. Gusnard, D. A., Akbudak, E., Shulman, G. L., and Raichle, M. E. (2001), Medial prefrontal cortex and self-referential mental activity: Relation to a default mode of brain function, *Proc. Natl. Acad. Sci. U.S.A., 98*, 4259–64, doi:10.1073/pnas.071043098, https://doi.org/10.1073/pnas.071043098; and Wicker, B., Ruby, P., Royet, J. P., and Fonlupt, P. (2003), A relation between rest and the self in the brain? *Brain Res. Brain Res. Rev., 43*, 224–30, doi:10.1016/j.brainresrev.2003.08.003, https://www.sciencedirect.com/science/article/abs/pii/S0165017303002108?via%3Dihub.

2. https://healthybrains.org/brain-facts/.

Chapter 14

Dialogues in Delphi
(November 6, 1990)[1]

Jean Klein

Our teaching is essentially based on understanding and what understanding means in the context of truth. Truth here is our real nature, which cannot be objectified. The understanding required to approach truth is thus different from the usual way we understand the world of referents and objects. So the first step is to see the difference between what is understandable—objects— and what is beyond conventional understanding—the objectless.

On the level of the mind, ordinary understanding, the nearest we can come to objectless truth is a clear perspective, a vision of the objectless. I often call this a geometrical representation. The contents of this representation are what could be called the facts of truth: that the mind has limits; that truth is beyond the mind; that truth, our real nature, cannot be objectified, just as the eye cannot see itself seeing; that truth, consciousness, was never born and will never die; that it is the light in which all happenings, all objects, appear and disappear; that in order for there to be understanding of truth, all representation must dissolve. When this representation, the last of the conventional subject-object understanding, dies, it dissolves in its source—the light of which the mind was informed but could not comprehend. In other words, understanding dissolves in being understanding. We no longer understand, we are the understanding. This switchover is a sudden, dramatic moment when we are ejected into the timeless.

To say that truth is one is a mental conjecture that calls for objectification. Because we cannot objectify truth, it can only be spoken of in terms of what it is not. As it is beyond subject and object, we call this way non-dual, advaita.

Understanding, then, calls for complete openness. When we look from the point of view of the male or female, we only see from the level of gender. When we look from the point of view of the personality, the "I-concept," all is personal, in object-object relationship. But when we take a stand in globality, consciousness, awareness, then there is only consciousness. From the point of view of gender, or the "I-concept," we occupy a mere fraction of being. But when we are in our wholeness, we see only the global. The moment we knowingly occupy our globality, or even have a glimpse of it, the chess board is completely changed. From this point of view, which is no longer a *point* of view, we see things related to one another, because everything now refers to awareness, to silence. All that is phenomenal, all that is objective, only has reality when it abides in, when it refers to, silence, to stillness. So the changing of the chess board is a result of having the foretelling, or a sudden glimpse, of reality.

Do you have something to say?

Once one is ejected into the timeless, when the geometrical understanding dissolves in being understanding, can one only speak, think, function from the totality? And so, how can one teach those who do not function in totality?

Only wholeness can teach wholeness. The teacher lives in the totality, and this is itself the teaching.

How then is it possible to teach or relate to those who think from the point of view of time?

As I have often said, the mind cannot change the mind. Only the timeless in me can awaken the timeless in you. The teacher does not refer to the "I," to psychology. It is meaningless to teach at the psychological level about what is beyond the "I."

But surely a certain amount of teaching at the psychological level is helpful.

Helpful for what? Helpful to whom? There are many psychologists in the world but few teachers.

I would like to ask, please, about the role of memory, the function of memory in our lives.

Our memory functions primarily to maintain the "I-concept." We refer very often to the past to create the future and maintain the "I." Up to 80 percent of our waking time is spent in pampering the "I" through daydreaming. We waste all our energy in daydreaming. And by daydreaming, I mean all projecting, all strategy, all becoming. Free from the "I-concept," we no longer refer ourselves to the past. So we are free from psychological memory. But when the situation asks for functional memory, practical memory, of course we refer to the past. But this memory is not problematic. It belongs only to the circumstance, to the moment, the situation itself, and dies with the situation.

I would like to ask about the chess board you mentioned. I feel that many times in my life the pieces have merely shifted like a scenario played with small variations. I feel trapped in it. How can I free myself from the trap?

Generally, we function on the level of the male or female, or the "I-concept," and all our relations with our surroundings are from object to object. This is not creative living, it is repetitious. But when we have the forefeeling of what we really are, we are totally open, open to the openness, and the object "I" has no hold. We are openness, the ultimate subject, and we are no longer bound to our surroundings. We are not in our surroundings, but the surroundings are in us. In openness we discover elements in the situation that we never saw before, and we become creative. Then we see things as they are, free from personal interference, free from conflict, free from compulsion. Do you see what I mean?

Does this opening happen from the mind's point of view?

When the mind comes to a moment of helplessness, when the mind says, "I don't know," it means it has come to the end. Then, spontaneously, you are taken by openness. You know moments in life when things come unexpectedly to you and you are not able to refer back, because there is no reference to the past since the situation comes to you so unexpectedly. Then you are obliged to look without thinking, to see facts, to deal with facts. And in facing the situation so, you find yourself in spontaneity. You are the acting, but there is not an actor, there is only acting.

Can I come to know my real nature through art?

Absolutely. Because art is an expression of beauty, of love. Beauty can never be objectified. Beauty is an expression of your totality, of your globality, which, as an artist, you feel as an inner demand to share with the surroundings. You might express it in poetry, in painting, in sculpture, in music or architecture. But it is important to know how to handle the material.

But you are not only an artist when you produce sounds or colors. You are also an artist when, for example, you are looking at art. It is how to look, how to hear, how to touch, how to smell, how to taste, which makes the artist. In true art there is an empty space given by the artist, where the artist, the producer and the observer come together. When both come together, then it is really a beautiful work of art.

Dr. Klein, I have had a taste, I think, of what you are talking about, the stillness, the silence in which there is a kind of choiceless happening. But it seems that there is a connection back to my ego as a kind of insurance policy. My question is, how can I remove that insurance policy and trust fully?

As long as you take yourself for an independent entity, you are bound to the ego. The presence that is silence, stillness, is only in the absence of the person. So it is this deep-rooted idea of being somebody which takes you away from stillness, from silence. Practically speaking, familiarize yourself with listening, looking, hearing, without letting conceptualization interfere. Look, listen, without naming, judging, comparing, evaluating, justifying, and so on. Simply live in perception without conceptualization. Because in pure perception there is no room for the person, the "I."

But first be very clear about what you have understood by "I." It is memory, formed by society, belief, information from books, and so on. You have identified yourself with this image: "I am this, I am Mr. So-and-so." On the level of the "I-concept" there is no spontaneity, there is only repetition, acting in patterns. In the absence of the "I-concept" there is spontaneity, creativity, and invention. In other words, look at things, understand things, without selection. Choice is made by a chooser. Where there is no chooser, there is no choice.

If there is no one who stays open to the perspective of truth, what is it that is open?

It is consciousness which is open, because its nature is only openness. It is completely limitless, because it is not an object. Your real nature is not-knowing. You real nature is timeless. The moment knowing comes in, you create time. There is no weight in openness. The plane offers to carry your luggage in the hold, but sometimes I think you insist on carrying all your luggage yourself!

I think I understand the "I don't know." But, on the other hand, does not the desire to know come from our real nature?

The desire to know comes from what you desire. But what is the motive to know objects, to know situations? Really, objects, whether in functional daily life or in art, are a hallelujah to the ultimate. Every object points to the ultimate, because all the potential in the object is in the ultimate subject. There is no independent object, there is only the autonomous subject. Scientists may believe that there are objects outside us, but after years of understanding, you see that an object only has its reality in the subject. There are not two, there is only one.

What is important is that you are aware that there are spontaneous moments of knowing. When you say, "I understand," the understanding is already depleted, because in this moment you have conceptualized the understanding and made it an object. It is important that the knowing become being knowing, which means that it is completely absorbed in your totality. When this occurs, there is a transfer of energy, and your brain, the chess board as we said earlier, changes. You should know that you burn your hands when you say, "I know." Real knowing takes place in your totality, Otherwise, knowing is like collecting stamps.

The first words mentioned this morning were that the teaching has to do with understanding and that the mind must understand what it is not. Could you please talk on this?

The teaching is beyond knowledge. The discriminating mind can only understand what is understandable. The intellectual mind can never know what is beyond knowledge. But when the mind sees this clearly, it relaxes and dissolves into our totality. It then functions as the whole mind or consciousness. As it belongs to this totality, it belongs to reality, to truth, and can have a glimpse of reality. The mind can come to a global geometrical representation of the truth. When the mind is clear, there is no danger that the insight becomes confused in feeling.

You said that when knowing is absorbed in our totality, there is a transfer of energy, and our brain changes. Does this transfer happen suddenly, or is it a gradual process?

The understanding is instantaneous. The switchover from living in the fraction to living the global is also instantaneous. But our body-mind is accustomed to functioning in a fractional way, so it may continue to do so through habit for some time. But there is no longer any impetus in it, and it dies away in totality.

This morning on the mountain, watching the beauty in front of me, opening, hearing the sounds and seeing everything, I became aware that there were two: me looking at the beauty. When I saw this, it seemed as though I wasn't really seeing or hearing, and I didn't really know what was in front of me, and I felt completely lost. This is an observation. There is no question.

In looking, there is no looker, there is only looking. There is no "observer" and no "observed." An observed is only possible when there is an observer, but the observer is a creation of the mind. See that in looking at the mountains there is only looking. In any case, you are present. But a moment later your mind creates a witness. So eliminate the observer, and the observed automatically disappears too. Looking is then oneness; consciousness is one with its so-called object.

When you look at the mountains, your five senses must be open. You taste, smell, feel, touch, hear the mountain. You are in total receptivity. Because—and I know you can't say this in the Greek language—the seen is in the seeing, what you look at has its potentiality, its reality, in you as the ultimate looker.

When we speak of being open, we must be completely open. This is very important. The looking, the hearing, the listening, must become organic. By organic I mean that the body, the five senses, must be included. For example, when you look at this beautiful valley here and you go really into the valley with your tactile sensation, your body sensation, you feel yourself without any boundaries. Then there is a feeling of freedom which brings great joy, or when you are in front of a big green meadow and you go into every corner of the green, you bathe in the green, then you come out feeling completely fresh, because green has a very strong power, the power to emphasize existence, to make you feel more integrated, more alive.

Similarly, when you look at a beautiful stone, you may feel the quality of the stone, its stone-stillness. It lives in its stillness. The reason for its existence is its stillness. And so when you really go into the stone and feel its heaviness and follow all the variations of its form, its cavities and convexity, it brings you to stillness. Really looking at a stone, being one with it, makes you also still.

It sounds, from what you say, as though the senses are, in one way, the organs of knowledge and as if, through the senses, the qualities of things go into our essential nature.

Yes, when the object is received by the senses, it is a pure perception not captured by the mind. Only in pure perception free from any mental qualification can an object give its secret to us completely. The perceived dissolves in perceiving.

And this is the secret, to bring us back to the perceiving?

Absolutely. The perceiving is our real nature, consciousness, the home ground of all objects.

Can we have a break for a few minutes?

When we say that we must come to the end of the mind, that we must exhaust the mind, is it a necessary process, something which must happen, or is it possible to have an insight without the mind being exhausted? And secondly, is this process itself a meditation, or does meditation begin at the end of the mind?

When the mind goes to its end—and it goes to its end when it thinks of the unthinkable—we can call it meditation, because in thinking the unthinkable, we are silent. Our thinking no longer starts from thinking, it starts from silence. When the mind comes to the end of its potentiality, it is a relaxed mind. This means that when there is something to think, it thinks, and the rest of the time it is in nonthinking, that is, a natural state of relaxed, nondirected attention. If we do not come to the end of the thinking mind, we will be bound to it, so that even when there are moments when there is nothing to think, we are still in the mind and live in constant agitation. The relaxed mind functions in discontinuity. Only when it functions like this can we be aware of the continuity behind all functioning. The continuity is timeless meditation. It is this presence which gives life and reality to all "appearings."[2] Any other so-called meditation you might do has no flavor. But really, meditation is praying, praying without someone who prays or is prayed to. Real praying is thanking for the joy of being. It is expressed at every moment. Experiences like joy, transcendence, peace, and holiness are all expressions borrowed from the mind. But the meditation we are talking about here is without any qualification. Its only quality is that it is without qualifications. It is the extinction of everything that could be a state.

As long as the mind is not exhausted, it will still be an obstacle to any real insight. Because the uninformed mind—that is, the mind which does not know its limits—will continue to try to understand what is beyond it. It will be driven by will or unconscious reflex, in the old patterns of becoming and attaining. The mind will still be looking for freedom, but in trying to attain it, it goes further away from it. Because there is no way to go to freedom, for there is nobody to go to it. When the mind remains in the reflex that there is something to attain, something to become, something to achieve, it cannot come to the only useful perspective for the mind, the perspective of living in not-knowing. When the mind abides in not-knowing, when it is, at every moment, open to the unknown, it is a tool of higher reasoning. Any other use of the mind is a nuisance.

The important thing is to realize that what we are looking for is the looker, is our presence. To achieve something in the phenomenal realm we must, of course, refer to something we already know. But regarding that which can never be an object, we must go away from it. We must come to the organic memory of the body. This is important, because through this organic memory we will come to the absolutely relaxed state, where we have all our energy in our hand, so to speak. In this relaxed state the body and the mind come more or less together. There is no more duality. As we have said before, the relaxed body is dynamic, not passive. Passive relaxation is still in duality. It is not integrated because there is still emphasis on the object, relaxation.

Even in a relaxed state, the mind automatically creates pictures, or thoughts. How can we exhaust the mind?

These are residues, and these residues must also come to their exhaustion. When we let them come to their exhaustion, we have a forefeeling of the "I am." Don't go into the images or thoughts of these residues. Some teachers say to observe them, listen to them, but don't go in, don't follow them. My experience is that we must not observe or listen or follow them, because the moment we look at them we feed them by creating a witness to them. Take your stand in the void, the "I am." From here, you ignore them. But I think that when you become aware of the body, not the concept body but the feeling body, and you are at one with the feeling, in this becoming aware of the true body feeling, the residues of images and words and language have no more power. You are, of course, still in subject-object relation, the perceiver and the perceived body feeling, but there comes a moment where there is only the "I am."

When we are living in our tactile, global body, we are no longer in our foreheads. Generally, we live in our foreheads, and this localization prevents all global sensation. When we remain in our foreheads, we are in the hands of the devil. So we must become free from the brain. In the beginning there may be some difficulty to be free from the brain, because it is partly activated by the taking and grasping of the eyes, which are very connected with the brain. It is important, therefore, to consciously relax the eyes, to sense the hollows of our eyes, their heaviness. When this part is sensitive, there is a deep relaxation in the brain. Some scientists don't believe we can sense our brain, but they are studying medicine in a superficial way. We can sense and change our brain. For when the brain becomes relaxed, we feel ourselves no longer localized in the thinking factory of the forehead, but we feel ourselves behind, in the upper cervical vertebrae. When we feel ourselves behind, in our neck, we can no longer see from the point of view of the individual which projects individual objects. Because the individual is a thought construct which comes from the frontal area. From behind there is no longer any concretization. There is only a vague cloud of objectivity. Then this subtle localization behind in the neck dissolves down into the heart, and the heart is the last door, the last expansion. Finally, we become free also from the heart. We become emptiness, emptiness without border and without center. We are the universe and the universe is us.

But I would say, take note of all this and immediately forget it.

NOTES

1. Jean Klein, *Open to the Unknown, Dialogues in Delphi*, ed. Emma Edwards (Salisbury, UK: New Sarum Press, 2020). Content reproduced with permission.
2. Editor's quotation marks.

Chapter 15

John Doe, the Actor[1]

Francis Lucille

(Questioner): I would like to know if you have seen your original nature.

(*Francis Lucille*): Why would you like to know that?

I would like to know because I think that a person who has seen his original nature could be a teacher for me.

Your teacher has to be discovered in your heart. You have to find out by yourself. When you find out, you discover your real nature.

In fact, there is no teacher. There is a teacher only for as long as one takes oneself to be a student. In the same way, as long as an infant needs breastfeeding, there is a breastfeeding mother. But from the vantage point of the so-called teacher there is no such distinction. There is only welcoming, oneness, happiness.

The student and teacher are one and the same.

Absolutely.

I just read an article in a publication on yoga. The thrust of it was that gurus and teachers are, perhaps, the biggest impediment on the planet. The author suggested that we retain our personal freedom and simply find out who we are, instead of remaining a student and following somebody around, reading books, or ceaselessly looking for another teacher.

As long as you take yourself for a personal entity, you may assume two positions: one in which you want someone to help you, or one in which you want to find the truth by yourself and don't want to be taught. Even if someone is helping, you need to, at least, complete the work. That is why a good teacher doesn't give you everything already made, predigested. He gives you stuff to work on and understand by yourself. This universal principle applies to any kind of teaching, including spiritual teaching. If you take either of these two positions, you are right. In the first case, because the desire to find a spiritual teacher comes from a deep desire to find your

Self, and in the second case, because there is a desire for independence, for autonomous understanding, which emanates from your own autonomy, your own independence. As long as you don't feel a desire for a teacher, don't worry about it. Everything, every person, every event in your life is your teacher. At some point something you read, or hear, or a person you meet may provide an insight that will make it clear to you that there is a possibility to live free of the notion of being a person—to live knowingly in your own freedom and your happiness. In the beginning, you may be open to this possibility of a creative life, then doubts may arise. In this case, you may want to meet someone who lives in freedom. It was in this spirit that I started looking for a spiritual teacher in my early years, and I didn't regret it. Another reason for seeking a teacher is to find answers to questions you may have. There are many good reasons to meet a teacher. But in fact, there is only one: to meet yourself—your Self. You are looking for your Self. Your Self is not limited by, or to, this body and this mind. Your Self is immense, beautiful, and immortal. Be open to that possibility, be open to the source of all possibilities.

You spoke of the possibility of not being a person, but being free and happy. Could you please elaborate?

The actor on stage who plays Hamlet today, Macbeth tomorrow, and King Lear the next day doesn't take himself for Hamlet, Macbeth, or King Lear. He takes himself for John Doe, the actor. But this doesn't prevent him from being Hamlet, Macbeth, or King Lear on stage. When you know that you are awareness, and not a man or a woman, a spouse or a parent, this knowledge doesn't prevent you from playing all these parts one after another. But because these parts aren't permanent, they aren't you, because what you are is continuous. These various characters you play are like garments. You put them on, you take them off, and you get new a garment. What you are is always present.

Does the playing of roles somehow contribute to our identification with the personal entity? Is there a reason why we are playing roles?

You can play whatever role the current circumstances in your life require, but without identifying yourself with it, with the personal. Now, if you are asking if there's any reason for identifying yourself with a personal entity, the answer is no. There is no good reason. Just don't do that. Don't even say that there is no good reason. Just don't do that.

The second question was "Is there a reason why we are playing roles?" Well, it would be boring otherwise. Diversity is part of beauty. It is a celebration. What we are, our true nature, is not a blank. It isn't nothingness. It contains everything. Everything is our Self, therefore, your Self from moment to moment.

Everything you see, everything you touch, everything you think is you. Just after the thought, after the perception, after the feeling, you say, "I was there as a person and I was having this thought, this feeling, this perception." But that isn't true, because at the time of the thought, feeling, or perception there was no thinker, feeler, or perceiver, and there was no object thought, felt, or perceived. There was only thinking, feeling, perceiving. So from moment to moment there is only oneness. And this is what you are. This is the real you. As such you are not here or there. "I am here" is a thought. When you eliminate this thought, where are you?

I was with you up until the last part.

Are you with yourself?

What do you mean?

Are you with yourself? Or is your Self separate from you?

I am separate.

You are separate from yourself?

I am working on myself.

How do you know that you are separate from yourself?

It's a long story.

How do you know now that you are now separate from yourself without going into the past? Not yesterday or tomorrow, but now. Are you separate from yourself? On what basis can you say that?

Keep going because I think I am . . .

Try to find whether you are really separate from yourself. Try to find out for sure. What I feel is that I'm always with myself. I am my best companion. How could I be separate from myself?

Maybe it is just that I think I am separate.

Yes. But where does your thought that you are separate appear?

In myself.

Right. So you are not separate from yourself.

I don't know. I have to think about it.

Think about it.

So separateness is something we do in thinking, not in reality?

Absolutely.

If we could all stop thinking, we would all be very happy.

We don't need to stop thinking. We can't actually end thinking as a result of effort, because the effort itself would involve thinking. There's a story about a king who was very ill. He sent for a famous physician and told him, "Cure me or I'll have your head cut off." Seeing that the king was dying, the physician said, "I can save you, but you have to follow my instructions carefully, otherwise the medicine will be ineffective." The king agreed. The physician gave him some medicine and asked him not to think about a gray monkey whenever he took it. Of course, this turned out to be very impossible. So the king died, and the physician saved his own life. This story tells you that if you try to stop thinking, your trying requires thinking, so you can never achieve your goal.

Do thoughts stop? I guess what I am trying to express is that thoughts are helpful in our role-playing but don't necessarily help us to be who we are.

The kind of thoughts that are not useful are thoughts that derive from the notion of being a person. Such thoughts bring about hatred, separateness, fury, desire, and so on. They are conducive to negative emotions. If I am convinced that I am this limited body-mind, born a few years ago and bound to die within a few years, there is no way I can prevent the myriad thoughts that originate from this belief from coming up. If I make an effort to prevent them from coming up, pressure will build up inside me, and I may end up in jail or in a mental institution. There is no way of preventing these thoughts from arising as long as their root has not been cut. If I want to get rid of leaves on a tree, because they are littering my front yard, I can try to remove the leaves one by one, but next spring they will be back again. The real solution is to cut the trunk or, better, uproot the tree. The root of these thoughts and negative emotions is the notion that I am a personal entity, that I am separate. The uprooting of the tree is the understanding that my actual experience, the eternal now, is devoid of such a separation.

How do people make the shift of consciousness from identifying with their separate personality to become aware of the truth?

There is nothing the person can do to see that "personness" is a fake. The person persistently adheres to his identity as a person, but there are moments of freedom from this identity. In these moments there is an opportunity to take some distance and have a glimpse of this presence that we all are—awareness.

What is our most precious good? It isn't any part of our body. This is evidenced by the fact that people will submit to having a body part amputated, if necessary, to save their life. Our most precious good is not even the body in its totality. What we really love is consciousness. The real question is: Is consciousness in the body or is the body in consciousness? We have been conditioned by our surroundings, by our teachers, by the prevalent materialism to believe that our body is in the world, our brain is in the body, and consciousness is a function of the brain. From the vantage point of nonduality, the picture is just the opposite: the ultimate reality is awareness, within which there is the mind. The body, the thoughts, and the rest of the universe all appear in the mind. Now, how am I going to decide, from these two positions, which one is true? It is important to understand with our logical apparatus, the mind, that this question can't be decided by the mind. If I choose one of these positions rather than the opposite, it is a belief, an act of faith. If I see that clearly, I am already free from the concept that I am in the world, that I am my body. I understand that existence in the world is an act of faith, not an absolute truth, and I am now open to the other possibility. The mind can't decide because it knows only that which is within itself. What is beyond the mind cannot be known by the mind. All it can do is understand that it cannot decide. When it understands that it can't find the ultimate answer, it becomes quiet. In this stillness there is the possibility for our true nature to take us. We can't take it. We can only be open and welcome it.

NOTE

1. Francis Lucille, *Eternity Now*, ed. Alan Epstein (Temecula, CA: Truespeech Productions, 2006 and 2009). Content reproduced with permission.

Chapter 16

Putting an End to the Discriminating Mind and To Study the Way Is to Study the Self[1]

Sekkei Harada

PUTTING AN END TO THE DISCRIMINATING MIND

The zazen in which by watching the breath you forget you are breathing is something you cannot see with the eye or know directly. So let me explain what it means to truly see something.

Consider a vase of flowers. On seeing these flowers—in the first instant you perceive them—you probably did not think "beautiful" or "these flowers suit me" or "these are such and such kinds of flowers." You simply saw them. This is what we call "right seeing," the most correct way of seeing. But then thoughts arose, such as "they're beautiful" or "I don't like these flowers." This second perception arises incredibly quickly. Such conscious perceptions as "beautiful" and "ugly" have no relation to the thing seen. As they have absolutely no relation to the flower itself, discriminations such as "like/dislike" or "beautiful/ugly" only arise from within your own mind. As long as we continue to make such discriminations with our minds, it will not be possible to see the flower as it is.

Human beings have six sense functions: seeing, hearing, smelling, tasting, touching, and thinking. Although these functions are all different, we are never confused by them. They are mysterious functions. No matter how complicated a thing may be, at once we can see it, hear it, think it. It is impossible to see it mistakenly or to hear a sound mistakenly. Moreover, there is no guiding center inside that gives us orders such as "see this" or "hear this" or "feel this." This means the condition of allowing these six functions to be as they are is the most peaceful condition for human beings.

There is a method of zazen called "shikantaza," which means "to sit single-mindedly." Shikantaza is to sit entrusting yourself to thoughts as they arise.

147

It is to sit in a dignified manner, without being moved by what is seen, heard, or thought; shikantaza is to sit without being bothered in any way by these things, by continuing to entrust yourself in this way to the six sense functions as they are, it is possible to know that you are one with things. This is what we call "casting off body and mind."

In China, Dogen practiced with Zen Master Nyojo, and he cast off body and mind doing this kind of zazen. He went to Nyojo and said, "I have cast off body and mind." Nyojo said, "No. It must be 'body and mind cast off.'" The reason why "cast off body and mind" is not correct is that from the beginning, body and mind have already been cast off. Consequently, Nyojo explained that casting off body and mind is wholly unnecessary.

TO STUDY THE WAY IS TO STUDY THE SELF

Without being aware of it, you have come to perceive "this thing" as yourself. That you have done this for a long time poses a big problem. "This thing" belongs to no one. If, in fact, "this thing" were you, the word "you" would itself become unnecessary. "This thing," which you don't really understand, can clearly perceive on hearing or seeing something. That it can perceive or be conscious of something is the reason that delusion arises. Delusion arises at that point because there is both that which is understood and that which is not understood. It is mistaken to think something exists that, in fact, does not exist. This is the case with the ego-self, which though it does not exist, is thought to be "you." Since "this thing," which is not really understood, is perceived to exist, when things don't go as you wish, they become the cause of feelings of dissatisfaction or lack. Accordingly, Dogen had this to say:

> To study the Way is to study the Self.
> To study the Self is to forget the ego-self.
> To forget the ego-self is to be enlightened by all things.
> To be enlightened by all things is to cast off body and mind both
> of oneself and others.

Dogen is asking you to look at "this thing" that you perceive to be yourself and then to ask yourself, "What is the true Self? Who *am* I anyway?" He is saying that to pursue and investigate these questions is the practice of the Way of Buddha. "This thing" is nothing more than a symbol of you. If you can just forget "this thing," this symbolic ego-self, the division between it and other things will disappear. To "cast off" means that "this thing" becomes one with all things, that the body and mind of yourself as well as others have been cast off. All things have disappeared, they have become empty. It is the realization that already everything has been cast off, that everything is one and already empty. It is not a matter of *becoming* one, becoming "Mu" (nothingness), or becoming "ku" (emptiness) as a result of practice.

NOTE

1. © 2008 Sekkei Harada, *The Essence of Zen: The Teachings of Sekkei Harada.* Reprinted by arrangement with Wisdom Publications, Inc., wisdompubs.org.

Chapter 17

Who Is Thinking? Satsang with Papaji[1]

H. W. L. Poonja (Papaji)

Question: *I'm not clear how to make the best use of you as my teacher. I want to make the best use of my time here, but I'm not clear how I should use my time. What should I be doing that I am not doing at home?*

Papaji: Take care of the purpose for which you have come. First, clarify your purpose. A relationship is not really necessary. That we can look after later. Purpose is the foremost, the most important thing. When you are thirsty, you go to the river. Your purpose is to quench your thirst. It is not to ask the river what kind of relationship you have with it. You don't need a relationship; you only need a purpose. You came here the day before yesterday and your purpose is to find out who you are. Find this out. Know who you are. If you first know who you are, then you will automatically know who I am. So, your first priority is the question "Who am I?" Once you have discovered that, you will know the real nature of all the other things and people that you see. First start with this question "Who am I?" We started on this question the day before yesterday. You need to recognize yourself. Now, what was that question I asked you to ask?

Q: *Who?*

P: Yes, what was the full question?

Q: *Who is thinking?*

P: Yes, this was the question I gave you. I told you to find the answer to this question. I asked you to return home to the Self through asking this question, and then to come back and tell me what you saw there.

Q: *What do I see there?*

P: Yes, what do you see there? [There was a pause while Papaji wrote "who" on a piece of paper and showed it to the questioner.] What do you see here?

Q: *I see a word on a piece of paper.*

P: This simple word is your question.

Q: *What do I see in here?*

P: Anywhere. Wherever the "who" is. Your question is, "Who is thinking?"

Q: *I can see the question.*

P: Can you see where the question comes from? Focus on this question and look to see where it arises from. Return back to the "who." What do you see there?

Q: *I see arising. I see things arising, one from another.*

P: Something arose that is the predicate. Now, what is the subject? Who is thinking? Return from this predicate of thinking and focus on the "who." This is the finish. Now you are at the root, aren't you? Find out who this "who" is. What is its shape? What is the shape of this "who"? What is its form? How is it? What does it look like? [Long pause] What is happening?

Q: *The question just arises out of nothing, out of emptiness, and disappears back into emptiness.*

P: That's right. You say this question disappeared into the emptiness. The question was, "Who is thinking?" For thinking you need a mind, don't you? Now, the process of thinking has been arrested. It happened when you put the question "Who is thinking?" Now the process has been arrested. Then you said, very correctly, that the question disappears, that's what you said. "There's emptiness." What else do you say?

Q: *It's just emptiness; just space.*

P: OK, it's emptiness; it's space. Emptiness is there; space is there. This is your inherent nature. You can call it presence or space or anything else. It is obstructed by desire and by thinking. It is always obstructed by desire. Emptiness is just the lack, the absence of thoughts and desires. When you have a burden on your shoulder, you are restless. Let us say that you are holding onto two hundred pounds and that you want to get rid of this trouble, this burden. When you drop it, you have not gained anything. You have not attained some new state that was never there before. You have simply thrown something away that was troubling you and returned to your inherent nature, the inherent state that was there before you loaded yourself up with this weight. This thinking process, this burden, is a desire that we always carry with us. I am showing you how to drop this unwanted burden. When you ask the question, "Who is thinking?" you arrest the process of thinking and return back to your true nature, your spontaneous nature, and this is what you are always. The mind does not enter here. Time does not enter. Death does not enter. If you stay there, there will be no fear. If you step out of it, you step into *samsara*, manifestation, and there you are in trouble all the time.

Q: *I think I have a desire to make a much bigger deal of it.*

P: What?

Q: *I think I had expectations that it would be some big, great experience, but actually the experience of it is very ordinary. It just feels very clear, very ordinary, and very empty.*

P: Yes, from emptiness everything arises. From emptiness all this cosmos has arisen, all this manifestation comprising millions of planets and solar systems. All of these millions of planets hanging in space arose from just one thought that arose from this particle of emptiness. This can happen without affecting the emptiness at all.

Q: *Should I try to stay in the emptiness? Thoughts arise in the emptiness. Some of them are attractive; some make me afraid; and some of them are repugnant. I find myself latching on to thoughts and identifying with them. I become those thoughts. I lose sight of the emptiness and the presence until I can remind myself again.*

P: If you remind yourself at that time, all is over, all is gone. The best position to take is that of not forgetting. Just play your role, but don't forget that it is all just a drama on the stage. Imagine a drama company is putting on a play. The person who has to play the servant of the king falls sick at the last moment and cannot come. No other actors are available, so the proprietor of the company steps in to play the role. In the play, the king, who is one of the employees of the proprietor, orders the servant around: "Fetch my shoes. I want to go for a walk." The proprietor meekly obeys and carries out the orders, but does he ever forget that he is the owner of the company? He is happy to act the role of the servant because all the time that this role is being portrayed, he knows that he is really the proprietor. If you live like this, knowing that you are the Self, you can act anywhere. If you know this, all your activities will be very beautiful, and you will never suffer. Once you have had a glimpse, a knowledge of this emptiness, you will be happy all the time because you know that all manifestation, all *samsara*, is your own projection. Where does all this manifestation rise from? When you are asleep, there is nothing there, is there?

Q: *There's another kind of dreaming then?*

P: I am not speaking of dreaming. We can talk about that state later. For now, I'm talking about slumber, deep sleep. A few years ago, I met a team in Rishikish. Twenty-five people had come from all over the world: psychologists, physiologists, even parapsychologists. They had a very original proposition that they're trying to test: that there are only two states, waking and dreaming. They said that man is either awake or dreaming and that there was really no such state as sleep. In India we say that there are five states: waking, dreaming, sleeping, *turiya*, and *turiyatita*. One of them told me, "That is what we are discovering in the West. When we put an EEG on a sleeping person's brain we find that dreaming is going on all the time, even during what appears to be deep sleep."

Q: *What is the last one?*

P: *Turiyatita.* Waking, dreaming, and sleeping are states you understand. After this there is *turiya*, the fourth state. This is the state in which the previous three appear and disappear. Beyond that is *turiyatita*, which means "beyond the fourth." These scientists were going from ashram to ashram, looking for swamis to test with their equipment. Some of the scientists were part of the astronaut-training program. Apparently, astronauts were not sleeping well in space, so research was going on, looking for ways to improve their sleeping. There was a theory that some kind of meditation or yoga might improve their sleeping patterns.

These scientists were looking for swamis to test. They wanted to put electrodes on their heads while they were meditating to see what happened to the brain waves during meditation. They tried many people and eventually ended up with a man called Swami Rama. When they arrived, he was gardening in his ashram. I was not there at the time, so I got this story secondhand. They approached him very respectfully and explained their purpose. Then they asked him if he would sit or lie down and meditate while they checked out his brain waves.

He replied, "You can attach your wires while I am watering my garden. I don't need to sit down to meditate." If you are knowingly established in the substratum, any amount of activities can go on, and you won't need the mind to do them. The Self will take care of all these things and you will remain in peace at all times. The scientists put wires on his head and discovered that, as the swami had said, his mind was not working while he was engaged in his daily gardening chores. They were so impressed, they took him off for further tests.

Let us go back to the three states—waking, dreaming, and sleeping—and the underlying fourth state of emptiness. The three states are projected onto that substratum, that background in which sleeping comes and goes, dreaming comes and goes, and waking comes and goes. There is some substratum, some basic foundation on which they all revolve. That foundation, that presence, that space is always there, but while you are preoccupied with outside things, you forget it.

Now, there are three classes of people. In the first category there are those who never ever forget. Under all circumstances, they know that everything is taking place in this substratum. These people are the *jivanmuktas*, which means that they are fully liberated while they are still alive in their bodies. The second category get themselves into trouble because sometimes they remember and sometimes they forget. Awareness of emptiness may be there for a while, but then the memory of a friend who has died may rise up and suddenly they are in grief. They have lost the awareness of that emptiness by attaching themselves to a thought. This kind of emptiness is not abiding: it depends on the whims of mental activities. The people in the third category are suffering all the time. They never have a glimpse of that original space, that emptiness, and so they suffer endlessly. For them, *samsara* never ends or even stops briefly.

If you are a member in the very exclusive number one club, you know that whatever manifests is an appearance in your own Self. When you wake up, manifestation arises, but you know that it is all a projection. When you sleep, no manifestation is present, but you, your Self, will still remain. Something will still be there while you sleep, and that something is your own Self.

Q: *I am not aware of that presence while I am asleep.*

P: Yes, that is because "you" are not present. It is the "you" that you live through that desires these matters. For "you" presence is only felt when there is some obstruction to the awareness of the presence.

Q: *When there's obstruction, I can feel presence, but when there isn't, I can't. This sounds very paradoxical.*

P: Your sense of being a person is the obstruction. Everything, all your experiences, or lack of them, are mediated through this idea of individuality. This obstruction rises from the presence, and you either feel the presence through it, or you are aware of its absence. The presence is there all the time, but you don't feel it in your deep sleep state because this mediator, this "I," is not there. You don't know how to be aware of anything when this "I" is absent, so you declare, "Presence is not there when I sleep."

You use this obstruction to validate all your experience, but it has no inherent validity of its own. *Shanti*, peace, was there before the obstruction arose, and when the obstruction subsides, *shanti* still prevails. Your inherent nature is this *shanti*. It is there both when the experiencer is there and when the experiencer is absent.

Q: *Yes, it's obvious. A fish swims in water all its life, but it doesn't know anything about water. If you want to teach it about water, you take it out of the water, and immediately it understands what water is and how important it is. What you are saying is that if there is nothing to interfere with the presence, there's nothing to contrast the presence to. And that means there is no means to know the presence.*

P: Here we speak of the fish that is still in the river and which cries, "I am thirsty." It is ignorance of the underlying substratum that creates the idea of suffering. That space, that emptiness, is your inherent nature. It is always there.

Q: [begins to laugh uncontrollably]

P: He's a doctor of . . . [Papaji also starts to laugh].

Q: *What a relief!* [Everyone in the room laughs] *I can't believe it's so simple. Hmm. Thank you. Thank you very much. I seem to remember now.*

Q: [new questioner, addressing the laughing man] *Did you forget? I watch myself and I ask myself questions such as "Who is getting upset?" but I forget all the time.*

P: When you say, "I have forgotten," you are not forgetting, you are suddenly remembering. Every time the thought, "I have forgotten" arises, that is remembrance.

Q: *But there is also a point when you are not even aware that you have forgotten. You just get angry, for example, with no thought of forgetfulness or remembrance.*

P: You have a relationship with this entity that is forgetting or remembering. There must be a person who is forgetting. There is a person who is the same whether she has forgotten or remembered. So, the person remains the same throughout the process of remembering and forgetting. Find out the "I" who has the forgetfulness and you will discover the "I" that never forgets. The real "I" is consciousness itself. It will not forget anything. If light is everywhere, nothing can be hidden because there is no area of darkness where things are not clear. When you return to consciousness, everything will be very clear. Nothing will be forgotten or hidden. There is the sleep state in which you have dreams, and there is the waking state. These are known to you. But there is something beyond them, and that is consciousness. This is your true nature. You don't have to acquire it, gain it, attain it, achieve it, or aspire for it. Since you have never lost it, you don't have to run after it to get it back. It is here now, and it will always be here. It can't be lost. If it is not here now, what is the use of trying to get it? Whatever you newly acquire you will someday lose. So look for that which is never lost, which is permanent, abiding, natural and always there, here and now. Look into "now." Look into presence. Look into space. Look into your own emptiness. The whole cosmos is there, the whole cosmos. It emerges from there. Return and see the source of all phenomena. Then, enjoy life.

NOTE

1. *The Fire of Freedom, Satsang with Papaji*, ed. David Godman (Boulder, CO: Avadhuta Foundation, 2007). Used with permission.

Chapter 18

On Dying to Self

Retreat, End of Day[1]

Vimala Thakar

QUESTION: I have realized that it is necessary to die to the image of self, but the dying does not take place. I keep on thinking about dying, but it does not occur.

VIMALA: I realize the necessity of dying to the image or images of self . . . what does that imply? Dying is not destruction, is it? Why is it necessary to die to the images? When my house is on fire, do I have to think about getting out, or jumping out? Do thought, ideas about methods, or techniques enter my consciousness when I see that the house is on fire? Is there an intervention of thought at all? Is there a time lag between perception and action? When the house is flooded there is no time lag between perception and action, because perception at the sensual level of the flooded house results instantaneously in the mobilization of organic intelligence. Perception instantaneously gets converted into understanding and understanding leads to spontaneous action. Is that not what happens?

Do I realize that the images that I have, or that people have about me and that I have accepted, prevent me from living? Have I realized that images isolate me from life? Living is relating to that which is, interaction with life is living. Images prevent me from perceiving the facts, leaving aside interacting with life. Could it be that the perception of a psychological fact does not activate, does not mobilize intelligence in us, as it does at the sensual level?

Is it because of our defective upbringing through untold centuries, having been drugged by thought and knowledge, by the gathering of ideas, the thinking about how to use them, bargaining with them to such an extent that we have lost that spontaneous movement of organic intelligence? That is the question. Not why dying does not take place, but why perception of a psychological fact, perception not at the sensual level but perception through sensitivity at the psychological level, does not activate intelligence.

Should we ask the question how to bring up children, how to bring ourselves up so that the same activation of intelligence that takes place at the
sensual level will take place at the psychological level also? And is this
activation at all dependent on the realization that images will not allow me to
live, just as the fire does not allow me to live in the house? Please do see that
it is the urge to live that makes me jump out of the window, even break the
window, if the house is on fire, I jump out instantaneously.

So I have to realize that images will not allow me to live. The jumping out
of the images, the enclosures, the isolation that the images have built up could
occur if we perceive actually, not as a piece of knowledge, not as an idea, but
as a fact that we are not living. I wonder if you recollect that we had asked
this question of ourselves on the very first day: "Are we alive, are we living,
or are we under the illusion that we are living?"

Could it be that the word "dying," the use of the term "dying" stimulates an
unverbalized resistance, and the intelligence gets blocked by that resistance,
because death is something negative for us, because dying and death are
mistaken for destruction.

When the form of a flower has exhausted the potential of manifesting its
creativity, the petals of the flower dry up and drop away. In autumn the leaves
of a tree dry up, they become a beautiful yellow, like ripe old age in a human
body, having its own glory; you know the smile that shines through the
wrinkles in ripe old age, it has as much beauty and ecstasy as the smile on an
infant or a child's face. So the leaves drop away. They do not die away, they
fall to the earth and get converted into manure, revitalizing the earth. Though
the form disintegrates, the energy is recycled and converted into another form
and continues. Life knows no death.

The human form disintegrates, either having exhausted the biological
potential it withers away, or having been contaminated by sickness, the
movement of energy gets terminated. That is not the end of life, maybe the
discontinuity of a particular form, a particular expression.

Could it be that the word dying to self, dying to ego, sends a shiver down
the spine, and provokes an unverbalized resistance or fear within us? If this
is so, let us put away the word "dying." Religious exploration is not an ordeal
in which we must torture ourselves with words, fears, and resistances. The
investigation or exploration is a joyous adventure involving the seriousness
of the whole of life. Seriousness can be joyous, it need not be depressive,
sad, cynical, or fearful. So let us put away the word "dying." Let us say the
discontinuity of this occupation with image building. Shall we now reword
the question? I realize that the discontinuity of building images is vitally necessary, and that does not happen.

It does not happen because I have not been trained for that. Shall I begin
with myself, this moment, here and now to go through relationships and

experiences without building up images about myself and others? It is possible, learning is possible until the last breath, that is the beauty of being born in a human form. It is quite a benediction to be born a human being.

How can we move through events and incidents of daily living, of relationships, without building images? An image is built upon a value judgment, is it not? It is based on a conclusion, a categorical conclusion, an irreversible conclusion. Supposing I learn to register and record facts without converting my understanding into rigid conclusions.

I understand the facts, I respond to them as for the requirements of the situation, as for the work that I have to do. I act on the understanding of the challenge, the understanding of the situation. I do not move naively, ignorantly, or casually, there is no time in life for being casual. If I am casual, absentminded, or distracted, then I will miss the opportunity of meeting life, of partaking of its intelligence, I will miss the opportunity of living.

Sensually I perceive, sensitively I understand, verbally I grasp the implications. I respond to the situation, and there is a full stop. There is no conclusion, theory, or dogma to be deduced and transferred to memory. I do not want any defense mechanism against tomorrow, because tomorrow does not exist, it is only in the mind. In the present I do not need any defense mechanism, I need spontaneity, I need intelligence, I need the willingness to expose myself.

Why should I take the trouble of drawing conclusions, of making value judgments, of building up ideas, introducing rigidity in my consciousness? You see, there is a way to learn with no memory to be added. And in this way I learn to move through relationships without drawing rigid conclusions or building images about other people against the tomorrows: if I know how that person is, then I will know how to deal with that person!

When I have learned to live without creating new memory, I find that without drawing conclusions, without building images, it is possible to live, to share life, to communicate, to move through relationships. And there is a freshness about it. Referring to memory and behaving on the basis of that memory makes me stale, there is no vitality, there is no freshness. So I learn to be fresh at every moment, I do not refer to the past.

If I learn to live that way, and it becomes an enjoyable way of living, then the old images lying stored in memory become irrelevant and defunct without any conscious effort on my part at all. Please do see this. If you like to call that dying of the images, you may. But why use a term that stinks of negativity to the conditioned consciousness? You know, spirituality is a science of life and living, and there is so much to learn. Knowledge creates the illusion that there is wisdom in us, that there is understanding in us, and that we need not move a finger, just use the knowledge stored in memory, and that is all to living.

If one can get disillusioned about the role of knowledge, about the efficacy of knowledge, then I think learning becomes possible. Sadhana or self-education is learning, discovering, and living from moment to moment in the light of your own understanding.

There are two things to learn. One is sharpening the sensitivity, so that perception of a psychological fact activates intelligence, as it does at the sensual level. And secondly to live without drawing conclusions or formulating value judgments about people and about ourselves. Is that not an alternative civilization, an alternative human culture?

If the basis of culture, which today is knowledge, thought, and thinking, gets replaced by learning and understanding, the very complexion of human relationships will go through a qualitative change. Then I will not keep thinking about dying, because thinking is not going to bring about dying, thinking is not committing suicide, is it? Setting ourselves free of the habit of building up images is not committing suicide. As this is a very basic and fundamental question, we are going into it rather deeply.

Thirdly, when the perception, the understanding of the mental movement enables me to see that there is nothing like an individual mind, an individual ego, that it is only a cultural contrivance of the human race, that this verbalization, this ideation and conceptualization is only a cultural contrivance for social living, then the importance we attach to the movement of thought will no longer be there. It will be like any other means to be used. Thinking will no longer be equated with the act of living.

Preoccupation with the mental movement will terminate the moment we realize that though this idea, this concept, this thought structure is needed to deal with the man-made world, with the man-made structures, if and when necessary, we need not be imprisoned in it, so that a sense of freedom, not only from images but from the whole thought movement, emerges out of that understanding. Could it be that if I am preoccupied with the movement of thought and I want to get rid of the image-making occupation, it may not be possible?

Let me take one step further and see the limitations built into the thought structure, see its limited utility, so that the importance of the constant movement of thought is not there anymore, the necessity to interpret and build a value judgment on the behavior of other people, or on my own behavior, is no longer there. This sharpens the sensitivity, gives it a depth and intensity that it did not have before, because it was entangled in the movement of thought. Now that sensitivity is free from the strain and stress of the thought movement.

Therefore, as soon as there is perception, the organic intelligence, the creativity contained in the human body, gets activated. There is no longer a difference between sensual and psychological perception. You see the beauty of it. Liberation is holistic maturity, it is a holistic growth into another dimension of consciousness, a transformation in the total way of living, physical, verbal, psychological, individual, and social. That is called a revolution. It is not bringing about a patchwork of changes here and there, as per the need of the hour.

NOTE

1. Originally published in *Life as Teacher* by Vimala Thakar (Bookfund Vimala Thakar Holland, 1991), https://vimalathakar.world/wp-content/uploads/2017/09/LifeAsTeacher.pdf. Copyright 1993 by Bookfund Vimala Thakar. Reprinted with permission.

Chapter 19

No Trace[1]

Shunryu Suzuki

When you do something, you should burn yourself completely, like a good bonfire, leaving no trace of yourself.

When we practice zazen, our mind is calm and quite simple. But usually, our mind is very busy and complicated, and it is difficult to be concentrated on what we are doing. This is because before we act, we think, and this thinking leaves some trace. Our activity is shadowed by some preconceived idea. The thinking not only leaves some trace or shadow, but also gives us many other notions about other activities and things. These traces and notions make our minds very complicated. When we do something with a quite simple, clear mind, we have no notion or shadows, and our activity is strong and straightforward. But when we do something with a complicated mind, in relation to other things or people, or society, our activity becomes very complex.

Most people have a double or triple notion in one activity. There is a saying, "To catch two birds with one stone." This is what people usually try to do. Because they want to catch too many birds, they find it difficult to be concentrated on one activity, and they end up not catching any birds at all! That kind of thinking always leaves its shadow on their activity. The shadow is not actually the thinking itself. Of course, it is often necessary to think or prepare before we act. But right thinking does not leave any shadow. Thinking which leaves traces comes out of your relative confused mind. Relative mind is the mind which sets itself in relation to other things, thus limiting itself. It is this small mind which creates gaining ideas and leaves traces of itself.

If you leave a trace of your thinking on your activity, you will be attached to the trace. For instance, you may say, "This is what I have done!" But actually, it is not so. In your recollection you may say, "I did such and such a thing in some certain way," but actually that is never exactly what happened. When you think in this way you limit the actual experience of what you have done. So if you attach to the idea of what you have done, you are involved in selfish ideas.

Often we think what we have done is good, but it may not actually be so. When we become old, we are often very proud of what we have done. When others listen to someone proudly telling something which he has done, they will feel funny, because they know his recollection is one-sided. They know that what he has told them is not exactly what he did. Moreover, if he is proud of what he did, that pride will create some problem for him. Repeating his recollections in this way, his personality will be twisted more and more, until he becomes quite a disagreeable, stubborn fellow. This is an example of leaving a trace of one's thinking. We should not forget what we did, but it should be without an extra trace. To leave a trace is not the same as to remember something. It is necessary to remember what we have done, but we should not become attached to what we have done in some special sense. What we call "attachment" is just these traces of our thought and activity.

In order not to leave any traces, when you do something, you should do it with your whole body and mind; you should be concentrated on what you do. You should do it completely, like a good bonfire. You should not be a smoky fire. You should burn yourself completely. If you do not burn yourself completely, a trace of yourself will be left in what you do. You will have something remaining which is not completely burned out. Zen activity is activity which is completely burned out, with nothing remaining but ashes. This is the goal of our practice. That is what Dogen meant when he said, "Ashes do not come back to firewood." Ash is ash. Ash should be completely ash. The firewood should be firewood. When this kind of activity takes place, one activity covers everything.

So our practice is not a matter of one hour or two hours, or one day or one year. If you practice zazen with your whole body and mind, even for a moment, that is zazen. So moment after moment you should devote yourself to your practice. You should not have any remains after you do something. But this does not mean to forget all about it. If you understand this point, all the dualistic thinking and all the problems of life will vanish.

When you practice Zen, you become one with Zen. There is no you and no zazen. When you bow, there is no Buddha and no you. One complete bowing takes place, that is all. This is Nirvana. When Buddha transmitted our practice to Mahakashyapa, he just picked up a flower with a smile. Only Mahakashyapa understood what he meant; no one else understood. We do not know if this is a historical event or not, but it means something. It is a demonstration of our traditional way. Some activity which covers everything is true activity, and the secret of this activity is transmitted from Buddha to us. This is zen practice, not some teaching taught by Buddha, or some rules of life set up by him. The teaching or the rules should be changed according to the place, or according to the people who observe them, but the secret of this practice cannot be changed. It is always true.

So for us there is no other way to live in this world. I think this is quite true; and this is easy to accept, easy to understand, and easy to practice. If you compare the kind of life based on this practice with what is happening in this world, or in human society, you will find out just how valuable the truth Buddha left us is. It is quite simple, and practice is quite simple. But even so, we should not ignore it; its great value must be discovered. Usually when it is so simple, we say, "Oh, I know that! It is quite simple. Everyone knows that." But if we do not find its value, it means nothing. It is the same as not knowing. The more you understand culture, the more you will understand how true and how necessary this teaching is. Instead of only criticizing your culture, you should devote your mind and body to practicing this simple way. Then society or culture will grow out of you.

NOTE

1. Shunryu Suzuki, excerpts from *Zen Mind, Beginner's Mind*. Protected under the terms of the International Copyright Union. Reprinted by arrangement with the Permissions Company, LLC, on behalf of Shambhala Publications Inc., Boulder, Colorado, shambhala.com.

Appendix

Shohaku Okumura's Translation of Dog's Buddha-Nature Part of Busho

第12章狗子還有佛性也無

(100)趙州眞際大師にある僧とふ、「狗子還有佛性也無」。 A monk asked Great Master Zhenji of Zhaozhou, "Does a dog have buddha-nature or not?"

(101) この問の意趣あきらむべし。 We should clarify the intention of [the monk who is asking] this question.
狗子とはいぬなり。 Gouzi means "a dog."
かれに佛性あるべしと問取せず、なかるべしと問取するにあらず。
[The monk] is neither asking if [a dog] has buddha-nature, nor asking if [a dog] has not buddha-nature.
これは、鐵漢また學道するかと問取するなり。 He is asking if an iron man also studies the Way.
あやまりて毒手にあふ、うらみふかしといへども、三十年よりこのかた、さらに半箇の聖人を みる風流なり。 Although [the monk] may deeply **regret** having being seized **unexpectedly** by [Zhauzhou's] poison hand, he did it in the excellent style of **finally** seeing half a sage after thirty years.

(102) 趙州いはく、「無」。 Zhauzhou said, "It does not have. (*mu*)"

(103)この道をききて、習學すべき方路あり。 Hearing this saying, there must be a path to study [we should follow].
佛性の自稱する無も恁麼道なるべし、狗子の自稱する無も、恁麼道なるべし、傍觀者の喚作の 無も恁麼道なるべし、その無わづかに消石の日あるべし。 The "*mu*" that buddha-nature itself speaks must be said in such a way; the "*mu*" that the dog itself speaks must be said in such a way;

the "*mu*" that a bystander **cries out** must be said in such a way. The "*mu*" will have **a day when at the very least it melts stone**.

(104)僧いはく、「一切衆生皆有佛性、狗子為甚麼無」。 The monk said, "All living beings, all of them have buddha-nature, why does the dog not have?"

(105) いはゆる宗旨は、一切衆生無ならば、佛性も無なるべし、狗子も無なるべしといふ、その宗旨 作麼生、となり。The essential principle is that, if all living beings are "*mu*," buddha-nature also must be "*mu*," and the dog also must be "*mu*." [The monk is asking] what is such an essential principle like?
狗子佛性、なにとして無をまつことあらん。 Why should the dog's buddha-nature need wait for "*mu*."

(106)趙州いはく、「為佗有業識在」。Zhauzhou said, "Because it has karmic consciousness."

(107)この道旨は、「為佗有」は「業識」なり。 What this saying means is that "being for the sake of others" is [being] with karmic consciousness.
「業識有」、「為佗有」なりとも、狗子無、佛性無なり。 Even if "being (*u*) with karmic consciousness," or "being (*u*) for the sake of others," the dog is "non-being (*mu*)," and buddha-nature is "non-being (*mu*)."
業識いまだ狗子を會せず、狗子いかでか佛性にあはん。 Karmic consciousness has not yet understood the dog; how could the dog meet with buddha-nature?
たとひ雙放雙收すとも、なほこれ業識の始終なり. Whether we let go of the two ["being (*u*)" and "non-being (*mu*)"] or take in the two, it is still beginning and end of karmic consciousness.

(108)趙州有僧問、「狗子還有佛性也無」。 A monk asked Zhauzhou, "Does a dog have buddha-nature or not?"

(109)この問取は、この僧、搆得趙州の道理なるべし。 This question is about the principle for this monk to get hold on Zhauzhou.
しかあれば佛性の道取問取は、佛祖の家常茶飯なり。 Therefore, expressing and asking buddha-nature is ordinary tea and rice of the buddha-ancestors.

(110) 趙州いはく、「有」。
Zhauzhou said, "It has (*u*, being)."

(111) この有の様子は、教家の論師等の有にあらず、有部の論有にあらざるなり。
The way this "being (*u*)" exists is not the same with "existence" of the commentary masters in the teaching schools; is not the same with "existence" discussed in Sarvastivadin (Existence School).

すすみて佛有を學すべし。 We should further advance and study buddha-being (*butsu-u*). 佛有は趙州有なり、趙州有は狗子有なり、狗子有は佛性有なり。 Buddha-being is Zhauzhou-being; Zhauzhou-being is dog-being; dog-being is buddha-nature-being.

(112) 僧いはく、「既有、為甚麼却撞入這皮袋」。 The monk said, "Since [the dog] already has it, why did it enter forcibly into this skin-bag?"

(113) この僧の道得は、今有なるか、古有なるか、既有なるかと問取するに、既有は諸有に相似せり といふとも、既有は孤明なり。 In asking if what this monk expresses is present-being, ancient-being, already-being; although already-being resembles various beings, already-being is solitary and bright.

既有は撞入すべきか、撞入すべからざるか。 Should already-being enter forcibly, or not enter forcibly?

撞入這皮袋の行履、いたづらに蹉過の功夫あらず。 The action of entering forcibly into the skin-bag is not a vain mistaken effort.

Index

171

About the Contributors

Lucy Biven trained in child and adolescent psychotherapy at the Anna Freud Center in London, United Kingdom. She was head of child and adolescent psychotherapy in Leicester, United Kingdom. Biven has coauthored *The Archaeology of Mind* with Jaak Panksepp in 2012 and wrote *A Short-Cut to Understanding Affective Neuroscience* in 2022. She has lived much of her adult life in England and currently resides in Maryland.

David Bohm, PhD (12/20/1917–10/27/1992), was an American Brazilian British scientist who has been described as one of the most significant theoretical physicists of the twentieth century and who contributed unorthodox ideas to quantum theory, neuropsychology, and the philosophy of mind. Bohm advanced the view that quantum physics meant that the old Cartesian model of reality—that there are two kinds of substance, the mental and the physical, that somehow interact—was too limited. To complement it, he developed a mathematical and physical theory of "implicate" and "explicate" order. He also believed that the brain, at the cellular level, works according to the mathematics of some quantum effects and postulated that thought is distributed and nonlocalized just as quantum entities are.[*]

Ben Connelly is a Soto Zen teacher and Dharma heir in the Katagiri lineage. He also teaches mindfulness in a wide variety of secular contexts and brings his practice to climate justice activism. Ben is based at Minnesota Zen Meditation Center, travels to teach across the United States, writes for *Tricycle* magazine, and is author of five books for Wisdom Publications, including *Inside the Grass Hut*, *Inside Vasubandhu's Yogacara*, and *Mindfulness and Intimacy*.

Charles Eigen is a psychotherapist, teacher, and long-time meditation practitioner in Milwaukee, Wisconsin. He was a founding member of the Mindfulness Community of Milwaukee and a past president of both the C. G. Jung Center of Milwaukee and the Milwaukee Zen Center. He has been a lecturer at the University of Wisconsin–Milwaukee in both the Department of English and the Department of Human Kinetics. Chuck Eigen has been a practitioner of craniosacral therapy, Rolfing Structural Integration, and Rolfing Movement, as well as Internal Family Systems Therapy and the Focusing method. He has also been a Progoff Intensive Journal Workshop leader. His previous book is *Inner Dialogue in Daily Life* (Jessica Kingsley).

Gangaji was born in Texas in 1942 and grew up in Mississippi. After graduating from the University of Mississippi in 1964, she married and had a daughter. In 1972, she moved to San Francisco where she began exploring deeper levels of her being. She took bodhisattva vows, practiced Zen and Vipassana meditation, helped run a Tibetan Buddhist Meditation Center, and had a career as an acupuncturist in the San Francisco Bay Area.

Despite her successes, Gangaji continued to experience a deep and persistent longing for fulfillment. In 1990 the answer to her prayer came unexpectedly, taking her to India and to the meeting with Sri H. W. L. Poonja, also known as Papaji. In this meeting, Gangaji's personal story of suffering ended and the promise of a true life began to flower and unfold. Today, Gangaji travels the world speaking to seekers from all walks of life. A teacher and author, she shares her direct experience of the essential message she received from Papaji and offers it to all who want to discover a true and lasting fulfillment. Through her life and words, she powerfully articulates how it is really possible to discover the truth of who you are and be true to that discovery.

Eugene T. Gendlin, PhD (12/25/1926–5/1/2017), taught at the University of Chicago from 1964 to 1995. His philosophical work is concerned especially with the relationship between logic and experiential explication. He was a founder and editor for many years of the Clinical Division Journal *Psychotherapy: Theory Research and Practice*. His books and articles include *Experiencing and the Creation of Meaning, Focusing, Focusing-Oriented Psychotherapy, Let Your Body Interpret Your Dreams, A Process Model*, and *Language beyond Post-Modernism: Saying and Thinking in Gendlin's Philosophy (edited by David Levin)*. Gendlin's numerous honors include the Viktor Frankl Prize, awarded by the city of Vienna and the Viktor Frankl Family Foundation, and lifetime achievement awards from both the World Association for Person-Centered and Experiential Psychotherapies and from the US Association for Body Psychotherapy. The American Psychological

Association's Clinical Division awarded him the "Distinguished Professional Psychologist of the Year" in 1970. His book *Focusing* has sold over 500,000 copies and is translated into seventeen languages.

Temple Grandin, PhD, is a Distinguished Professor of Animal Science at Colorado State University. Her main research interests are animal behavior and welfare. Equipment she has designed is used by major companies in the meat industry. She has also served as a consultant on animal welfare for companies such as McDonalds and Tyson. Some of the books she has authored are *Animals in Translation*, *Thinking in Pictures*, and *Livestock Handling and Transport*. Her new book, *Visual Thinking*, was a *New York Times* best seller. At age three she had no language, and she overcame the challenges of autism with the help of her mother and many good mentors. She was inducted into the Women's Hall of Fame in 2017.

Frederick R. Gustafson, DMin (4/4/1941–7/17/2018), was a graduate of the C. G. Jung Institute of Zurich, Switzerland, and one of the founding members of the C. G. Jung Institute of Chicago. He was employed in private practice as a Jungian analyst and as a pastoral counselor. For over twenty years Doctor Gustafson was involved in the ceremonial life, including the Sun Dance, of the Brule branch of the Lacota people. He is the author of *Dancing between Two Worlds: Jung and the Native American Soul* and *The Black Madonna of Einsiedeln, An Ancient Image for Our Present Time* and editor of *Moonlit Path: Reflections on the Dark Feminine* and *Pierre Teilhard de Chardin and Carl Gustav Jung: Side by Side.*

Thich Nhất Hanh (10/11/1926–1/22/2022) was a Vietnamese Buddhist Zen master, poet, scholar, and human rights activist. In 1967 he was nominated by Martin Luther King Jr. for the Nobel Peace Prize. He is author of more than one hundred books, sixty in English, including *Being Peace*, *Present Moment Wonderful Moment*, and *Calming the Fearful Mind*. He lived at Plum Village, his meditation center in France, and traveled worldwide, leading retreats on the art of mindful living. Ordained as a monk at age sixteen in Vietnam, Thich Nhất Hanh soon envisioned a kind of engaged Buddhism that could respond directly to the needs of society. He was a prominent teacher and social activist in his home country before finding himself exiled for calling for peace. In the West he played a key role in introducing mindfulness and created mindful communities (sanghas) around the world. His teachings have impacted politicians, business leaders, activists, teachers, and countless others.

Sekkei Harada (1926–2020) was the abbot of Hosshin-ji, a Soto Zen training monastery and temple in Fukui Prefecture, near the coast of central Japan. He was born in 1926 in Okazaki, near Nagoya, and was ordained at Hosshin-ji in 1951. In 1953, he went to Hamamatsu to practice under Zen Master Inōe Gien (1894–1981) and received inkashomei (certification of realization) in 1957. In 1974, he was installed as resident priest and abbot of Hosshin-ji and was formally recognized by the Soto Zen sect as a certified Zen master (shike) in 1976. Since 1982, Harada traveled abroad frequently, teaching in such countries as Germany, France, the United States, and India. He also led zazen groups within Japan, in Tokyo and Saitama. From 2003 to 2005, he was director of the Soto Zen Buddhism Europe Office located in Milan.

Jean Klein (October 19, 1912–February 22, 1998), was a French author, spiritual teacher, and philosopher of Advaita Vedanta (Nondualism).[1] According to Jean Klein, it is only in a "spontaneous state of interior silence that we can open ourselves to our true nature: the 'I Am' of pure consciousness." Jean Klein was born in Berlin and spent his childhood in Brno and Prague. He studied musicology and medicine in Vienna and Berlin, becoming a physician. Having left Germany in 1933 for France, he secretly worked with the French Resistance in the Second World War. After the war, Klein again left for India to study Yoga and Advaita Vedanta for three years. During those three years he met a spiritual teacher of Advaita, Pandit Veeraraghavachar Rao, a scholar at the Sanskrit College in Bangalore, and returned to the West to become a spiritual teacher himself.*

Jiddu Krishnamurti (5/12/1895–2/17/1986) is regarded as one of the greatest philosophical and spiritual figures of the twentieth century. Krishnamurti claimed no allegiance to any caste, nationality, or religion and was bound by no tradition. His purpose was to set humankind unconditionally free from the destructive limitations of conditioned mind. In his talks, he pointed out to people the need to transform themselves through self-knowledge, by being aware of the subtleties of their thoughts and feelings in daily life, and how this movement can be observed through the mirror of relationship. His books include *The Ending of Time*, *Freedom from the Known*, *Commentaries on Living*, *Education and the Significance of Life*, *The Awakening of Intelligence*, and *The First and Last Freedom*. (From KFA website.)

Francis Lucille. Francis Lucille is a spiritual teacher in the tradition of Advaita Vedanta. A longtime friend and disciple of Jean Klein, whom he met in 1975, Francis transmits the ancient wisdom of nonduality, the common ground of Advaita Vedanta, Cha'an Zen Buddhism, Taoism, and Sufism. His teachings reflect his teacher's appreciation for humor, art, music, and poetry while integrating his own passion for the sciences, stemming from his training in mathematics and physics at the Ecole Polytechnique. His pedagogical approach is characterized by its distinctive intellectual rigor and an emphasis on investigation of the body and its sensations.

More information on retreats and other events is available on his website: francislucille.com.

Pierre Morin, MD, PhD, was for many years the copresident of the International Association of Process-Oriented Psychology (IAPOP) and is a faculty member at the Process Work Institute of Portland Graduate School. As a physician in Switzerland, he worked in the fields of coma and brain injury recovery and psychosocial medicine. He worked for twenty years as a clinical director and supervisor in a community outpatient mental health program that works with refugees and trauma survivors. He is the author, with Gary Reiss, of *Inside Coma* and author of *Health in Sickness—Sickness in Health, Big Medicine*, and *Communal Medicine*, three books that advocate for a new, ethical sensitivity toward people that experience emotional and physical health challenges and describe a cutting-edge mind-body treatment. Pierre can be reached at pierre@creativehealing.org (www.creativehealing.org).

Jac O'Keeffe is a theology graduate from the Pontificate University of Ireland with postgraduate studies in adult and community education. From 1997 to 2007 Jac pursued a spiritual path that was eclectic and disciplined. From 2007 she served as an independent spiritual teacher, guiding people in the unfoldment of their own spiritual journey. In her books, teachings, talks, and retreats she supports the empowerment of individuals who are done with seeking, done with hiding, done with outsourcing their spiritual awakening to gurus. Her books include *Born to Be Free* and *How to Be a Spiritual Rebel*. In 2023, Jac made the shift from working with students of spirituality to supporting spiritual teachers and leaders. Drawing from fifteen years of experience as an international spiritual teacher together with certifications in Leadership Skills for Women in Management, Financial Coaching, and as a Right Use of Power educator, she supports both spiritual and personal development in her clients. Jac is a founding member of the Association for Spiritual Integrity and is the current sitting president of the board of directors. For more information about Jac visit jac-okeeffe.com and the Association for Spiritual Integrity

Shohaku Okumura, Roshi, is an ordained priest and Dharma successor of Kosho Uchiyama Roshi in the lineage of Kodo Sawaki Roshi. He was the director of the Soto Zen Buddhism International Center in San Francisco from 1997 to 2010. His published books of translation include *Opening the Hand of Thought, Realizing Genjokoan: The Key to Dogen's Shobogenzo, Zen Teachings of "Homeless" Kodo*, and several others. He is the founding teacher of the Sanshin Zen Community, based in Bloomington, Indiana, where he lives with his family.

Sri Harilal W. Poonja (Papaji) (10/13/1990–9/6/1997). His mother was the sister of Swami Rama Tirta, a well-known sage and poet. Poonjaji was eight years old when he first experienced the unstoppable bliss of his own infinite nature. As a young man Poonja served in the Indian army. After resigning his commission, he began a spiritual quest in search of God, which took him all over India. Everywhere he went he was disappointed, finding only "businessmen disguised as sadhus." Finally, when he was in his early thirties, Bhagavan Sri Ramana Maharshi appeared in a vision and directed him to go to Tiruvannamalai. There, in the presence of Bhagavan, his master, he ended his search. After the partition of India, Papaji settled his family in Lucknow. It was there, toward the end of his life, that he began to be discovered by Western devotees.

Shunyru Suzuki, Roshi (May 18, 1904–December 4, 1971), was a Sōtō Zen monk and teacher who helped popularize Zen Buddhism in the United States and is renowned for founding the first Zen Buddhist monastery outside Asia (Tassajara Zen Mountain Center). Suzuki founded the San Francisco Zen Center that, along with its affiliate temples, comprises one of the most influential Zen organizations in the United States. A book of his teachings, *Zen Mind, Beginner's Mind*, is one of the most popular books on Zen and Buddhism in the West.[*]

Raymond Tallis, FRCP, is a philosopher, poet, novelist, cultural critic, and a retired physician and clinical neuroscientist. He has published over thirty widely acclaimed books on the philosophy of mind, metaphysics, philosophical anthropology, and literary and cultural criticism. He has been awarded honorary doctorates by four British universities, two for contributions to the humanities and two for contributions to medical science. His most recent books include *Of Time and Lamentation: Reflections on Transience* (2017, 2019), *Freedom: An Impossible Reality* (2021), and *Prague 22: A Philosopher Takes a Tram through a City* (forthcoming, 2024).

Vimala Thakar (4/15/1921–3/11/2009) was an Indian social activist and spiritual teacher. She pursued a strong interest with meditation and spiritual practices throughout her youth. Later she became active in the Bhoodan (Land Gift) Program. This program, led by Vinoba Bhave, persuaded landlords to give land to poor farmers. Through the 1950s, several million acres of farmland were so redistributed. She traveled India to its length and breadth. In 1958, Thakar attended talks given by, and met with, the philosopher Jiddu

Krishnamurti. This meeting was to change her life. She left the Land Gift movement to dedicate herself to what she called "the internal problem"—the spiritual liberation of the individual.[3] She dedicated herself to teaching meditation and philosophy, traveling between India, the United States, and Europe. In 1979, she rekindled her passion for social activism, traveling through India and founding centers to educate villagers in agro-centered industries, sanitation, local self-government, and active democratic citizenship. Her teachings came to emphasize balancing "inner" spiritual development with "outer" social development, an evolution reflected in her 1984 book *Spirituality and Social Action: A Holistic Approach.**

*From Wikipedia.